The Defiant Muse

FRENCH FEMINIST POEMS FROM THE MIDDLE AGES TO THE PRESENT

THE DEFIANT MUSE
Series Editor, Angel Flores

The Defiant Muse: French Feminist Poems from the Middle Ages to the Present
Edited and with an introduction by Domna C. Stanton

The Defiant Muse: Hispanic Feminist Poems from the Middle Ages to the Present
Edited and with an introduction by Ángel Flores and Kate Flores

The Defiant Muse: German Feminist Poems from the Middle Ages to the Present
Edited and with an introduction by Susan L. Cocalis

The Defiant Muse: Italian Feminist Poems from the Middle Ages to the Present
Edited by Beverly Allen, Muriel Kittel, and Keala Jane Jewell and with an introduction by Beverly Allen

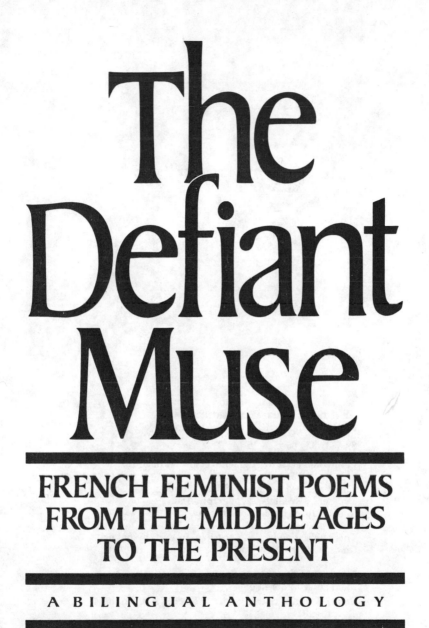

The Defiant Muse

FRENCH FEMINIST POEMS
FROM THE MIDDLE AGES
TO THE PRESENT

A BILINGUAL ANTHOLOGY

EDITED AND WITH AN INTRODUCTION BY
DOMNA C. STANTON

89 88 87 86   6 5 4 3 2 1

Permission acknowledgments begin on page 207.

Cover and text design by Gilda Hannah
Typeset by Weinglas Typography Inc.
Manufactured by Banta Company

This publication is made possible, in part, by public
funds from the New York State Council on the Arts.

Library of Congress Cataloging-in-Publication Data
Main entry under title:
French feminist poems from the Middle Ages to the
    present.
    (The Defiant Muse)
    English and French.
    1. Feminism—Poetry.   2. French poetry—
Women authors—Translations into
English.   3.French poetry—Women
authors   4.English poetry—Translations from
French.
I. Stanton, Domna C.   II. Series.
PQ1170.E6F68 1985   841'.009'9287   85-16270
ISBN 0-935312-46-3
ISBN 0-935312-52-8 (pbk.)

To my mother

CONTENTS

PUBLISHER'S PREFACE

The Feminist Press is proud to publish this set of anthologies of feminist poetry, the first bilingual collection of its kind. When Domna C. Stanton proposed the project to The Press in 1983, I immediately responded that it was "a natural" for The Press, and a critical publication in women's studies that was long overdue. To be sure, the idea for the series and the actual work began years earlier. In 1976, Kate Flores urged Ángel, her husband, to collaborate on an anthology, not simply of women's poetry, which had been sporadically included in the more than twenty volumes of verse he had edited, but specifically of feminist poetry, which had never been done. However, as the enormity of the undertaking became apparent, they enlarged the original scope from one to four volumes, each to be devoted to a major language, and contacted Domna C. Stanton for French, Susan L. Cocalis for German, and Beverly Allen and Muriel Kittel for Italian. In common, these editors agreed upon the general conception of the volumes; independently, over a period of several years, they did extensive research in libraries at home and in the countries of origin. That arduous process led to a "re-vision" of poets whose feminism had been ignored or suppressed. Far more important, it led to the discovery of numerous poets whose work remains unknown in their own country to this day. Thanks to these editors, the poetry can now have the audience it deserves.

Reading each volume produces the exciting awareness of a strong national tradition of feminist poetry, dating back to "the dark ages." Together, the anthologies confirm the existence of many common themes and threads that connect women beyond differences of class and culture, time and place. For that inspiring vision, the editors of this series, like those of us at The Feminist Press, can be proud...and joyful.

Florence Howe

INTRODUCTION

"Go therefore back in the house, and take up your own work,
The loom and the distaff, and see to it that your handmaidens
Ply their work also; but the men must see to discussion,
All men, but I most of all. For mine is the power in this household."
  Penelope went back inside the house, in amazement,
For she laid the serious words of her son deep away in her spirit.[1]

The admonitions of Telemachus to his mother dramatize the gender divisions that confine women's work to "the loom and the distaff," and condemn the second sex to silence. Neither to be seen nor heard, woman is denied power and authority, which are transmitted from father to son, and are identified in this Homeric scene with "discussion," public discourse, indeed, poetry. For Penelope's "crime" is to ask the celebrated poet, Phemius, for a different lyric, more consonant to her needs; chastised, she acquiesces, returning to the epic weaving that exemplifies her fidelity to (a) man. How much more "criminal," then, would Penelope have seemed had she dared sing her own lyric in the public arena. How monstrously she would be depicted, like one of those Sirens whose land "is piled high with [the] boneheaps of men" enchanted and destroyed by "the melody of their singing" (XII, 44-46). Better by far, says this seminal poem, for man to plug his ears and stay upright, lashed to the phallocratic mast.

Siren and Penelope, like Eve and Mary, the monster and the angel, are symbols of the bad and the good woman in our system. In effect, that set of antitheses also marks the difference between the speaking/writing female subject and the speechless, spoken female object. As feminist scholarship has shown during the past fifteen years, perhaps most thoroughly in Sandra Gilbert and Susan Gubar's *The Madwoman in the Attic* (1979), those symbols have haunted, or as Virginia Woolf would say, "distorted" women's writing. But as Gilbert and Gubar emphasize in their preface to *Shakespeare's Sisters* (1979), the system that brands all female authors as deviant creates even more formidable obstacles for the woman poet than for the prose writer.

Enshrined as the highest, most esoteric language in Western thought, poetry has been considered the property of a priestly figure whose gifts derive from or refer back to the godhead. Homer's Phemius may be the first incarnation of the poet who sings "with a voice such as gods have" (I, 336), and who has been called bard or *vates*, genius or prophet. In fact, "the divine singer" (I, 371) has often been identified with the Adam of Genesis 2:19, the sole beneficiary of God's power to name.[2] Down through the Judeo-Christian ages, this priestly figure has enjoyed a privileged connection to inspiration and enthusiasm—the breath and voice of the transcendental Father. In turn, he initiates neophyte sons into the secret knowledge of ancient glyphs and tongues, laws and rules, codes and conventions. As a result, and as Suzanne Juhasz has observed,[3] the rebellious Penelope has been treated as monstrously presumptuous if she attempts to steal those patriarchal secrets, and monstrously laughable if her songs do not possess them; at any rate, hers can be dismissed as the trifles of a mere poetess, dilettantish, minor, trivial, feminine.

From this perspective, it is understandable why the inferior, vulgar, indeed prosaic language of prose offered women comparatively greater freedom; more specifically, why the short story and especially the novel, lacking a venerated tradition of rules and conventions, count the "inferior sex" among their earliest practitioners and innovators. As Woolf remarks in *A Room of One's Own* (1929), "all the older forms of literataure were hardened and set by the time she became a writer. The novel alone was young enough to be soft in her hands."[4] Thus Woolf's essay centers on fiction, while it enumerates the obstacles that thwarted "the expression of poetry in women." For the singing Penelope she calls Judith Shakespeare, Woolf can only envision a destiny of madness and death in anonymity.

Following Woolf's lead—or so it would seem—feminist literary critics in the 1970s focused on fiction, the novel in particular, and elaborated important theories of women's writing and gendered reading. As a consequence, however, the post-Woolfian scholarship we call women's studies continued to plug its ears to female poets. To be sure, the relative visibility and accessibility of women's fiction played a part in this phenomenon, over and beyond the generalized resistance to poetry in contemporary culture. Nevertheless, in the late 1970s, a happy few began to wonder with Gilbert and Gubar why "the problems as well as the triumphs of women poets in England and America still remain inexplicably obscure."[5] And they bemoaned, with Margaret Homans, "this critical blindness to women poets...[which] demonstrates that the same conditions that originally restricted most women writers to the novel still obtain" (p.7). So saying, the texts of Homans, Gilbert and Gubar, Juhasz, and others proposed a new critical agenda for the 1980s featuring the specificity of women's poetic practices. And yet, these and subsequent studies have dealt almost exclusively with nineteenth- and twentieth-century British and American poets, chiefly with Elizabeth Barrett Browning, Christina Rossetti, Emily Dickinson, Sylvia Plath, Anne Sexton, and Adrienne Rich. In what regrettably appears to be another manifestation of cultural centrism in women's studies, female poets from other places and ages have remained unexplored, unknown, silenced like Homer's Penelope. To promote for these eccentric poets a movement "out of silence...into the glare and vulnerability of print," as Rich puts it,[6] thus also means to endorse a worldwide feminist practice that embraces heterogeneity.

The compilation of an anthology of poetry by French—or other non-English-speaking—women represents an initial, but important, step in this far-reaching enterprise. Predictably, anthologies of French poetry in translation include few women; *The Penguin Book of French Verse* (1975), for instance, admits only Christine de Pisan, Pernette du Guillet, Louise Labé, and Catherine Pozzi. More understandably, recent international anthologies of women poets also contain but a small sampling of French writers. The very useful *Penguin Book of Women Poets* (1978), which spans 3,500 years and 40 literary traditions, includes 20 short poems by French authors.[7] And the more circumscribed *Twentieth-Century Women's Poetry in Translation* (1976) provides only a few texts by the poets Marguerite Clerbaut, Anne Hébert, and Simone Weil.

The present anthology of French feminist poetry does not include those three contemporary authors. That discrepancy, however, should not simply be ascribed to the partialness or incompleteness of every anthology. Rather, it reflects the partiality, the particular ideological point of view of this editor who, like all editors, determines by the texts selected for inclusion what image of a poetic tradition is created. The bias that has typified and stigmatized compilations of French women's poetry to date is nowhere more apparent than in Jeanine Mounin's *La Poésie féminine* (1963–66), the most massive contemporary work of its kind.[8] In an extended preface that explores the existence of a poetic tradition by French women, Mounin iterates the stereotypes of femininity and the clichés of feminine writing that pervade traditional literary histories.[9] The principal preoccupations of this poetry, she claims, are conjugal and maternal happiness, and a desire for love that is couched in passive emotionalism. Often insipid, derivative and repetitive, *la poésie féminine* is not the expression of a literary vocation, since, according to Mounin, the "socio-physiological need to propagate" renders such ambition less acute in women than in men (p. 62). The writing, more instinctive than rigorous, serves instead to compensate for a failed emotional life, expressing the fear and bitterness of solitude. Rarely, then, does this poetry evince a capacity for abstract thought beyond conventional religious views or flights into mysticism; rarely does it highlight involvement in political and social problems. The tone, says Mounin, "is almost never one of revolt or anger, humor or sarcasm, but of disenchantment, a kind of chronic depressiveness...devoid of a desire to react" (p. 37), much less to express "resentment against male dominance" (p. 57); "women do not revolt and assert themselves in adversity" (p. 62). The specific forms of male dominance or female adversity remain a mystery, however, since Mounin's version of French literary history aims to show that women writers suffered no hindrances after the seventeenth century. Rejecting the need for "an aggressive feminism" at the close of her preface (p. 64), just as she denies the feminism of her investigation at the outset, Mounin welcomes the absence of "all traces of antagonism between the sexes" in contemporary women's writing (p. 64), and points to the future disappearance of *la poésie féminine*.

In opposition to this image of women's poetry, whose disappearance can only be welcome, the present volume affirms its feminist bias. The desire to combat the notion—and its self-fulfilling proof by the verse selected—that women's cultural productions confirm patriarchal clichés make this an "a-mazing" anthology, to use Mary Daly's term for feminist demystification. The volume is born in negativity, in an affirmation of the proposition, " 'that's not it,' 'that's still not it,' " which Julia Kristeva has called the crux of female dissidence.[10] More specifically, this project began with the determination to exclude poems that privilege *kinder, kirche, küchen*, extol conjugal bliss, passively bemoan seduction and abandonment, and seek escape into transcendent saintliness or the beauty of flora and fauna. Conversely, the decision was made to include poems that showed an awareness of the scenes and acts of "the femininity plot," and opposed or tried to subvert them with a different script. To be sure, some verse, by its ambiguity, resists such classification. More problematic by far, however, were the residual meanings of "feminist" in the notion of "feminist poetry," since no canonical definition of the term and genre exists, nor, for that matter, should exist. Indeed, although the importance of exposing a deviant poetic practice seemed beyond question, the apparent need to establish a limited and somewhat arbitrary set of criteria for "feminist poetry" was disturbing, perplexing. In pragmatic terms, however, the process of selection required a constant negotiation between ideological and idealistic preconceptions, on the one hand, and on the other, the concrete poems that could be found over a finite period of time. This work was in some senses both Odyssean and Penelopean: it involved a wandering from text to text looking for signposts of a definitional map, then evolving, through continual unraveling and revision, a set of criteria that were finally woven in the poetic fabric of the volume.

More than Penelope's weavings or Odysseus's wanderings, the metaphor for this work is archeological. For the key to the probe lay in unearthing names of women poets, beyond the few already well known in literary history. First, new names were ferreted, one by one, out of anthologies of French women's poetry, and of these, Mounin's was unquestionably the most useful source, although only 15 of her 100 authors appear in the present volume. Subsequently, names were dug out of compilations listed under "Women, Poetry by" and "French, Poetry;" volumes of selected verse from individual periods of French literature; literary histories; even voluminous biographical dictionaries of authors.[11] As their number expanded, the names provided access to sources that could be mined for other names, texts, and sources, more obscure, less "feminine" than the canonized and anthologized. In the recesses of

American libraries and through interlibrary loans, ultimately in the byzantine Bibliothèque Nationale in Paris, volume after volume of poetry was examined; collections of writing by women were scanned; journals surveyed. Many were the fallow periods when no text seemed worth retaining. Still, by bits, by fits, with the help of friends and strangers, texts began to accumulate, gaps started to fill, and another map of French women's poetry emerged—a repressed, feminist practice.[12]

Contrary to what Mounin would have us believe, this *poésie féminine* is informed first and foremost by a condemnation of the patriarchal institutions and attitudes that oppress women. The opening texts in the anthology, written in the Middle Ages by Anonymous—who, as Woolf pointed out, was "often a woman"—decry matrimony, the main event in the femininity plot. The bondage of marriage, what Christine de Pisan (1364–c.1430) calls its "martyrdom," is analyzed and denounced from Madeleine Des Roches in the sixteenth century to Natalie Clifford Barney and Marguerite Grépon in the twentieth. And the travails of pregnancy, which Catherine Des Roches (1550–1587) bemoans, lead to a refusal to propagate in Louise Geneviève de Sainctonge (1650–1718), Lucie Delarue-Mardrus (1880?–1945), and Barney (1877–1972). Devoid of stereotypical maternal bliss, this corpus contains but a few inscriptions of the mother-daughter bond—most positively in Madeleine Des Roches (c. 1530?–1587); more ambivalently in Thérèse Plantier (1911–); and on a symbolic level, in Marie-Anne Du Boccage (1710–1802) and Charlotte Calmis (?–1970), who envision a noble race of women, indeed a different order.

Outside of marriage, the love relation represents an ongoing problem for women who resent masculine domination. To be sure, poems of the medieval courtly tradition argue for the equality, even the preeminence of the lady (Marie de Ventadour, ?–c. 1222). More radically, the Comtesse de Die (twelfth century) asserts woman's right to sexual pleasure, a theme that recurs in a sensualist eighteenth-century text by the anonymous Mme de C***. Typically, however, the impossibility of loving arrogant men who only desire admiring slaves is highlighted in this poetry, in tones ranging from mild accusation to violent hatred for "Men-Sex" (Monique Buri, 1928–); from playful irony to bitter sarcasm against creatures in the "droopy drawers of supermen" (Joyce Mansour, 1928–). Thus, starting with Pisan's refrain, "I love not love, nor want its woe," freedom is sought from the entrapment of masculine desire. And solutions are sometimes found in the solitary safety of virginity (Mlle de ***, seventeenth century), the militancy of an amazonian community (Du Boccage), and the love of another woman (Renée Vivien, 1877–1909; Barney; Delarue-Mardrus).

Transcending the individual and the personal, this poetic practice indicts the institutions that perpetuate women's oppression by "the first sex." The sociopolitical and juridical implications of love and marriage in a phallocratic system are first underscored by Pisan's defenseless widow.

And they are revealed through various other figures in more explicitly political verse after the revolution of 1789; the adulterous wife whose murderous husband is innocent, according to man-made laws ("Epistle to the Emperor Napoleon," Constance-Marie de Salm-Dyck, 1767–1845); the unwed mother victimized by societal prejudice (Camille Bélot, c. 1900); the woman who kills herself and her child in despair (Louis Colet, 1810–1876); and the prostitute, the pariah embraced as a sister in "Injustice" (Delarue-Mardrus). The policies and prejudices of governments—be they monarchic, imperial, republican, or democratic—number among the sources of female servitude in a system that Monique Buri depicts as a "train to hell," with no end or transformation in sight.

Over and beyond the sociopolitical sphere, religious and cultural forces of subjugation are denounced as well. "Trust me, I am the way to happiness," says the guardian angel in a dialogue by Amable Tastu (1798–1885), which dramatizes the nefarious consequences of conforming to feminine destiny. In her pessimistic "Revolt," Adine Brabart Riom (1818–1899) censures the Lord's approval of man's tyranny over woman, which leaves no solution but death for the exiled sex, the outcast who, like an allegorical "She-Fox" (Claire Goll, 1891–1977), is hunted down by male predators. Although especially visible in nineteenth-century texts, the prejudices of patriarchal religion are exposed much earlier, for instance, through Pisan's misogynistic clerics who malign the female, from Eve on, as the source of evil. Religion, however, is but part and parcel of a system that ascribes all negative traits to women. "Men still hate you and run you down," declares the Muse to her female interlocutors in Mlle de ***'s "Fair Sex Avenged by the Fair Sex" (1701), citing after Pisan, the "hundreds of critics, hundreds of bilious authors [who]...spill floods of ink against our mores."Conversely, man "venerates us only for our nothingness," exclaims the speaker in Salm-Dyck's "Letter to Women," a culminating protest against denying women the gift of reason, the strength of intellect, the right to education and enlightenment. By that denial, the cultural and religious, the political and familiar perpetrators of the patriarchy strive to keep women ignorant ("Agnodicia," Catherine Des Roches) and to maintain their dominion (Colet).

Of necessity, the poetic practice herein called feminist specifically confronts and combats woman's oppression in relation to language. During the *ancien régime*, Anne de La Vigne (1634–1684) writes in her "Reply to the Shade of Descartes" that men's laws make it a female duty "to speak but rarely and to have no knowledge," although in republican times, the Salic law excluding women from authority can still rule the world of letters (Philippine de Vannoz, 1775–1851). In complicity with the law, parents insure against female writing by imposing the spindle and taking the quill away, husbands by demanding unceasing duties from their wives ("First Ode," Madeleine Des Roches). Moreover, if women break the writing interdiction, "a thousand voices blame our daring/Complaining, disturbed, astonished, they menace" (Salm-Dyck); or they "denounc[e] the mania...the piteous derangement" (Vannoz), heaping ridicule upon female babblings (Mlle de ***). Inevitably, such actions and attitudes have a debilitating effect on the aspiring poet—"my feathered pen was broken 'ere I flew," we read in Madeleine Des Roches's ode—and lead her, well into the nineteenth century, to deny she desires or deserves glory, to forego singing "songs magnificent," to be "pleased with lower harmonies." In more precise generic terms, the fearful, rule-bound speaker in de La Vigne's "Reply to the Shade of Descartes" leaves the "artful exposition" of philosophical principles to "our foremost sages"; but she becomes Descartes's exponent as she sings his praises, and she highlights the capacities of other, more daring women. Similarly, although satire is pronounced a dangerous craft, whose usurpation is intolerable to men (Mlle de ***), the mode pervades this poetic corpus from beginning to end. Thus the repressive laws of gender and genre are bemoaned but broken, as women appropriate male-identified forms and insert/assert the female speaking subject; these include the drinking song (Sainctonge); the heroic narrative of society's liberation from its conquerors ("The Deliverance of Argos," Adelaïde-Gillette Dufresnoy, 1765–1825); and, most especially, the love poem to a woman.[13] From Anne de Rohan (1584–1646) to Barney and Delarue-Mardrus, in a "lesbian continuum," to use Adrienne Rich's term, that ranges from casual friendship to intense eroticism, this poetry overturns the androcentric imperative alienating woman from woman, and affirms the many different threads that connect the female sex in pain and pleasure. In that process, appropriation leads to the transformation of traditional themes, the exploration of different scenes—women's bodies and desires (Vivien), women's activities in their colloquial dailiness (Cathy Bernheim, 1946–)—and beyond, to the strong suggestion that other, secret, shadowy forms and meanings exist, impenetrable to the masculine obsession for order and elucidation (Yanette Delétang-Tardif, 1907–). "Am I not the lacemaker of shadow...?" asks Charlotte Calmis's emblematic woman.

Doubly deviant, this feminist poetry does not merely make a man the monstrous object of attack, it also celebrates the qualities, capacities, and accomplishments of women. To be sure, the celebration is sometimes haunted by a sense of inadequacy that comes from the absence of a woman-centered language and tradition, an absence identified and deplored by Marie de Romieu (1545?–1590?) in "Brief Discourse: That Woman's Excellence Surpasses Man's":

What tongue exists to laud the female merits?
What voice is there that could thus sing their praises?
What pen would dare commit to memory
The glory unrivaled of their valiant minds?...
For if I tried to perfect a work so noble
My lowly style would then lose heart and power.

Paradoxically, this self-effacement and the discursive void underlying it are effaced by the very existence of the poem, which makes the solitary ''I'' heroic. Starting with the sixteenth century, however, the poet is supported and inspired by the muses, sometimes re-etched in feminist traits to personify the gynocentric woman free from marital or amorous bonds to pursue art and learning (Pernette Du Guillet, c. 1520–1545).[14] Or, then, as de La Vigne's ode to Mademoiselle de Scudéry indicates, the role of the muse is often assumed by the woman who serves as a poem's addressee. Even more significant, poems highlight lists of celebrated foremothers and contemporaries as objects of inspiration and veneration. In Romieu's ''Brief Discourse,'' for instance, the speaker cites Leontia, Eustochion, Sappho, Corinne, Armille Angosiole, indeed, ''legions'' of women in Germany, Italy, and Spain, before turning to her native France. Like a woman in a garden of magnificent blooms, she does not know which to pick for her ''anthology''; finally, the selected are cited:

Come, my Countess de Retz, sister of the Muses
The fourth charity, come to be inscribed
First within my verse. Greek is known to you;
From your mouth comes a special parlance
That pleases kings and courts magnificent...
Come next Morel, Charamont, Elisenes,
Des Roches de Poitiers, Graces of Pierie,
And you who hold the sceptre of Navarre...
To praise you worthily, my ladies,
One would need borrow the knowledge and the voice
Of a Valeria, or the fine speech,
Ornament of ancient Italy, of a Cornelia.
Not strong enough is my own voice. But if one of you
Brought this to perfection, before the eyes of all,
Soon it would be judged, without appeal, that we
From dawn of time to now, are more than men.

Such a list bespeaks the effort to create a female literary tradition and the desire to bring forth the poetry in women. ''Women, take up your pen and brush again,'' exhorts the speaker in Salm-Dyck's late eighteenth-century epistle. By contrast, nineteenth- and twentieth-century poems do not feature these ''feminaries''—to use Monique Wittig's term—possibly because the existence of a sisterhood is assumed. This is suggested by the pronoun ''we'' in texts by Bélot, Vivien, Delarue-Mardrus, Goll, Angèle Vannier (1917–), and Bernheim, and confirmed by Calmis's poem (''V'') addressed to the French women's movement. And yet, if poets of the modern period rehearse the personal, professional, and political problems of their predecessors; if the ''I'' still feels ''struck with exile,'' robbed of her being, like a ghost (Vannier), or even ''the dead woman in a poem'' (Marie-Françoise Prager, 1925?–), it is perhaps, not solely because of the enduring oppressiveness of the partriarchal order. Women's plight may also result from the lost knowledge, the repression of an empowering poetic tradition of their own.

To be sure, the feminist tradition that this "eccentric," "unrepresentative" anthology reconstitutes is richer in certain periods than others; or so it seems at the close of this preliminary investigation. In researching this book, feminist poems of the Middle Ages, the sixteenth century, and the period from the Revolution of 1789 to 1850 proved to be more plentiful, more accessible than those of the seventeenth, eighteenth and twentieth centuries—a phenomenon that raises troubling questions. For instance, that the earliest periods represented in this anthology, when few women were literate, should provide a richer body of feminist poetry than our own runs counter to an evolutionary view of history, which holds to progressively greater freedom and boldness of expression. As Joan Kelly has suggested, however, traditional (or male) theories of periodization and evolution do not necessarily obtain for women's history.[15] Indeed, the *ancien régime* saw aristocratic or economically privileged women rule medieval courts of love; establish the leading salons of the seventeenth and eighteenth centuries; and wield power in the royal court, as mistress of the king and mother to his illegitimate children; women even become queen-regents in fifteenth-, sixteenth-, and seventeenth-century France. By comparison, the post-Napoleonic era was governed, until 1965, by a Civil Code that tied the female firmly to the family, and made her a minor, legally and economically dependent on a man.[16] And yet, there is no simple causal correlation between history and literature.[17] In point of fact, the stronger, feminist verse in this anthology does not fall conveniently on the earlier side of 1789: that Revolutionary period and the turbulent half-century following it contributed the most explicitly political poetry to the volume, the two centuries preceding it, the least powerful.

Perhaps, then, some explanation for the apparent waxing and waning of feminist poetry can be found in the events and trends of literary history. The most pertinent and pervasive of these is unquestionably the *querelle des femmes*, the debate on women's roles, qualities, and capacities that first pitted misogynists against feminists at the dawn of the fifteenth century. In this anthology, Christine de Pisan represents the first inscription of the *querelle*, which becomes more marked in the sixteenth century, as feminist poets emphasize woman's need for education, and proclaim her talents in the arts, her moral worth, indeed, her superiority to man. As Germaine Brée has observed, however, the *querelle des femmes* "has gone on more or less heatedly, ever since [the Middle Ages], surfacing in times of social unrest—during and after the French Revolution, for example, and again in our own time."[18] In fact, while some seventeenth- and eighteenth-century poets iterate the terms in which the debate was couched in earlier centuries,[19] at the time of the revolution they affirm more radically and concretely their inalienable rights to equality with men, in the spirit of

Olympe de Gouges's Declaration of the Rights of Women (1792). And nineteenth-century poems, in keeping with the dominant intellectual and social preoccupations of the period, focus on the plight of working-class or marginal women, and the devaluation of the female in philosophical and religious systems.

The relative paucity of feminist verse in our time, however, as in the seventeenth and early eighteenth centuries, may also be related to the comparative status of prose and poetry as privileged modes of writing. French literary historians have traditionally disparaged the poetry of the so-called "classical period," with one or two notable exceptions, and have highlighted instead its innovations in prose—the novel and the short story, memoirs and letters, essays and treatises. Accordingly, when literary historians do cite women of the period, it is invariably prose writers— Scudéry, Lafayette, and Sévigné in the seventeenth century, Graffigny, Riccoboni and Du Deffand in the eighteenth. Although the distinctions between poetry and prose have broken down in the twentieth century, nevertheless no female poet associated with surrealism or modernism can compare with the celebrity attained by the prose of Colette, Beauvoir, Wittig, Sarraute, Duras, Cixous, Irigaray, and Kristeva. Indeed, in a diachronic perspective, most of the well-known French women writers have authored prose,[20] with the exception of Christine de Pisan, included in this anthology, and four poets who have been excluded: Marie de France in the twelfth century, Louise Labé in the sixteenth, Marceline Desbordes-Valmore in the nineteenth, Anna de Noailles in the twentieth. To be sure, this phenomenon may well be the sign of a generalized prejudice against female poets, and, in relative terms, the greater acceptability of female prose writers. And yet, the more productive periods of feminist verse in this volume tend to coincide with canonical highpoints of French poetry—the Middle Ages, the Renaissance, Romanticism. Does this mean that periods that privilege poetry thereby also promote the production of feminist verse? Or does it mean that literary history's privileging of those periods has promoted the survival of more plentiful feminist verse? But then, how can we explain the comparative thinness of feministy poetry in the post-Romantic tendencies known as symbolism, surrealism and modernism?[21]

While answers to such questions must await further study, research for this book revealed that many French women writers produced "feminist" prose and "feminine" poetry. This dichotomy, which also warrants closer examination, nonetheless suggests that in contrast to prose, the conventions of poetry, the noblest, the priestly language, may have a repressive impact on women's writing. In opposition to theories of the revolutionary force of poetry, this would imply that its various generic, thematic, figural, and prosodic conventions serve to hamper the possibility of more radical discourse and meaning. A case in point is the celebrated

Louise Labé (1525–1566), whose work was ultimately excluded from the volume, after considerable hesitation. The prose preface to her love poems, addressed to her friend, Clémence de Bourges, is decidedly feminist by this anthology's criteria:

Because I cannot personally do justice to the good intentions I feel toward our sex—the desire that it surpass or equal men not only in beauty but in learning and virtue—I can do no more than beg valiant and virtuous ladies to elevate their minds beyond the distaff and the spindle, and to strive to make the world understand that if we are not born to command, we must not be disdained as mere companions in private and public affairs by those who govern and are obeyed.[22]

The sentiments expressed in one of her typical love sonnets to a man, however, differ sharply:

When I catch sight of your fair head
garlanded with living laurel,
making your sad lute sound so well
that you compel to rise and be your followers
rocks and trees—when I see you adorned
in virtues legion, chief in honour among men,
then does my passionate heart suppose
that by such virtue as you are beloved,
esteemed by all, so you could love,
and to such worthy virtue could you amend
the virtue of taking pity,
and the virtue of being aroused
sweetly and slowly by my love.[23]

Labé's passionate and tortured verse is not "feminist" in content (the level of the signified), although an analysis of the subtle ways in which she reworks Petrarchan conventions (on the level of the signifier) could provide the basis for a feminist reading.

The instance of Labé and other "fine" poets excluded from this volume raises the well-rehearsed issue of the tensions between "poetic quality" and ideology.[24] To be sure, this is, in many ways, a false dichotomy, since any definition of "poetic quality" inevitably contains ideological preconceptions. Putting the argument, then, in different, albeit still value-laden terms, it could be said, for example, that the criteria used for this feminist anthology principally concern the message (or the denotative function), rather than the form of the message for its own sake, which Roman Jakobson has defined as the poetic function.[25] From this perspective, some texts in the volume will seem didactic and prosaic, most especially in translation. Was it not Robert Frost who declared all poetry lost in translation—a loss of semantic and figural play all the more acute in an anthology that has favored literal translations, even at the expense of meter and rhyme? Still, the problems of translation do not obviate the fact that the poems in French often betray what Marianne Moore termed "the pull of the sentence," an impulse toward the broader discursive space of prose. This deviation from the highly concentrated, elliptical, or hermetic language, traditionally associated with superior poetry, could be viewed as a defect or lack. This writer would argue, instead, that it suggests an unwillingness to be confined within the bonds of what Gertrude Stein called "patriarchal poetry." It betokens a deviant practice that self-consciously breaks down man-made oppositions, not only between genders, but also between the genres of prose and poetry and the realms of politics and poetics. Indeed, some of these "prosaic" poems are impelled by a desire to "protest, to preach, to proclaim an injury"; they are "deformed" by anger, which the author of *A Room of One's Own* thought incompatible with great "incandescent" verse (pp. 58-59). However, Woolf's ideological views contain their own denial of the poetic power of protest and rage. As Salm-Dyck stated two centuries ago in her "Letter to Women," "Anger is enough and worthy of Apollo." And yet, beyond the expression of an anger charged with political and discursive meanings, the feminist voice in this corpus also celebrates her position as a woman speaking for and to other women. In that dual process, the a-mazing "I" refuses to sing "in steady docile iambs" ("Couplets," Barney), and affirms the value of a more "careless" dance (Delétang-Tardif).

Isn't it time, then, to re-view this deviant poetic figure? As Hélène Cixous urges, "You only have to look at the Medusa straight on to see her. She's beautiful and she's laughing."[26] Unlike Judith Shakespeare, the singing Penelopes who comprise this volume were not silenced by the interdictions and the representations of sons and fathers. Their resonant verse should inspire and empower us to rediscover defiant "women of all the ages," guided by the spirit of Andrée Chédid's closing words:

These immemorial Women
        through clay and stones
        parting the husks of time
Clear a path to the present.

From the subsoil of centuries
delivering the spirit . . .

They raise echoes, words
and questions of today.

NOTES

Many individuals deserve thanks for their contributions to this book, most especially Margaret Waller for her painstaking research at the Library of Congress, and her unstinting assistance in revising translations and preparing the manuscript. A special acknowledgment is due to the translators: without their work, however frustrating it may have been, half of the volume would literally not exist. With the exception of six texts, previously published by Carl Hermy, Albert Herzing, Muriel Kittel, Naomi Lewis, and Patricia Terry, all translations were especially prepared for this volume by Beth Archer, Dorothy Backer, Mary Ann Caws, Martha Collins, Joan M. Ferrante, Serge Gavronsky, Barbara Johnson, Muriel Kittel, Sarah Spence, and Patricia Terry.

1. Richard Lattimore, trans. *The Odyssey of Homer*, (New York: Harper Colophon, 1965), I, 356–61.
2. See Margaret Homans, *Women Writers and Poetic Identity* (Princeton: Princeton University Press, 1980), pp. 29ff.
3. Suzanne Juhasz, *Naked and Fiery Forms: Modern American Poetry by Women, A New Tradition* (New York: Harper and Row, 1976), pp. 1-6.
4. Virginia Woolf, *A Room of One's Own* (New York: Harcourt, Brace and World, 1929), p. 80.
5. Sandra Gilbert and Susan Gubar, eds., *Shakespeare's Sisters: Feminist Essays on Women Poets* (Bloomington: Indiana University Press, 1979), p. xvi.
6. Adrienne Rich, Foreword to *Twentieth-Century Women's Poetry in Translation*, ed. Joanna Bankier, et al. (New York: Norton, 1976), p. xix.
7. The figure is comparable in Aliki Barnstone and Willis Barnstone's *A Book of Women Poets from Antiquity to Now* (New York: Schocken, 1980).
8. Jeanine Mounin, *La Poésie féminine*, 2 vols. (Paris: Seghers, 1963-66). In French, the adjective *féminine* does not necessarily have stereotypical connotations; thus the contemporary writer and theorist Hélène Cixous uses the term *écriture féminine* to herald the advent of radical, gynocentric writing. Other anthologies of women's poetry include: Marcel Béalu, *Anthologie de la poésie française de 1900 à nos jours* (Paris: Stock, 1953); Alphonse Séché, *Les Muses françaises*, 2 vols. (Paris: Louis Michaud, 1908). The phrases quoted in this critique of Mounin are the present author's translations.
9. For example, Jean Larnac, *Histoire de la littérature féminine en France* (Paris: Kra, 1929).
10. Quoted in *New French Feminisms*, ed. Elaine Marks and Isabelle de Courtivron (Amherst: University of Massachusetts Press, 1980), p. 137.
11. To illustrate the problem: not a single woman poet appears in J. Bersani, et. al., *La Littérature française depuis 1945* (Paris: Bordas, 1970), which cites 350 male and 12 female authors.
12. That the feminist poetic practice represented in this anthology is essentially limited to "metropolitan" French writers suggests the even greater invisibility of Francophone poets from Canada, the Carribean, and Africa, and underscores the need for exploration of their work. Even within the confines of metropolitan French literature, the difficulties of finding bio-bibliographical information about women poets, not to mention any interpretation of their work, are apparent in several short entries in the Notes on the Poets. However fragmentary the results of this research may seem, the Notes is nonetheless a beginning, which will, one hopes, be filled in/out by others.

13. If poetry is the property of men, then all the genres practiced by women are "appropriated," beginning with the courtly love lyric, which must be rewritten when the "I" is female and the love object a man; next, the early modern sonnet, ode, and epistle, inspired by classical and Italian models; the *mondain* or *galant* verse developed in seventeenth- and eighteenth-century salons; the dramatic narratives of the nineteenth century; down to the modernist subversions of poetic genre. From this perspective, the only French poetic genres with distinctly female associations are the *chanson de la mal mariée* (song of the mismarried woman) and the *chanson de toile* (weaving song) of the Middle Ages.

14. In what constitutes an exception, the speaker in Mlle de ***'s "The Fair Sex Avenged by the Fair Sex" (1701) chastises the phallic muse who inspires men's satires against women.

15. Joan Kelly, "Did Women Have a Renaissance?," *Women, History and Theory* (Chicago: University of Chicago Press, 1984), pp. 19-50.

16. For instance, French women did not obtain the vote until 1944.

17. Of course, there is also a lack of correlation between historical "events," as they have traditionally been defined, and the "facts" of feminist history, as their juxtaposition reveals in *New French Feminisms*, op. cit., pp. 3-27.

18. Germaine Brée, *Women Writers in France: Variations on a Theme* (New Brunswick: Rutgers University Press, 1973), p. 7. Although brief, this work is a useful feminist antidote to traditional literary histories.

19. For that reason, poems by Fanny de Beauharnais (1737–1813) and Anne-Marie Beaufort d'Hautpoul (1763–1837), for instance, were not included in the volume. Joan Kelly has argued that "women on the feminist side of the *querelle* repeated rather than advanced their ideas because of both "the repetitiveness to which they were responding" and "the lack of an underlying social movement to carry their thought forward." This second condition changed during the Revolution of 1789 when women of different classes came together in a common struggle that mutually advanced the scope of feminist practice and theory. See "Early Feminist Theory and the Querelle des Femmes," in Joan Kelly, *Women, History and Theory*, pp. 65-109.

20. To be sure, both "well-known" female prose writers and the far more numerous ones that remain outside the canon need to be the focus of feminist analysis. Additional names and information regarding French feminist writers can be found in *Histoire du féminisme français*, ed. Maïté Albistur and Daniel Armogathe, 2 vols. (Paris: Éditions des femmes, 1977).

21. According to literary historical categories, the verse of Vivien and Barney would be classified as decadent rather than symbolist poetry, although the periods with which those styles are identified overlap. Joyce Mansour is the only poet in this anthology clearly associated with Surrealism. In general, there is a particular dearth of information on French women's poetry in the period ranging from Symbolism through Surrealism.

22. Louise Labé, *Oeuvres poétiques* (Paris: Le Club Français du Meilleur Livre, 1967), preface, p. 12; translation, this author's.

23. The sonnet, translated by Judith Thurman, appears in *The Penguin Book of Women Poets*, ed. Carol Cosman, Joanne Keefe, and Kathleen Weaver (New York: Penguin, 1978), p. 109.

24. Among the "fine" contemporary poets excluded are Edith Boissonnas and Anne Hébert. For a recent discussion of this issue, see Richard Jones, ed., *Poetry and Politics, An Anthology of Essays* (New York: Quill, 1985), especially the essays of Robert Bly and Denise Levertov, who question the prevailing post-romantic identification of the poetic and the lyrical, which predicates

against the political. Although the volume includes important essays by Adrienne Rich, June Jordan, and Carolyn Forché, none deals specifically with the issue of literary quality and feminist ideology. Indeed, it is a question that feminist criticism has largely avoided, as Lillian Robinson emphasizes in "Treason Our Text: Feminist Challenges to the Literary Canon," *The New Feminist Criticism: Essays on Women, Literature and Theory*, ed. Elaine Showalter (New York: Pantheon, 1985), pp. 105-21.

25. In other words, it could be said that the criteria used are primarily oriented toward the signified, rather than the play of the signifier, the notion featured in latter-day definitions of poeticity.

26. Hélène Cixous, "The Laugh of the Medusa," *SIGNS: Journal of Women in Culture and Society*, Vol. I, No. 4, p. 255.

The Defiant Muse

FRENCH FEMINIST POEMS
FROM THE MIDDLE AGES
TO THE PRESENT

CHANSON DE TOILE

En un vergier lez une fontenele,
Dont clere est l'onde et blanche la gravele,
Siet fille a roi, sa main a sa massele:
En sospirant son douz ami rapele.
5   «Aé, cuens Guis amis!
La vostre amors me tout solaz et ris.

«Cuens Guis amis, com male destinee!
Mes peres m'a a un viellart donee,
Qui en cest mès m'a mise et enserree:
10 N'en puis eissir a soir n'a matinee.
      Aé, cuens Guis amis!
La vostre amors me tout solaz et ris.»

Li mals mariz en oï la deplainte,
Entre el vergier, sa corroie a desceinte:
15 Tant la bati qu'ele en fu perse et tainte.
Entre ses piez por pou ne l'a estainte.
      Aé, cuens Guis amis!
La vostre amors me tout solaz et ris.

La bele s'est de pameson levee,
20 Deu reclama par veraie pensee:
«Bels sires doulz, ja m'avez vos formee,
Donez moi, sire, que ne soie obliee,
Ke mes amis revengne ainz la vespree.»
      Aé, cuens Guis amis!
25 La vostre amors me tout solaz et ris.

Et Nostres Sires l'a molt bien escoutee:
Ez son ami qui l'a reconfortee.
Assis se sont soz une ante ramee:
La ot d'amors mainte larme ploree.
30   Aé, cuens Guis amis!
La vostre amors me tout solaz et ris.

ANONYMOUS BALLADS AND SONGS
(TWELFTH–THIRTEENTH CENTURIES)

WEAVING SONG

In an orchard a little fountain flows,
Shadowless ripples over white stones.
There a king's daughter, her head bowed low,
Remembers her sweet love and her sorrows.
5   "Alas, Count Guy! The cost
Of loving you is joy and laughter lost.

"Count Guy, my love, how cruel is my fate!
The old man my father gave me for mate
Keeps me in his house and locks every gate,
10 Nor can I leave it early or late.
    Alas, Count Guy! The cost
Of loving you is joy and laughter lost."

The cruel husband hears her, and soon
Appears in the orchard, his belt removes,
15 And beats her until she is so badly bruised
She falls at his feet in a deathlike swoon.
    Alas, Count Guy! The cost
Of loving you is joy and laughter lost.

The lady arose from her faint and prayed.
20 Her thoughts cried to God without constraint.
"Most gracious Lord, by whom I was made,
Let me not be forgotten! Oh, may
I see my love before nightfall today!"
    Alas, Count Guy! The cost
25 Of loving you is joy and laughter lost.

And Our Lord listened. Before the day's end
She had the sweet comfort of her friend.
Beneath a great tree whose branches bend,
Many tears for their love have fallen.
30 Alas, Count Guy! The cost
Of loving you is joy and laughter lost.

—*Patricia Terry*

MOTET

Hé Dieus! je n'ai pas mari
   Du tot a mon gré:
Il n'a cortoisie en li
   Ne joliveté!
5 Jone dame est bien traïe,
Par la foi que doi a Dé,
Qui a vilain est baillie
Pour faire sa volenté;
Ce fu trop mal devisé.
10 De mari sui mal païe:
D'ami m'en amenderai,
Et si m'en savoit mal gré
Mon mari, si face amie,
Car, voelle ou non, j'amerai!

NA CARENZA AL BEL CORS AVINEN

Iselda: Na Carenza al bel cors avinen,
donatz conseil a nos doas serors,
e car sabetz meils triar lo meillors,
conseillatz mi segon vostr' escïen:
5   penrai marit a nostra conoissenza?
o starai mi pulcela? e si m'agensa,
que far filhos no cug que sia bos;
essems maritz mi par trop angoissos.

Carenza: N'Alais i na Iselda, ensenhamen,
10   pretz e beltat, joven, frescas colors
conosc qu'avetz, cortez' e valors
sobre totas las autras conoissen;
per qu'ie.us conseil per far bona semenza
penre marit Coronat de Scienza,
15   en cui faretz fruit de filh glorïos:
retengud' es pulcel' a qui l'espos.

Iselda: Na Carenza, penre marit m'agenza,
mas far enfantz cug qu'es grans penedenza,
que las tetinhas pendon aval jos
20   e.l ventrilhs es cargatz e enojos.

MOTET

O God! I have no husband
  Suitable for me:
He shows me no courtesy
  Nor is he merry!
5 They do wrong to a young girl
When they give her to a churl
And leave her at his mercy—
By my faith in God, I swear
That is really too unfair!
10 Since I know I'm worth much more,
I shall even up the score
With a friend, and so should he;
For like it or not, I say
My loving heart won't fail to have its way!

—*Patricia Terry*

LADY CARENZA, WITH THE LOVELY, CHARMING BODY

Iselda: Lady Carenza, with the lovely, charming body,
      give us, two sisters, advice,
      for you know best what is best;
      with your knowledge advise me:
5   Should I take a husband of our acquaintance
      or remain a virgin? That appeals to me
      because I don't think having children is good;
      and being married seems far too distressing.

Carenza: Lady Alais and Lady Iselda, education,
10   excellence and beauty, youth, fresh color,
      I know you have; courtesy and valor,
      wisdom beyond all others;
      so I advise you, if you would sow good seed,
      to take as husband the Crown of Learning,
15   by whom you will bear fruit of glorious offspring;
      who marries him remains a virgin.

Iselda: Lady Carenza, taking a husband suits me,
      but having children is, I think, great punishment;
      for the breasts hang far down,
20   and the womb is laden and heavy.

Carenza: N'Alais i na Iselda, sovinenza
ajatz de mi, i lumbra de ghirenza;
quan i seretz, prejatz lo glorïos
qu'al departir mi retenga pres vos.

MOTET

Je sui joliete,
Sadete, pleisans,
Joine pucelete:
N'ai pas quinze ans,
5 Point mamelete
Selonc le tans:
Si deüsse aprendre
D'amors et entendre
Les samblans
10 Deduisans;
Mès je sui mise en prison.
De Diu ait maleïçon
Qui m'i mist!
Mal et vilanie
15 Et pechié fist
De tel pucelete
Rendre en abiete.
Trop i mefist, par ma foi;
En religion vif en grant anoi;
20 Dieus! car trop sui jonete;
Je sens les doz maus desoz ma ceinturete:
Honis soit de Diu qui me fist nonnete!

Carenza: Lady Alais and Lady Iselda, remember me,
and be the light of my salvation;
when you are there, pray to the glorious one
that at my departure he will keep me near you.

—*Joan M. Ferrante*

MOTET

I am merry,
Pretty, pleasing,
A young maiden;
Not quite fifteen;
5 Little breasts swelling
In keeping with the season;
I should indeed be learning
Of love, and discovering
Its charming
10 Face.
But I am put in prison.
God's curse on
Him who put me in this place!
Evil and villainy
15 And sin did he
To send to a nunnery
Such a maid as I.
I'faith, he did too great a wrong;
In religion I live in misery,
20 O God, for I am too young.
I feel beneath my belt the sweet pain:
May God curse him who made me nun.

—*Muriel Kittel*

ESTAT AI EN GRAN COSSIRIER

Estat ai en gran cossirier
Per un cavallier qu'ai agut,
E voill sia totz temps saubut
Cum ieu l'ai amat a sobrier;
5 Ara vei qu'ieu sui trahida,
Car ieu non li donei m'amor,
Don ai estat en gran error
En leit e quand sui vestida.

Ben volria mon cavallier
10 Tener un ser en mos bratz nut,
Qu'el s'en tengra per ereubut
Sol qu'a lui fesses cosseilier;
Car plus m'en sui abellida
No fetz Floris de Blancaflor.
15 Mon cor ieu l'autrei e m'amor,
Mon sen, mos oillz e ma vida.

Bels amics, avinens e bos,
Cora us tenrai en mon poder?
E que jagues ab vos un ser,
20 E qu'ie.us des un bais amoros!
Sapchatz, gran talen n'auria
Qu'ie.us tengues en luoc del marrit,
Ab so que m'aguessetz plevit
De far tot so qu'ieu volria.

COMTESSE DE DIE (TWELFTH CENTURY)

I HAVE BEEN IN GREAT DISTRESS

I have been in great distress
Through a knight that was my own;
Always I wish it to be known
How I loved him to excess;
5 Now I see I am betrayed,
For I did not give my love,
Wherein I made an error grave,
In bed and when in clothes arrayed.

I should like to hold my knight
10 Naked in my arms at eve,
That enraptured, he'd not leave
If be his pillow then I might;
I take greater pleasure in my love
Than Floris took in Blancheflor:
15 I granted him my heart, my love,
My mind, my eyes, my life itself.

Dear friend, so handsome and so good,
When shall I hold you in my power?
And loving kisses on you shower
20 When one night I lie with you!
Know how much I would desire
To have you in a husband's stead,
Provided you a vow had said
To do all I should desire.

—*Muriel Kittel*

TENSON

V.—Gui d'Ussel, be'm pesa de vos
  Car vos estz laissatz de chantar;
  E car vos i volgra tornar
  Per que sabetz d'aitals razos
5 Vuoill qe'm digatz si deu far egalmen
Dompna per drut, can lo quier francamen,
Cum el per lieis tot cant taing ad amor
Segon los dreitz que tenon l'amador.

U.—Dompna Na Maria, tenssos
10   E tot cant cujava laissar;
  Mas aoras non puosc estar
  Qu'ieu non chant als vostres somos;
E respon vos de la dompna breumen
Que per son drut deu far comunalmen
15 Cum el per lieis ses garda de ricor:
Qu'en dos amics non deu aver major.

V.—Gui, tot so don es cobeitos
  Deu drutz ab merce demandar,
  E dompna deu l'o autreiar,
20 Mas ben deu esgardar sazos;
E'l drutz deu far precs e comandamen
Cum per amig' e per dompn' eissamen,
E dompna deu a son drut far honor
Cum ad amic, mas non cum a seignor.

25 *U.*—Dompna, sai dizon de mest nos
  Que, pois que dompna vol amar,
  Engalmen deu son drut onrar,
  Pois engalmen son amoros;
E s'esdeven que l'am plus finamen,
30 E'l faich, e'l dich en deu far aparen,
E si ell'a fals cor ni trichador,
Ab bel semblan deu cobrir sa follor.

V.—Gui d'Ussel, ges d'aitals razos
  Non son li drut al comenssar,
35 Anz ditz chascus, can vol prejar,
Mans jointas et de genolhos:
«Dompna, voillatz que us serva francamen
Cum lo vostr'om» et ell' enaissi'l pren;

MARIE DE VENTADOUR (?–c. 1222)

DIALOGUE

V.—Gui d'Ussel, it disturbs me
    That you have ceased to sing;
    I would like you to begin again,
    Since you know the arguments.
5 I want you to tell me if a lady should
Treat her lover as her equal, when he asks openly,
As he does in all that pertains to love,
Under the law that lovers obey.

U.—Lady Maria, debates and
10   All song, I thought I had left behind,
    But now I cannot resist
    Singing at your request;
And I answer you, briefly, that the lady
Should treat her lover as he does her,
15 Without any thought of wealth,
For between two such friends there should be no master.

V.—Gui, all that he desires
    A lover should ask by her mercy,
    And the lady should promise it,
20 But she must choose her time;
The lover should beg and command
From friend and lady in the same way;
The lady should honor her lover
As a friend, but not as a lord.

25 *U.*—Lady, here among us they say
    That if a lady wants to love
    She should honor her lover equally,
    Since they are equally in love;
And if it happens that she loves more truly,
30 Her deeds and words should show it;
But if she has a false, deceiving heart,
She should cover her folly with a good semblance.

V.—Gui d'Ussel, those are not the arguments
    Of lovers as they begin;
35   Rather, when one starts to plead
    On his knees, with joined hands, he says:
"Lady, allow me to serve you openly
As your man"; and so she takes him;

Ieu lo jutge per dreich a trahitor,
40 Si's rend pariers ei's det per servidor.

  U.—Dompna, so es plaith vergoignos,
      Ad ops de dompn'a razonar
      Que cellui non teigna per par
      Ab cui a faich un cor de dos;
45 O vos diretz, e no us estara gen,
    Que'l drutz la deu amar plus leialmen,
    O vos diretz qu'il son par entre lor;
    Pois ren no'lh deu drutz mas quant per amor.

BALADE

    Cent balades ay cy escriptes,
    Trestoutes de mon sentement.
    Si en sont mes promesses quites
    A qui m'en pria chierement.
5   Nommée m'i suis proprement;
    Qui le vouldra savoir ou non,
    En la centiesme entierement
    En escrit y ay mis mon nom.

    Si pry ceulz qui les auront littes,
10 Et qui les liront ensement,
    Et partout ou ilz seront dittes,
    Qu'on le tiengne a esbatement,
    Sanz y gloser mauvaisement;
    Car je n'y pense se bien non,
15 Et au dernier ver proprement
    En escrit y ay mis mon nom.

    Ne les ay faittes pour merites
    Avoir, ne aucun paiement;
    Mais en mes pensées eslittes
20 Les ay, et bien petitement
    Souffiroit mon entendement

I judge him a real traitor who presents himself
40 As an equal, when he offered himself as a servant.

    U.—Lady, it is a shameful case
      When a woman argues
      That she holds him her equal
      With whom she has made one heart of two;
45 Either you will say, and this would be unworthy of you,
That the lover should love more faithfully,
Or you must say that they are equal, and thus
The lover owes no more than what he gives in love.

—*Joan M. Ferrante*

CHRISTINE DE PISAN (1364–c. 1430)

BALLAD

A hundred ballads I have written,
All of my own feelings.
Thus I have kept my promise
To the one who pressed me dearly.
5 I have named myself properly;
Whether this one wants to know it or not,
In this the hundredth,
I have set my name in writing.

I beg those who have read them,
10 And those who will read them,
Wherever they are recited,
That they be taken as entertainment,
Without bad glossing;
For I intend only good by it,
15 And in the last verse, properly,
I have set my name in writing.

I did not do them for reward,
Nor for any payment,
But from among my thoughts
20 I have chosen, and very gently
Breathed into them my understanding

Les faire dignes de renom,
Non pour tant desrenierement
En escrit y ay mis mon nom.

de *L'EPISTRE AU DIEU D'AMOURS*

En vers dient, Adam, David, Sanson,
Et Salemon et autres a foison
Furent deceuz par femme main et tart;
Et qui sera donc li homs qui s'en gart?
5 Li autres dit que moult sont decevables,
Cautilleuses, faulses et pou valables.
Autres dient que trop sont mençongieres,
Variables, inconstans et legieres.
D'autres pluseurs grans vices les accusent
10 Et blasment moult, sanz que riens les excusent.
Et ainsi font clers et soir et matin,
Puis en françois, leurs vers, puis en latin,
Et se fondent dessus ne sçay quelz livres
Qui plus dient de mençonges qu'uns yvres.
15 Ovide en dit, en un livre qu'il fist,
Assez de maulz, dont je tiens qu'il meffist,
Qu'il appella le Remede d'amours,
Ou leur met sus moult de villaines mours,
Ordes, laides, pleines de villenie.
20 Que telz vices aient je le luy nye,
Au deffendre de bataille je gage
Contre tous ceulz qui giter voldront gage;
Voire, j'entens des femmes honnorables,
En mes contes ne metz les non valables.
25 Si ont les clers apris tres leur enfance
Cellui livret en premiere science
De gramaire, et aux autres l'aprenent
A celle fin qu'a femme amer n'emprenent.
Mais de ce sont folz et perdent leur peine,
30 Ne l'empeschier si n'est fors chose vaine.
Car, entre moy et ma dame Nature,
Ne souffrerons, tant com le monde dure,
Que cheries et amées ne soient
Maugré touz ceulz qui blasmer les vouldroient,

To make them worthy of renown;
Not without good reason, therefore,
I have set my name in writing.

—*Joan M. Ferrante*

from *THE EPISTLE TO THE GOD OF LOVE*

Adam, David, Samson, Solomon,
And myriad others say in verse
They were deceived by woman, early and late:
What man then can protect himself?
5 Some say that many women are deceitful,
Wily, false, of little worth;
Others that too many are liars,
Fickle, flighty, and inconstant;
Still others accuse them of great vices,
10 Blaming them much, excusing them nothing.
Thus do the clerics, night and day,
First in French verse, then in Latin,
Based on who knows what books
That tell more lies than drunkards do.
15 Ovid in a book he wrote and called
Love's Remedy speaks of many faults,
But I believe he gravely erred.
He assigns to women base habits,
Makes them unclean, ugly, villainous.
20 I deny they have such vices;
In their defense I'll wage battle
With any who'll accept the challenge;
Of course, I mean honorable women;
The unworthy have no place in my tales.
25 Everything clerics learned from early
Childhood in grammar-school primers
And then teach to others is designed
To keep them from loving a woman.
But they are fools and waste their efforts;
30 Preventing it is hopeless.
Between me and my Lady Nature,
So long as the world lasts, we will not allow
Women to be uncherished and unloved,
Despite all those who would slander them,

35 Et qu'a pluseurs meismes qui plus les blasment
   N'ostent les cuers, et ravissent et emblent.
   Sanz nul frauder ne faire extorsion,
   Mais tout par nous et nostre imprecion,
   Ja n'en seront hommes si accointiez
40 Par soubtilz clers, ne pour touz leurs dittiez,
   Non obstant ce que mains livres en parlent
   Et les blasment que assez pou y valent.
   Et s'aucun dit qu'on doit les livres croire
   Qui furent fais d'ommes de grant memoire
45 Et de grant sens, qui mentir ne daignerent,
   Qui des femmes les malices proverent,
   Je leurs respons que ceulz qui ce escriprent
   En leurs livres, je trouve qu'ilz ne quistrent
   En leurs vies fors femmes decepvoir;
50 N'en pouoient yceulz assez avoir,
   Et tous les jours vouloient des nouvelles,
   Sanz loiaulté tenir, nez aux plus belles.
   Qu'en ot David et Salemon le roy?
   Dieu s'en courça et puni leur destroy.
55 D'autres pluseurs, et meismement Ovide
   Qui tant en voult, puis diffamer les cuide;
   Et tous les clers, qui tant en ont parlé,
   Plus qu'autre gens en furent affolé,
   Non pas d'une seule mais d'un millier.
60 Et, se tel gent orent dame ou moillier
   Qui ne feïst du tout a leur vouloir
   Ou qui meïst peine a les decevoir,
   Quel merveille? Car il n'est nulle doubte
   Que, quant uns homs en tel vilté se boute,
65 Il ne va pas querant les vaillans dames
   Ne les bonnes prisiées preudes femmes,
   Ne les cognoist, ne il n'en a que faire:
   Fors ceulz ne veult qui sont de son affaire;
   De filletes se pare et de pietaille.
70 Est il digne d'avoir chose qui vaille
   Un vilotier qui toutes met en conte
   Et puis cuide trop bien couvrir sa honte,
   Quant plus n'en puet et qu'il est ja vieulz homs,
   D'elles blasmer par ses soubtilz raisons?
75 Mais qui blasmast seulement les données
   Aux grans vices et les abandonnées,
   Et conseillast a elles non suivir
   Comme ilz ont fait, bien s'en pourroit suivir
   Et ce seroit chose moult raisonnable,

35 Nor let those who slander them most
   Take their hearts, steal and ravish them.
   Without any fraud or extortion,
   By us alone and our influence,
   Men will never again be so swayed
40 By subtle clerics nor by all their speeches,
   And despite what many books say,
   Defaming those deserving it so little.
   And if anyone says we must believe
   Books written by men of great minds
45 And intellect, who wouldn't stoop to lie
   When proving the malice of women,
   I reply to them who in their books
   Thus wrote that they strive in their lives
   For naught but deceiving women.
50 Those men can't get enough of it
   And every day wish for more, with no
   Loyalty, even to the loveliest.
   What of David and King Solomon?
   God, enraged, punished their wickedness.
55 As for others, Ovid in particular,
   Who has a grudge against women, wants to slander them,
   And all the clerics who've talked so much,
   More than others have they been driven mad,
   Not by a single woman but by a thousand.
60 If such men had a lady or a wife
   Who didn't do exactly as they wished
   Or went to lengths to deceive them,
   What's the wonder? For without a doubt
   When a man ferrets out such villainy
65 He does not seek ladies honorable,
   Good, cherished, virtuous women;
   He doesn't know them, has no use for them,
   Wants only those who'll satisfy his needs,
   Surrounds himself with nymphets and wenches.
70 Is he worthy of anything of value,
   This libertine telling tales on them all,
   Who thinks he's hidden his own shame well
   By defaming women with subtle arguments,
   When he's old in fact and can't do it any more?
75 But whosoever reproaches only
   Great sinners and shameless women
   And counsels others not to do
   As they have done, we would do well to listen.
   It would be a most reasonable lesson,

80   Enseignement digne, juste et louable,
     Sanz diffamer toutes generaument.
     Et a parler quant au decevement,
     Je ne sçay pas penser ne concevoir
     Comment femme peust homme decevoir:
85   Ne le va pas ne cerchier ne querir,
     Ne sus son lieu prier ne requerir;
     Ne pense a lui, ne ne lui en souvient,
     Quant decepvoir l'omme et tempter la vient.
     Tempter comment?—Voire par tel maniere
90   Qu'il n'est peine qui ne lui soit legiere
     A endurer et faissel a porter.
     A aultre riens ne se veult deporter
     Fors a pener a elles decevoir,
     Pour y mettre cuer et corps et avoir.
95   Et par long temps dure la trioleine,
     Souventes fois avient, et celle peine,
     Non obstant ce que moult souvent y faillent,
     A leurs esmes ja soit ce qu'ils travaillent.
     Et de ceulz parle Ovide en son traittié
100 De l'Art d'amours; car pour la grant pitié
     Qu'il ot de ceulz compila il un livre,
     Ou leur escript et enseigne a delivre
     Comment pourront les femmes decevoir
     Par faintises et leur amour avoir;
105 Si l'appella livre de l'Art d'amours;
     Mais n'enseigne condicions ne mours
     De bien amer, mais ainçois le contraire.
     Car homs qui veult selon ce livre faire
     N'amera ja, combien qu'il soit amez,
110 Et pour ce est li livres mal nommez,
     Car c'est livre d'Art de grant decevance,
     Tel nom li don, et de fausse apparence.
     Et comment donc quant fresles et legieres,
     Et tournables, nyces et pou entieres
115 Sont les femmes, si com aucuns clers dient,
     Quel besoing donc est il a ceulz qui prient
     De tant pour ce pourchacier de cautelles?
     Et pour quoy tost ne s'i accordent elles
     Sanz qu'il faille art n'engin a elles prendre?
120 Car pour chastel pris ne fault guerre emprendre.
     Et meismement pouëte si soubtil
     Comme Ovide, qui puis fu en exil,
     Et Jehan de Meun ou Romant de la Rose,
     Quel long proces! quel difficile chose!

80 Worthy, just, and laudable teaching,
That doesn't condemn women as a whole.
And speaking of deceptiveness,
I can't conceive or imagine
How a woman can deceive a man:
85 It isn't she who seeks and looks for him,
Nor begs below her station, nor implores,
She doesn't think or reflect on him:
It's the man who comes tempting and deceiving her.
She, tempt him how? Only in a way
90 That for him all burdens become
Easy to endure and bear.
Men have no interest in other things
Except deceiving women to make them give
Their heart, body, and all wealth.
95 Man's Lenten season may last awhile,
As it often does, but this hardship
(Though it often fails to work for many)
Is used solely for their own advantage.
And of these men speaks Ovid in his treatise
100 On the Art of Love; out of great pity
For them did he compile a book
Wherein he writes and teaches openly
How they can deceive women
And gain their love by pretense.
105 He called the book the Art of Love,
But teaches neither rules nor customs
Of loving well, the opposite instead.
A man who wishes to go by this book,
However much he's loved, will never love,
110 And so this book is badly named,
For it's the Art of Great Deception;
That other name creates a false impression.
Besides, how is it that if women are
As frail, frivolous, changeable,
115 Naive, and imperfect as clerics say,
That certain men have such a need
To pursue this collection of wiles?
And why, if women never agree,
Does one need arts or snares to capture them?
120 To capture a castle one need not wage a war.
But even in works of poets as subtle
as Ovid, sent into exile,
Or Jean de Meun in the Romance of the Rose,
What a drawn-out affair! What an ordeal!

125 Et sciences et cleres et obscures
Y met il la et de grans aventures!
Et que de gent soupploiez et rovez
Et de peines et de baraz trouvez
Pour decepvoir sanz plus une pucelle,
130 S'en est la fin, par fraude et par cautelle!
A foible lieu faut il donc grant assault?
Comment peut on de près faire grant saut?
Je ne sçay pas ce veoir ne comprendre
Que grant peine faille a foible lieu prendre,
135 Ne art n'engin, ne grant soubtiveté.
Dont convient il tout de neccessité,
Puis qu'art convient, grant engin et grant peine,
A decevoir femme noble ou villaine,
Qu'elz ne soient mie si variables,
140 Comme aucun dit, n'en leur fait si muables.
Et s'on me dit li livre en sont tuit plein,
C'est le respons a maint dont je me plain,
Je leur respons que les livres ne firent
Pas les femmes, ne les choses n'i mirent
145 Que l'en y list contre elles et leurs meurs;
Si devisent a l'aise de leurs cuers
Ceulz qui plaident leur cause sanz partie,
Sanz rabatre content, et grant partie
Prenent pour eulx, car de legier offendent
150 Les batailleux ceulz qui ne se deffendent.
Mais se femmes eussent les livres fait
Je sçay de vray qu'autrement fust du fait,
Car bien scevent qu'a tort sont encoulpées,
Si ne sont pas a droit les pars coupées,
155 Car les plus fors prenent la plus grant part,
Et le meilleur pour soy qui pieces part.
Encor dient li felon mesdisant,
Qui les femmes vont ainsi desprisant,
Que toutes sont fausses seront et furent
160 N'oncques encor nulles loiaulté n'urent,
Et qu'amoureux telles, qui qu'elles soient,
Toutes treuvent quant les femmes essoient;
A toutes fins leur est le tort donné,
Qui qu'ait meffait, sur elles est tourné;
165 Mais c'est maudit; et on voit le rebours;
Car, quant ad ce qui afflert a amours,
Trop de femmes y ont esté loiales
Sont et seront, non obstant intervales
Ou faussetéz, baraz ou tricheries,

125 Learning both obscure and clear
   Does he insert, and great adventures!
   So many men implored and begged,
   So many labors and rules invented
   To deceive one simple maiden girl?
130 That's the goal through fraud and wile! Against
   A weak place does one need a vast assault?
   Why make a great leap from so nearby?
   I can't see this or understand
   That great effort is needed to take a weak place
135 Or art or snare or great subtlety,
   Which are deemed wholly necessary.
   Since artifice is needed, great contraptions,
   Great care to deceive women noble or base,
   They must not be as inconstant
140 As some say, nor their actions so changeable.
   And if I'm told books abound with such ideas,
   To that refrain I do object;
   I must reply: the books were not written
   By women, nor did they put in those things
145 One reads against them and their ways.
   Men imagine freely to their heart's content,
   Who plead their case 'gainst no opponent,
   Tell their tale without drawing in their horns
   And take the lion's share; for battlers
150 On a whim attack those who are defenseless.
   But if women had produced the books,
   I know the product would be different.
   They know well they are wrongly blamed.
   The parts are not rightly divided;
155 The mightiest takes the largest share
   And the best for him who doles out the pieces.
   Still more, these lying rascals
   Who go 'round maligning women say
   That all are false, will be and were,
160 Never did any loyalty possess;
   That even those women who love, whoever they are,
   So discover when loyal they try to be.
   One finds fault with them in every case;
   Whoever's done wrong, it's blamed on them.
165 But that's scandalous; it's just the reverse:
   For in fact it happens in love
   That too many women have been loyal
   Are and will be, despite the times
   They were victims of falseness,

170   Qu'on leur ait fait et maintes manteries.
       Que fut jadis Medée au faulz Jason?
       Trés loialle, et lui fist la toison
       D'or conquerir par son engin soubtil,
       Dont il acquist loz plus qu'autres cent mil.
175   Par elle fu renommé dessus tous,
       Si lui promist que loial ami doulz
       Seroit tout sien, mais sa foy lui menti
       Et la laissa pour autre et s'en parti.
       Que fu Dido, roÿne de Cartage,
180   De grant amour et de loial corage,
       Vers Eneas qui, exillé de Troye,
       Aloit par mer las, despris et sanz joye.
       Presque pery lui et ses chevaliers?
       Recueilli fu, dont lui estoit mestiers
185   De la belle, qu'il faussement deçut;
       Car a trés grant honneur elle receut
       Lui et ses gens et trop de bien lui fist;
       Mais puis après vers elle tant meffist,
       Non obstant ce qu'il lui eust foy promise
190   Et donnée s'amour, voire, en faintise,
       Si s'en parti, ne puis ne retorna,
       Et autre part la sienne amour torna;
       Dont a la fin celle, pour s'amistié,
       Morut de dueil, dont ce fu grant pitié.
195   Penelope la feme Ulixès,
       Qui raconter vouldroit tout le procès
       De la dame, trop trouveroit a dire
       De sa bonté ou il n'ot que redire:
       Trés belle fu requise et bien amée,
200   Noble, sage, vaillant et renommée.
       D'aultres pluseurs, et tant que c'est sanz nombre,
       Furent et sont et seront en ce nombre;
       Mais je me tais adès d'en plus compter,
       Car long procès seroit a raconter.[. . .]   (1.267–470)

205   Et ainsi sont les femmes diffamées
       De pluseurs gens et a grant tort blasmées
       Et de bouche et en pluseurs escrips,
       Ou qu'il soit voir ou non, tel est li crys.
       Mais, qui qu'en ait mesdit ou mal escript,
210   Je ne truis pas en livre n'en escript
       Qui de Jhesus parle ou de sa vie
       Ou de sa mort pourchacée d'envie,
       Et mesmement des Apostres les fais

170 Ruses, trickery, and many lies.
   How then was Medea with Jason the false?
   Most faithful; by her subtle artfulness
   He captured the golden fleece
   For which he gained more praises than a thousand men.
175 Through her was he renowned above all,
   And swore he'd be her loyal, gentle friend,
   Completely hers; but his pledge he broke,
   He left her for another and departed.
   What of Dido, queen of Carthage?
180 She had great love and faithful heart
   For Aeneas who, exiled from Troy,
   Seafaring, was dishonored, joyless, weary,
   Almost dead, he and his comrades.
   He was restored by the beautiful lady
185 Whose art this was, and whom he falsely deceived.
   She did receive him and his men
   With great honor; too good was she to him.
   Soon after he acted so wickedly
   Despite the faith he'd promised and the love
190 He'd given, love of course false-hearted.
   Then he left and never returned,
   But turned elsewhere the love that was hers.
   In the end then for his friendship
   She died of grief, and a great pity this was.
195 Penelope, wife to Ulysses,
   Whoever would recount that lady's
   Whole ordeal would find too much to say
   Of her goodness; it can only be retold:
   Very beautiful, desired and well loved,
200 Noble, wise, worthy, and renowned.
   So many others like these there were,
   Are and will be: they are countless;
   But I'll refrain from counting any more,
   For too long a tale 'twould be to tell.[...]

205 So it is that women are slandered
   By many men and wrongly blamed
   By word of mouth and many texts;
   True or not, it's the same accusation.
   But whatever malice has been said or written,
210 I do not find it in any book or writing
   That speaks of Jesus or his life
   Or his death pursued from envy;
   And surely not the Acts of the Apostles,

Qui pour la foy porterent maint dur fais,
215 N'euvangile qui nul mal en tesmoigne,
Mais maint grant bien, mainte haulte besoigne,
Grant prudence, grant sens et grant constance,
Perfaitte amour, en toy grant arrestance,
Grant charité, fervente volenté,
220 Ferme et entier corage entalenté
De Dieu servir, et grant semblant en firent,
Car mort ne vif oncques ne le guerpirent.
Fors des femmes fu de tous delaissié
Le doulz Jhesus, navré, mort et blecié.
225 Toute la foy remaint en une femme.
Si est trop folz qui d'elles dit diffamme,
Ne fust ores que pour la reverence
De la haulte Roÿne, en remembrance
De sa bonté, qui tant fu noble et digne,
230 Que du filz Dieu porter elle fu digne!
Grant honneur fist a femme Dieu le pere
Qui faire en voult son espouse et sa mere,
Temple de Dieu a la Trinité jointe.
Bien estre doit femme joyeuse et cointe
235 Qui autelle, comme Celle, fourme a;
Car oncques Dieux nulle rien ne fourma
De digneté semblable, n'aussi bonne,
Fors seulement de Jhesus la personne.
Si est trop folz qui de riens les ramposne
240 Quant femme est assise en si hault trone
Coste son filz, a la destre du Pere,
C'est grant honneur a femmenine mere.
Si ne trouvons qu'oncques les desprisast
Le bon Jhesus, mais amast et prisast.
245 Dieu la forma a sa digne semblance
Et lui donna savoir et cognoiscence
Pour soy sauver, et don d'entendement.
Si lui donna fourme moult noblement,
Et fut faitte de moult noble matiere,
250 Car ne fu pas du lymon de la terre
Mais seulement de la coste de l'omme,
Lequel corps ja estoit, c'en est la somme,
Le plus noble des choses terriennes.
Et les vrayes hystoires anciennes
255 De la Bible, qui ne puet mençonge estre,
Nous racontent qu'en Paradis terrestre
Fu formée femme premierement
Non pas l'omme; mais du decevement,

Who for the faith suffered many horrid blows.
215 Nor does any gospel attest to women's evil,
But rather great good, many lofty works,
Great prudence, constancy, intelligence,
Perfect love, true strength in faith,
Great charity, fervent will,
220 Firm and full heart made for serving God
That they displayed most visibly.
They never abandoned him, alive or dead;
Sweet Jesus, grieving, wounded, in agony,
Shunned by all, except for women.
225 In one single woman all faith lies
(It is thus madness to slander them);
For this exalted queen, in memory
Of her goodness, there was only reverence,
So noble and worthy was she,
230 Worthy enough to bear the son of God!
Great honor God the Father paid,
Who wished to make woman his wife and mother,
Temple of God joined to the Trinity.
Joyful and proud women should truly be,
235 Since they have the same form as she.
For never has God formed anything
As good or of like dignity,
Jesus the sole exception.
To reproach them for trifles is sheer madness
240 When a woman is seated on the highest throne,
Next to her son, to the right of the Father;
'Tis a great honor for woman as mother.
We never find good Jesus belittling women,
But rather loving and cherishing them.
245 God truly formed woman in his likeness
And granted her knowledge, intelligence,
Understanding for her salvation.
Thus he gave her a form most noble,
Of noblest matter making her,
250 And not at all of earthly clay,
But solely of the rib of man
Who already existed, the most noble,
The summit of earthly things.
And the authentic old stories
255 Of the Bible, which cannot be lies,
Tell us that in earthly Paradise
Woman was the finest creation;
It wasn't man. Of the deception

Dont on blasme dame Eve nostre mere,
260 Dont s'ensuivi de Dieu sentence amere,
Je di pour vray qu'oncq Adam ne deçut
Et simplement de l'anemi conçut
La parole qu'il lui donna a croire,
Si la cuida estre loial et voire,
265 En celle foy de lui dire s'avance;
Si ne fu donc fraude ne decepvance,
Car simplece, sanz malice celée,
Ne doit estre decepvance appellée.
Nul ne deçoit sanz cuidier decepvoir,
270 Ou aultrement decepvance n'est voir.
Quelz grans maulz donc en pevent estre diz?
Par desservir n'ont elles paradis?
De quelz crismes les peut on accuser?
Et s'aucuns folz a leur amour muser
275 Veulent, par quoy a eulz mal en conviegne,
N'en pevent mais; qui est sage s'en tiegne:
Qui est deceu et cuidoit decepvoir
Nulz fors lui seul n'en doit le blasme avoir.[...]   (1.558–628)

Par ces preuves justes et veritables
280 Je conclus que tous hommes raisonables
Doivent femmes prisier, cherir, amer,
Et ne doivent avoir cuer de blasmer
Elles de qui tout homme est descendu;
Ne leur soit pas mal pour le bien rendu,
285 Car c'est la riens ou monde par droiture
Que homme aime mieulz et de droitte nature.
Si est moult lait et grant honte a blasmer
La riens qui soit que l'en doit plus amer
Et qui plus fait a tout homme de joye.
290 Homs naturel sanz femmes ne s'esjoye:
C'est sa mere, c'est sa suer, c'est s'amie,
Et pou avient qu'a homs soit anemie;
C'est son droit par qui a lui est semblable,
La riens qui plus lui puet estre agreable,
295 Ne on n'y puet pris ne los conquester
A les blasmer, mais grant blasme acquester;
N'il n'est blasme si lait ne si nuisant
Comme tenus estre pour mesdisant,
Voire encor plus especialement
300 De diffamer femmes communement:
C'est un vice diffamable et villain,
Je le deffens a homme quant je l'aim;

For which Eve our mother is accused
260 And from which God's harsh sentence followed,
I say, in truth, she never deceived Adam,
But merely learned from the enemy
The word he gave her to believe.
She thought it earnest, true, and
265 Acting on that belief, told Adam;
Thus there was no deception or fraud
For simpleness that hides no malice
Must not be called deception.
No one deceives without wanting to deceive,
270 Or then 'tis not true deception.
What great evils can be said of women?
By serving don't women gain Paradise?
Of what crimes can one accuse them?
And if madmen want to trifle with
275 Their love, they never can, for evil
Will befall them: this the wise man avoids.
Whoever intended to deceive and is deceived
Has no one but himself to blame.[. . .]

By this evidence fair and true,
280 I conclude that all reasonable men
Should esteem, cherish, and love women
And have no desire to malign
Those from whom all men are born;
The good they do deserves not evil.
285 She's what man should love best in the world
By both rights and nature's laws;
Thus it's most vile and shameful
To slander the thing one most should love
And that gives all men joy. By nature
290 Man without woman feels no joy:
She's his mother, sister, lover,
And rarely ever his enemy;
It's her right, and in this she's like him,
She who is to man most pleasing.
295 By slandering them one can win
Nor praise nor renown, only great censure.
Nor is there censure so vile or harmful
As censure reserved for slanderers;
Indeed, ever so much more
300 For defaming women as a whole:
This vice itself is damnable and base.
I forbid it in a man I love,

Si s'en gard donc trestout noble corage,
Car bien n'en puet venir, mais grant domage,
305 Honte, despit et toute villennie;
Qui tel vice a n'est pas de ma maisnie.[...]   (1.721–748)

(1399)

NE TROP NE POU AU CUER ME SENS FRAPPÉE

VIII. LA DAME

Ne trop ne pou au cuer me sens frappée
Des dars d'Amours que on dit qui font grant guerre
A mainte gent, mais ne suis atrappée
La Dieu mercy! es las ne en la serre
5   Du dieu d'Amours.
Je ne lui fais requestes ne clamours,
Je vif sans lui en plaisance et en joye,
Par amour n'aim ne amer ne vouldroie.

Ne n'ay paour que je soie happée
10 Ne par regars, par dons ne par long erre,
Ne par parler mignot enveloppée,
Carl il n'est homs qui mon cuer peust acquerre;
   Ne a secours
N'y viegne nul, car escondit le cours
15 De moy seroit, et tantost lui diroie:
Par amours n'aim ne amer ne vouldroie.

Et beau mocquier m'ay de femme atrappée
En tel donger ou mieulx lui vaulsist querre
Pour soy tuer ou coustel ou espée,
20 Car perdu a du tout honneur sur terre.
   Pour ce a toujours
En cest estat je pense user mes jours,
A tous diray, s'il avient que on m'en proie:
Par amours n'aim ne amer ne vouldroie.

25 Prince d'amours, a vo Court que feroie?
Par amours n'aim ne amer ne vouldroie.

For a noble heart does no such thing;
No good comes of it, only great injury,
305 Shame, spitefulness, and baseness;
Who has this vice is outside my company.

—*Sarah Spence*

FROM DARTS OF LOVE THAT DO SUCH DOLE

VIII. THE LADY

From darts of Love that do such dole
I bear no wound, nor deep, nor small.
Many are scarred, but I am whole,
Unsnared, so Heaven be thanked! no thrall
5   In Cupid's chain.
No need for me to plead or plain.
In joy I live; alone I go;
I love not love, nor want its woe.

I have no fear, though men cajole
10 With glance, pursuit, gifts prodigal,
With sweet small words that charm the soul
For none shall win my heart at all.
   Then spare your pain;
Who comes to plead must plead in vain.
15 Begone, I'd say, for all must know
I love not love, nor want its woe.

Lost hearts! to me your doom is droll.
If in such plight one chance to fall,
Better for her the bell should toll,
20 For honor is gone beyond recall.
   So, I maintain,
In this fair state I shall remain;
To all who come, my word is No,
I love not love, nor want its woe.

25 Prince Love, your court I scorn. Why so?
I love not love, nor want its woe.

—*Naomi Lewis*

du *LIVRE DE LA MUTACION DE FORTUNE*

CI DIT DES INFORTUNES DES FEMMES

Mais pour ce que les destinees
Me semblent moult infortunees
Souvent avient dessus le sexe
Femenin, me plaist que j'ennexe
5   En mon dit un pou de la male
Fortune, qui femmes ravale,
Car Nature et pitié m'y tire,
Qui me fait plaindre leur martire.
Hé! Dieux! Quel dolente aventure
10 Avient a femme et qui moult dure,
Quant Fortune la fait embatre
A mal mari, qui la veult batre,
Et non pas veult tant seulement,
Mais le fait souvent, tellement
15 Qu'il y pert en dolente guise,
Ou pour pou de cause, et s'avise
Comment il pourra chagriner
Sa femme, par ymaginer
Riotes, ou n'a fons, ne rive;
20 Ne peut durer se il n'estrive,
Ou fait le jaloux, ou il l'est,
Par quoy quanqu'il voit lui desplaist,
Si n'est pas petite meschance!
N'a pas gaigné qui a tel chance!
25 Ou quant il jeue tout aux dez,
Ou de vin est souvent hourdez,
Puis rigne et gronce et veult tout batre,
Et les enfens brayent en l'aatre.
Ha! Dieux! Que c'est doulx paradis!
30 Et faut estre en crainte tousdis,
Car c'est ce qui parfait l'estraintte
Que la subgecion contrainte.
Les autres, par pou d'achoison,
Seront blasmees sanz raison
35 Par quelque faulce gorge gloute.
(Que mau feu toutes les engloute!)
Car par elles maintes diffames
Sont mises sur hommes et femmes,
Qui oncques n'en furent coulpables,
40 Ains sont bourdes non veritables.
Helas! Mais quel fortune amere
Cuert sus a femme, et quel misere,

from *THE BOOK OF FORTUNE'S CHANGES*

HERE ARE TOLD THE MISFORTUNES OF WOMEN

Because a destiny most
Unfortunate seems to me
Oft to befall the female sex,
To my poem I wish to add
5 A little about the ill
Fortune that oppresses women;
By nature I do this and by pity,
Which make me lament their martyrdom.
O gods! What sorrowful times
10 Come to pass, and how long-lasting
When Fortune has woman bound
To a wicked husband, who wants
To beat her, and not only wants to
But often does, so much
15 That he succumbs for a sorry excuse
Or for little reason, knowing
He can anger and aggrieve
Her by inventing quarrels
Unfounded and unending;
20 He can't exist if he doesn't bicker;
He either plays the jealous man or is one
And everything he sees irks him—
That's more than a little bad luck!
With luck like that, you've got nothing.
25 Whether he's betting all on dice
Or on wine is getting loaded,
He grumbles, groans, would strike everyone in sight,
And the children bray at home.
O gods! What sweet paradise!
30 One must always go in fear:
That's what makes perfect the constraint
That subjection imposes.
Other women, for little cause,
Will be blamed without reason
35 By some voracious throaty voices
(May hellfire devour them all!)—
By them many rumors slanderous,
Tales tall and untrue,
Are pinned on men and women
40 Who guilty never were.
Alas! What bitter fortune
And what misery rules o'er woman

Quant pert mari bon et paisible,
Qui preudoms l'avoit et sensible
45 Selon soy, et qui l'avoit chiere!
A bon droit en fait mate chiere!
Lors peut elle dire que seure
Lui queurt Fortune, car en l'eure
Lui sourdroit plais de toutes pars;
50 Se parens avoit, pour les pars
Playderont a la lasse femme;
S'ilz pevent, ja n'en sera dame
De chose qu'elle ait; et debteurs
Sourdront et desloyaulx menteurs,
55 Et diront que cil leur devoit,
Qui du sien presté leur avoit
Peut estre, mais n'y aura preuve,
Et ainsi la dolente veuve
Sera semonce et adjournee
60 En plusieurs cours et malmenee
Par cabusemens et plais querre
Contre elle, d'eritage et terre
Desheritee et desnuee;
Et tel l'a mainte foiz chuee
65 Et flatee, et honneur lui fait,
Et moult si offert en tout fait,
En temps que le mari vivoit,
Qui grant estat et bel avoit,
Qui a present le doz lui tourne
70 Et peut estre moult mal l'atourne
Par cautelles, et fait entendre
Que le mari, qu'i de cuer tendre
Amoit, estoit moult son tenu
Et que par lui a soustenu
75 Son estat, par prester avoir,
Si lui couvient le sien ravoir,
Et par quelque couleur monstrer.
La simple femme, qui entrer
Craindra en plait, fera accort
80 En payant, pour fuïr descort.
En plus, de mille guises sont
Les meschiefs, que les vesves ont,
Mais leur confort sont plours et larmes
Et, se parler comme clerc d'armes
85 Je doy, en ce cas, ce scet Dieux,
Qui leur vueille alegier leurs dieulx!
Mais s'il avient qu'ayent a faire,

When a good husband she does lose,
A gentleman, quiet and sensitive
45 Whom she felt held her dear,
And rightly made her his dear mate.
Then she can surely say
That Fortune has it in for her,
For soon claims press in from all sides.
50 If the weary woman has relatives,
They'll plead for their share.
If they can prevail, she will
Have nothing left; and debtors
And faithless liars will swarm, claiming
55 That such amount her husband owed them
For what he'd borrowed from them;
Perhaps, but no proof there'll be.
And so the sorrowful widow
Will be summoned, beleaguered
60 By false claims and pleas lodged
Against her in several courts,
Disinherited and
Divested of property and land.
And the man who many a time caressed
65 And flattered, paid her honor,
And offered so much in every way
While her husband with his great and
Beautiful estate was still alive,
Now turns his back on her
70 And against her speaks much ill;
And makes it understood by ruse
That the husband who loved with tender
Heart had been much in his debt,
Since the estate had been supported
75 By the many loans he had extended;
And so she should see things his way
And show it in some fashion.
The guileless woman fearing
A lawsuit will come to terms
80 And pay, all discord to avoid.
In a thousand different forms come
The troubles widows suffer;
But their only comfort is cries and tears;
And I must like a beadle speak
85 In this case, as God knows;
Who would lighten their sorrows!
But if it happens that they take

En cas qu'il leur soit neccessaire,
Pourchacier le leur pour le mieulx,
90 Par quoy frequantent en maint lieux,
Quieulx amis y trouveront elles?
Est il le temps que damoiselles
Ou dames ou femmes quelconques
Soustenoient roys, ducs ou contes
95 Et les portoient en leur droit?
Nennil, faillis est orendroit,
Et justice, qui favourable
Leur doit estre, n'est pas durable
Adés pour elles, se de quoy
100 Bien payer n'ont, mais en requoy
On leur dira belles leçons!
Se beaulx corps ou belles façons
Ont, ou jeunece seulement,
Bien seront et notablement
105 Conseillees, mais tel conseil
A nulle croire ne conseil,
Car conseil de honteux effect
Ne fait acroire en nesun fait.
Ainsi charité morte treuvent;
110 Ce scevent celles qui l'espreuvent!   (III, 1.6943–7052)

(1404)

du *TRIOMPHE DES MUSES CONTRE AMOUR:*
COMPLAINTE D'UNE DAMOISELLE

J'ai peur d'être dédit,
Ou n'avoir le crédit,
O Muses gracieuses,
De pouvoir répéter,
5 Et ici réciter
Vos forces vertueuses.

Or l'essai j'en ferai,
Et point ne cesserai
De publier, et dire

Action in a case where they must
Do for themselves as best they can
90 By frequenting many chambers,
What friends will they find there?
Is this a time when girls,
Ladies, or women of any sort
Find support in kings, dukes, or counts
95 To help them in their rights?
Not at all, not in these depraved days,
When justice, which should be
For them, does not prevail
If they've no money to pay.
100 Instead in secret chambers
Fine lessons they'll be taught!
If beautiful bodies or manners
They do have, or youth alone,
They'll be well and notably
105 Counseled, but such counsel
Is hardly to be credited,
For counsel with shameful ends
Brings credit to nothing whatever.
Thus is charity found dead—
110 As women who try it soon discover!

—*Sarah Spence*

PERNETTE DU GUILLET (c. 1520–1545)

from *THE TRIUMPH OF THE MUSES OVER LOVE:
A MAIDEN'S LAMENT*

I fear to be gainsaid
Or lack the credit,
O gracious Muses,
To reiterate
5 And here recite
Your powers so courageous.

But I'll make the attempt
And never cease
To publish and recount

10 Le merveilleux débat
     D'Amour, et le combat
     Contre vous et son ire.

     Mais par vous fut dompté,
     Et du tout surmonté,
15 N'ayant plus de puissance,
     Hélas! qu'il fut dépit
     Ce Dieu faible et petit,
     De voir son impuissance.

     Lui qui par ses efforts,
20 A vaincu les plus forts,
     Il est vaincu des Dames:
     Et par elles repris,
     Lié, mené, et pris,
     El souffre grands diffames.

25 Je l'ai vu promener
     Par la ville, et mener
     Ayant au cou la corde:
     Etant ainsi captif
     Cupido déceptif
30 Criait miséricorde.

     Amour outrecuidé
     Qui eût jamais cuidé
     Qu'eusses contre les Muses
     Onques voulu penser,
35 De guerre commencer,
     Vu qu'on connaît tes ruses.

     Craignais-tu point, hélas!
     De tomber dans les lacz
     De Pallas la Déesse?
40 Savais-tu pas combien
     Etait grand son lien,
     Sa force, et sa prouesse?

     Savais-tu point aussi,
     (Enfant sans nul souci)
45 Qu'Erato ma voisine
     Avait devant les yeux
     Honneur, qui vaut trop mieux
     Que toi, ni ta doctrine?

     Somme: Craignais-tu point
50 D'irriter en ce point
     Les Muses tant exquises?

10 The marvelous debate
   Of Love, of his campaign
   'Gainst you, and his anger.

   But beaten he was by you
   And utterly surpassed,
15 Having no more power,
   Alas! How chagrined was he
   This feeble little god,
   To behold his impotence.

   He who by his efforts
20 Conquered the strongest
   Is vanquished by Ladies,
   By them admonished,
   Caught, bound, and led away,
   Suffering great infamy.

25 I've seen him paraded
   Through town, and led
   With a rope 'round his neck;
   And in this captive state,
   Cupid, the deceiver,
30 For mercy would cry out.

   Who would have thought
   That you, o'erweening Love,
   Would ever dream
   Of starting up a war
35 'Gainst the Muses all,
   You whose tricks we know?

   Didn't you fear, alas!
   To fall into the nets
   Of Pallas the Goddess?
40 And didn't you know
   How great were her bonds,
   Her force, and her prowess?

   And didn't you know, besides
   (Child without a care),
45 That my neighbor Erato
   Had honor most in mind,
   Which has far greater worth
   Than you and your creed?

   In short: didn't you fear
50 That you'd irritate
   The Muses exquisite?

Tu pouvais bien savoir,
Que tu n'avais pouvoir
Contre leurs entreprises.

55 Or toutes t'ont laissé
Navré, captif, blessé,
Et sans force, et sans gloire:
Amour, va te cacher,
Tu ne dois plus tâcher
60 D'avoir d'elles victoire.

Après avoir fouetté
Et rudement traité
Ce faux dieu lunatique,
Elles ont bâti dessus
65 Le haut mont Parnassus
Un temple magnifique:

Excellent en beauté
Et ont à Loyauté
Consacré leur ouvrage.
70 Toutes les vis monter
Sur ce mont, et chanter
D'un merveilleux courage.

O quel plaisir de voir
En femmes tel savoir,
75 Et si douce harmonie!
O quel soulas d'ouïr
Tels accords, et jouir
De telle compagnie! [...]

Les Muses triomphaient,
80 Toutes philosophaient,
Disputant des sciences:
Et en ce sacré lieu,
Tenaient propos de Dieu,
Blâmant leurs consciences.

85 Au pied du mont, vaincu
Cupido, sans écu,
Caressait les aucunes:
Ses malheurs leur contait:
Mais aux Muses portrait
90 Toujours grandes rancunes.

Celles-là lui ont fait
Contentement parfait

Surely you could have known
That 'gainst their enterprises
You had no power.

55 So now they've left you,
Saddened, captive, wounded,
Without force or glory.
Love, go away and hide;
A victory over them
60 You must never try again.

Once they had thrashed
And treated harshly
This false, lunatic god,
They proceeded to build
65 A temple magnificent
On high Mount Parnassus.

This work of art,
Outstanding in beauty,
They devoted to Loyalty.
70 I saw them all ascend
This hill and sing
With wondrous heartiness.

What a pleasure to see
Such knowledge in women,
75 And so sweet a harmony!
What solace to hear
Such chords and enjoy
Such fine company![...]

The Muses were triumphant;
80 They all philosophized,
Discussing sciences.
And in this sacred place
Examining their conscience,
Words of God they spoke.

85 At the foot of the hill,
Vanquished Cupid, unshielded,
Caressed sundry women,
Told them his troubles,
Ever harboring 'gainst the Muses
90 Feelings of great rancor.

Those women made him
Perfectly contented,

Lui donnant jouissance
Des biens du corps, du coeur,
95 En le faisant vainqueur
De leur force et puissance.

Médisants envieux,
Qui dites en tous lieux
Que j'ai trop de louange
100 A nos Muses donné,
J'en suis tout étonné,
Et cela m'est étrange.

Contre moi réclamer
Devez, et me blâmer,
105 (Ainsi comme je pense)
De n'avoir par écrit
Assez leur bon esprit
Prisé, ni leur science.

Le loz de celles-ci
110 Est assez éclairci,
Selon ma fantaisie:
Mais le bruit et renom,
Et des autres le nom
Se voit en Poésie.

(1545)

ODE PREMIÈRE

Si mes écrits n'ont gravé sur la face
Le sacré nom de l'immortalité,
Je ne l'ai quis non plus que mérité,
Si je ne l'ai de faveur ou de grâce.

5 Je ne décris Neptune en sa tourmente;
Je ne peins pas Jupiter irrité,
Le vase ouvert, la fuite d'équité,
Dont notre terre à bon droit se lamente.

Giving him pleasures
Of the body and heart;
95 Thus they made him victor
Of their power and strength.

You spiteful gossips,
Who say all the time
That with too much praise
100 I've lauded our Muses,
I find this quite strange;
Truly I'm astonished.

You should rather blame me,
'Gainst me lodge protests
105 (Or so I believe)
For not having, by pen,
Valued nearly enough
Their minds or their knowledge.

In my imaginings
110 The glory of these women
Is abundantly clear;
But their fame and renown,
And names of others still,
Are inscribed in Poetry.

—*Dorothy Backer*

MADELEINE DES ROCHES (1530?–1587)

FIRST ODE

If my works are not visibly engraved
With the sacred name of immortality,
Neither have I sought nor earned that name,
Nor do I possess it by favor or by grace.

5 I do not paint Neptune in his torments,
Nor do I picture wrathful Jupiter,
The open vase, the flight of justice,
Which are lamented rightly here below.

L'enfant venu de Porus et Poenie,
10 Qu'on dit brûler le plus froid des glaçons,
Se plaît d'ouïr les superbes chansons,
Et je me plais d'une basse harmonie.

Mais qui pourrait, chargé de tant de peine,
L'espirit gêné de cent mille malheurs,
15 Voir Apollon révérer les neuf soeurs,
Et dignement puiser en leur fontaine.

Le ciel a bien infusé dedans notre âme
Les petits feux, principes de vertu;
Mais le chaud est par le froid combattu,
20 Si un beau bois n'alimente la flamme.

Nature veut la lettre et l'exercice,
Pour faire voir un chef-d'oeuvre parfait:
Elle bien sage en toutes choses, fait
Ses premiers traits limer à l'artifice.

25 Nos parents ont de louables coutumes,
Pour nous tollir l'usage de raison,
De nous tenir closes dans la maison,
Et nous donner le fuseau pour la plume.

Traçant nos pas selon la destinée,
30 On nous promet liberté et plaisir;
Et nous payons l'obstiné déplaisir,
Portant la dot sous les lois d'hyménée.

Bientôt après survient une misère,
Qui naît en nous d'un désir mutuel,
35 Accompagné d'un soin continuel,
Qui suit toujours l'entraille de la mère.

Il faut soudain que nous changions l'office,
Qui nous pouvait quelque peu façonner,
Où les maris ne nous ferons sonner
40 Que l'obéir, le soin et l'avarice.

Quelqu'un d'entre eux, ayant fermé la porte
A la vertu nourri du savoir,
En nous voyant, craint de la recevoir,
Pour ce qu'elle porte l'habit de notre sorte.

45 L'autre reçoit l'esprit de jalousie,
Qui, possesseur d'une chaste beauté,
Au nid d'amour loge la cruauté,
En bourrelant sa propre fantaisie.

The child brought forth by Porus and Poenia,
10 Who's said to burn the coldest blocks of ice,
Delights to hear those songs magnificent,
While I am pleased with lower harmonies.

But who could bear, burdened with such pain,
With mind disturbed by countless sufferings,
15 To watch Apollo laud the sisters nine,
Drawing from their fountain in manner dignified?

Heaven has instilled within our soul
Small fires, virtue's sources,
But warmth is often overcome by cold
20 If no fine wood there is to feed the flame.

Nature needs both practice and precision
In bringing forth a faultless masterpiece:
She, who is so wise in every way,
Has simple strokes with artifice perfected.

25 Our parents have customs laudable
To take away the use of reason;
They keep us locked inside the house,
And for the quill, we only get a spindle.

As they trace our steps along the path of fate,
30 Freedom and pleasure they promise us.
We bring a dowry under Hymen's laws,
And receive for it continuous displeasure.

Soon after there comes a misery,
Born in us of mutual desire,
35 Along with those unending cares
That ever grip a womb maternal.

We must at once reorder all the tasks
That gave our very days a certain shape,
For obedience, and care, and stinginess
40 Will soon become a husband's sole refrain.

One of these husbands, who closed the door
To virtue of the mind, fearing contamination,
Refuses to receive the learned being,
Because she wears the habit of the female kind.

45 Another is filled with jealousy,
And though possessed of beauty chaste,
Within the nest of love he lodges cruelty,
Feeding his own tormented fantasies.

Pyrrha choisit une claire semence
50 Pour repeupler le céleste manoir;
Et Deucalion sema le cailloux noir,
Dont le ciel même a fait expérience.

Mon Dieu! mon Dieu! combien de tolérance,
Que je ne veux ici ramentevoir!
55 Il me suffit aux hommes faire voir
Combien leurs lois nous font de violence.

Les plus beaux jours de nos vertes années,
Semblent les fleurs d'un printemps gracieux,
Pressé d'orage et de vent pluvieux,
60 Qui vont borner les courses terminées.

Au temps heureux de ma saison passée,
J'avais bien l'aile unie a mon côte;
Mais en perdant ma jeune liberté,
Avant le vol ma plume fut cassée.

65 Je voudrais bien m'arrêter sur le livre,
Et au papier mes peines soupirer;
Mais quelque soin m'en vient toujours tirer,
Disant qu'il faut ma profession suivre.

L'Agrigentin, du sang de Stesichore,
70 A dignement honoré le savoir;
Qui envers nous fait semblable devoir,
Pareil miracle on reverrait encore.

Dames, faisons ainsi que l'Amaranthe,
Qui par l'hiver ne perd sa belle fleur:
75 L'espirit imbu de divine liqueur,
Rend par labeur sa force plus luisante.

Pour supporter les maux de notre vie,
Dieu nous fait part de l'intellect puissant,
Pour le réduire à l'intellect agent,
80 Malgré la mort, la fortune et l'envie.

(1579)

Pyrrha chose a white-complected breed
50 To populate the manor in the skies;
But Deucalion, as heaven even knows,
For his part, a black stone sowed.

My God, my God, such endurance one does need,
I cannot even bear evoke it now!
55 It will suffice that I can show to men
How much their laws do violence to us here.

The loveliest days of our verdant years
Seem like the flowers of a gracious spring,
Buffeted by those storms and rainy winds
60 That narrow finally the course of life.

In the happy times of seasons past,
Strong winds had I truly at my side;
But when I lost the freedom of my youth,
My feathered pen was broken 'ere I flew.

65 How gladly would I linger over books,
And sigh my sorrows out on sheets of paper,
But always seems to come a care distracting
That tells me to pursue a wife's vocation.

Agrigentum, of Stesichorus' line,
70 Did honor knowledge worthily;
If we too were paid such homage,
It would create a miracle in kind.

Ladies, let's be like Amarantha,
Which loses not its flower in wintertime;
75 The mind, imbued with liquor of the gods,
By labor makes its power brightly shine.

To bear the miseries of this our life,
God imparts to us the strength of intellect,
Then mortals may make of it an active force,
80 In spite of death, fortune, and human envy.

—*Dorothy Backer*

RÉPONSE À SA FILLE, IV

J'aime plus que jamais mon vivre solitaire.
<blockquote>

la douce liberté!

ce que j'ai enfanté.

ma jeune secrétaire.
</blockquote>

5
<blockquote>

n'avoir aucun contraire.

l'honneur et la bonté.

la grâce et la beauté.

un agréable taire.

un discours à loisir.
</blockquote>

10
<blockquote>

un louable plaisir.

la dame bien apprise.

le labeur des neuf soeurs,
</blockquote>

Et de tes saints propos les mielleuses douceurs
Qui démontrent l'essaim de ta belle devise.

(1586)

BRIEF DISCOURS: QUE L'EXCELLENCE DE LA FEMME SURPASSE CELLE DE L'HOMME

Nous avons bien souvent à mépris une chose,
Ignorant la vertu qui est en elle enclose,
Faute de rechercher diligemment le prix
Qui pourrait étonner en après nos esprits.
5 Car, comme un coq qui trouve une perle perdue,
Ne sachant la valeur de la chose inconnue,
Ainsi, ou peu s'en faut, l'homme ignare ne sait
Quel est entre les deux sexes le plus parfait.
   Il me plaît bien de voir des hommes de courage,
10 Des hommes de savoir, le pouvoir; davantage,
Je me plais bien de voir des hommes la grandeur;
Mais puis, si nous venons à priser la valeur,
Le courage, l'esprit et la magnificence,
L'honneur et la vertu et toute l'excellence
15 Qu'on voit luire toujours au sexe féminin,
A bon droit nous dirons que c'est le plus divin,

REPLY TO HER DAUGHTER, IV

I love more than ever my solitary life.
                    sweet liberty!
                    the child I bore.
                    my young secretary.
5   having no obstacle.
                    honor and goodness.
                    grace and beauty.
                    delightful silence.
                    a leisurely chat.
10   a laudable pleasure.
                    the educated lady.
                    the nine sisters' labor,
And from your hallowed words the honeyed sweetness,
Mirroring the swarm upon your noble emblem.

—*Dorothy Backer*

MARIE DE ROMIEU (1545?–1590?)

BRIEF DISCOURSE: THAT WOMAN'S EXCELLENCE
SURPASSES MAN'S

   It often happens that we despise a thing,
When we know not the virtue it contains,
For want of seeking out the inner worth,
That in the end could seize the mind with awe.
5 For like a cock that finds a pearl long lost,
Grasping not the value of the thing,
So too can it be said that ignorant man
Knows not the sex more perfect of the two.
   I like to see power in men of courage
10 And men of knowledge; even more,
I like to see men's grandeur;
But then if we do really prize the valor,
Courage, mind, magnificence,
The honor, virtue, and all excellence
15 That shine forever in the female sex,
Justly we will call it the more divine.

Quelqu'un plein de dépit, tout coléré de rage,
Dira que je fais mal de tenir tel langage,
Et dira que la femme est remplie de maux,
20   D'inconstance et d'erreur, sur tous les animaux.
Quant à moi, je sais bien qu'entre nous femmelettes
On peut humainement trouver des fautelettes.
Mais cela ne fait pas que ne soit dû l'honneur
A la femme qui est pleine de tout bonheur,
25   Chasse-mal, chasse-ennui, chasse-deuil, chasse-peine,
L'assuré réconfort de la semence humaine.
        Si l'on veut balancer selon les saintes lois
Des hommes les péchés, d'un équitable poids,
Bientôt on trouvera que la juste balance
30   Contre l'homme don'ra la très juste sentence.
Pour prouver la grandeur je prends premièrement
De sa formation mon premier argument.
La matière de chair est-elle pas plus belle
(Dont ce corps féminin fut bâti sans modèle,
35   Suivant le saint vouloir du vrai Jupin tout bon)
Que n'est celle qui fut formée du limon?
Sans douter, il y a en l'une d'excellence
Plus qu'en l'autre n'y a de vertu ni puissance.
        Et comme le Soleil et les luisants flambeaux
40   Qui drillent dessus nous, comme tous animaux,
La nourricière terre, et comme le ciel même,
Bref tout ce qui fut fait de la main du suprême,
Devant l'homme mortel, n'est point si précieux,
Que l'homme est sur cela beaucoup plus glorieux,
45   Tout ainsi la femme est dessus l'homme plus digne,
Comme chef-d'oeuvre au vrai de la vertu divine.
        Aussi, quand Jupiter la voulut égaler
Aux citadins du ciel, les dieux fait appeler,
Afin que chacun fait offrande de la chose
50   Qu'il tenait dedans soi plus secrète et enclose.
Qui lui donna les mots d'un parler gracieux,
Qui lui quitta ses raies pour lui former les yeux,
Qui laissa son pouvoir, et qui son abondance,
Qui donna son honneur, qui donna la prudence.
55   Quelle langue pourra leurs mérites vanter?
Quelle voix pourra donc leurs louanges chanter?
Quelle plume osera laisser à la mémoire
De leurs braves esprits la nonpareille gloire?
Esprits vraiment constants en toute adversité,
60   Et non à tout moment comme l'autre irrité.
        Si l'on veut regarder de près toutes les choses,

One who is full of spite and choleric with rage
Will say that I do wrong to make such claims,
That woman, beyond all other creatures,
20 Is faithless, filled with faults and every evil.
I do admit that among us little women
There are some very human little faults.
But this doesn't mean that honor is not due
The woman who is fully blessed,
25 Bans all evil, worry, mourning, pain,
And is the certain solace of the human race.
    If all the sins of men, with even scale,
Were weighed according to the sacred laws,
We would soon find that in an honest weighing
30 The justest sentence would be passed 'gainst men.
To prove woman's greatness, I need only take
From her creation my first argument.
The stuff of flesh from which the female body
Was first designed by sacred will
35 Of good and truest Jupiter, is it not lovelier
Than that of man, formed from common clay?
Without a doubt, there is more excellence in one
Than in the strength or power of the other.
    Just as the Sun, that with bright torches
40 Doth beat down, just as the other beasts,
Nourishing earth, heaven itself,
In short, whatever the almighty hand has made,
Is not so precious, compared to mortal man—
Since man is much more glorious than the rest—
45 So too is woman far worthier than man,
Of God's virtue the truest masterpiece.
    Thus Jupiter, wishing her the equal
Of heaven's citizens, called upon the gods,
That each might offer her the very thing he held
50 Within himself most secret and enclosed.
One gave her words for graceful speech,
One released his rays to form her eyes,
One renounced his power, one his bounty,
One bestowed honor, another his prudence gave.
55   What tongue exists to laud the female merits?
What voice is there that could thus sing their praises?
What pen would dare commit to memory
The glory unrivaled of their valiant minds?
Minds truly constant in all adversity,
60 Not like the other, always aggravated.
    We should be willing to take a closer look

Qui sont divinement dedans elles encloses,
Argus n'y verra rien entre tant de vertus
Desquelles ces feuillets seront en brief vêtus:
65 Car de vouloir parfaire un si hautain ouvrage,
Mon bas style perdrait sa force et le courage.
Qu'on ne me vante plus des hommes les combats;
Qu'on ne me chante plus la force de leur bras:
Hé! quel homme osera, fut-il grand capitaine,
70 Parier sa vertu à la camillienne,
Camille qui jadis fut pleine de valeur,
En prouesse et conseil du monde seul honneur?
    Penthésilée quoi, ce foudre de la guerre,
De laquelle le nom demeure encor en terre
75 Et vivra pour jamais? Et quoi Sémiramis,
En qui Pallas avait sa plus grand' force mis?
Tant que les vents seront, jamais leur renommée
Glorieuse n'ira au gré de la fumée.
Valasque et Zénobie, en temps de nos aïeux,
80 Se sont acquis un nom toujours victorieux:
Mais le siècle ancien n'en a point tant de milles
Que le nôtre n'en ait encore d'aussi habiles.
    Allons donc plus avant, venons à la douceur
Et sainte humanité dont est rempli leur coeur.
85 S'est-il trouvé quelqu'un qui eut l'âme saisie
De semblable bonté, faveur et courtoisie?
Le ciel voûté n'a point tant de luisants brandons
Comme l'on comptera de féminins mentons
Qui ont abandonné leurs caduques richesses
90 Et se sont fait au ciel immortelles déesses,
Aux pauvres dédiées ont fait bâtir maint lieu,
Qui tout toujours était pour la gloire de Dieu;
Ont fait édifier mill' et milles chapelles,
Racheté prisonniers, y a-t-il oeuvres plus belles?
95 Jamais ne serait fait qui voudrait par menu
Raconter la pitié par elles maintenu.
    Lisez le fait hautain de cette noble dame,
De qui pour tout jamais courra ci-bas la fame,
Qui daigna recevoir d'une honorable main,
100 Libérale sans plus, tout le grand ost romain.
Tairai-je de Phriné le courage notable,
Sa libéralité sans cesse mémorable,
S'offrant à rebâtir les grands murs Thébéens,
Pour vivre seulement après soi quelques ans?
105 Ha! jamais ne sera que ma muse ne dicte
La grande charité qui était en Thabite,

At all the things divinely found in women.
Argus himself would not see the many virtues
That will adorn these pages e'er so briefly,
65 For if I tried to perfect a work so noble
My lowly style would then lose heart and power.
Let no one ever praise to me men's battles;
Let no one ever sing their strength of arms;
Ha! what man dares, be he the greatest captain,
70 Wager his virtue in the manner of Camille,
Camille, who, full of valor, long ago
In prowess and counsel, was the world's chief glory?
    What of Penthesilea, the thunderbolt of war,
Whose name yet does remain upon the earth,
75 And forever will endure? And what of Semiramis,
In whom Pallas placed her greatest force?
So long as winds exist, women's glorious fame
Will never go up in idle smoke.
Velasqua and Zenobia in our ancestors' days
80 Did for themselves acquire a name triumphant.
But olden times had not the many thousand
Women in our age so highly skilled.
    Let us go further, now turning to the sweetness
And saintly human kindness that does fill their hearts.
85 Has any man been found possessed of a soul
With like goodness, favor, courtesy?
There are fewer shining torches in the vaulted skies
Than there are women's chins here below,
Who abandoned their decaying riches
90 To become goddesses immortal in the heavens.
Devoted to the poor, they had countless shelters made
And always did these stand for God's true glory.
Chapels by the thousands they did also build
And ransom prisoners; are any works so wondrous?
95 Never would you finish if you ever wished
To recount in depth the pity they displayed.
    Read the lofty tale of that noble lady
Whose fame will last forever here on earth,
Who deigned to welcome, with an honorable,
100 Most liberal hand, the great armed host of Rome.
Shall I be silent on Phrine's noted courage,
Her liberality ever unforgettable,
Who offered to rebuild the grand Thebean walls,
But only a few years lived thereafter?
105 Ha! My Muse will never cease to tell
The great charity instilled in Tabitha,

Thabite qui portait tant d'honneur à son Christ
Qu'elle ne permettait que le pauvre souffrit.
Ce saint amour était caché dans sa poitrine
110 Tant qu'elle était sans plus à un chacun bénigne,
Aux pauvres orphelins, aux veuves mêmement,
Qui étaient sans secours, en disette et tourment;
Ainsi distribua tous ses biens de fortune,
N'ayant puis pour couvrir sa nature commune.
115 O amour non-ouï! ô sainte charité!
O coeur doux et bénin qui ta nécessité
Oublie pour aider à tes membres semblables!
Fait vraiment qui sera mise entre les notables
Et de qui parleront tous les siècles suivants,
120 En dépit de l'envie et de tous médisants.
     Le même est advenu à maintes damoiselles
Qui sont ores au ciel pour jamais immortelles,
Et de qui nous n'avons maintenant que le nom,
Le monde étant rempli de leur loz et renom.
125 Jà déjà j'ois crier quelqu'un à mes oreilles,
Qui me tance de quoi j'en dis tant de merveilles,
Et me dit: «Venez çà! ne savez-vous pas bien
Que nous ne faillons point que par votre moyen?
Savez-vous pas aussi que le mal qui nous presse
130 Vient de voir votre face et votre blonde tresse?
Si Pâris n'eut point vu d'Hélène les beaux yeux,
Troie n'aurait-ell' pas ses preux victorieux?
Encor tant de cités élèveraient leur têtes
Jusqu'au ciel, qui sont or l'habitacle des bêtes.
135 Abandonnez-vous pas pour un rien votre corps,
Qui est cause en après de tant de mille morts?
Ha qui voudrait de vous un gros volume écrire,
Il trouverait assez de sujet à médire.»
     Ainsi dit; mais, hélas! par là vous montrez bien
140 Que votre cerveau n'a ni bride ni lien,
Pauvres gens insensés, des bons esprits la fable!
Pourquoi avez-vous donc un' âme raisonnable?
Si vous n'en avez point, mes propos sont déçus:
Dieu vous a donc en vain d'une raison pourvus.
145 Ha! ce n'est pas ainsi, non ainsi ce n'est pas;
Vous ne vous trompez point par nos subtils appas.
C'est quelqu'une de nous, las! qui se laisse prendre
Dans les trompeurs filets que vous lui venez tendre.
     «Madame, dira l'un, vous savez que le Dieu
150 Qui commande à la terre, au ciel et en tout lieu,
Quand il veut décocher une flèche amoureuse,

That Tabitha who honored so her Christ
That never would she let a poor man suffer.
This holy love was hidden in her breast
110 And she was to everyone most justly kind,
To orphan children and to widows equally,
Who lay helplessly in want and torment.
She distributed all her fortune thus,
Leaving naught to cover her own body.
115 O love unheard-of! O saintly charity!
O heart benign and gentle that neglects
Its own needs to help its human kind!
Truly this deed will count among the celebrated,
Be spoken of for all centuries to come,
120 In spite of all the slanderers and their envy.
    The same has befallen so many damozels
Now in heaven, forevermore immortal;
While we now have nothing but their name,
The world is filled with their praises and fame.
125   Already I hear someone shouting in my ear,
Scolding me for speaking of their wonders:
"Look here!" he says. "Really, don't you know,
That we men fall only by your ways?
Don't you know that the evil driving us
130 Comes from your faces and your golden tresses?
If Paris hadn't seen the eyes of Helen
Wouldn't Troy still have its victorious heroes?
So many cities now inhabited by beasts
Would still raise their heads to heaven.
135 Don't you give your bodies for a trifle,
Which causes then a thousand deaths?
Ha! He who'd write on you a lengthy volume
Would find a lot of matter for contempt."
    So say you, but, alas, by this you clearly show
140 Your brain has neither bridle nor restraint.
Poor senseless folk, the laughingstock of wiser minds!
Why have you then a soul endowed with reason?
If you don't use it, my words are then for naught:
And God to you gave reason all in vain.
145 But that's not how it really is, no, not at all;
You are not fooled by our seductive lures.
Instead it's one of us, alas, who is seduced
By those deceptive nets you cast to trap her.
    "Madam," says one, "you know that God above,
150 Who rules the earth, heaven, everywhere,
When once a love arrow he chooses to shoot

L'on ne peut éviter la plaie dangereuse.
Je le sens maintenant, car vos perfections
Ont tellement navré mon coeur de passions
155 Que je ne sens en moi muscles, tendons ni veines,
Qui n'endurent pour vous innumérables peines;
Et si me plaît encor de vivre et d'y mourir,
Pourvu que vous daignez à mon mal secourir.»
    L'autre plus effronté dira: «Et bien, madame!
160 Y a-t-il quelqu'un ci-bas qui votre renom blâme?
Dites-le, je vous prie, je lui ferai sentir
Combien vaut d'acheter l'aune d'un repentir.
Je vous suis trop servant, j'aime trop votre face
Et le bénin accueil de votre bonne grâce.
165 Croyez assurément que tant que je vivrai,
Pour votre nom aimé ma vie je mettrai.»
L'autre, mieux embouché des mots de rhétorique,
Fera sembler le blanc être couleur libique,
Et, sous le voile feint d'un langage fardé,
170 Ornera son propos de tropes mignardé.
    «Si le ciel, dira-t-il, Madame, m'a fait naître
Pour vous être servant, comme je désire être,
Et si le même ciel vous a mis ici-bas
Pour sa bénignité ensuivre pas à pas,
175 Si vous n'avez le coeur d'une fière lionne,
Si à vous voir encor ne semblez félonne,
Pourquoi différez-vous à me donner secours,
Sans jouïr entre nous de nos douces amours?
Et pourquoi souffrez-vous qu'en mourant je m'écrie
180 Que je meurs pour aimer trop une fière amie?»
    Qui ne serait déçue à si mielleux propos,
Superbes, importuns, fâcheux, fiers, sans repos?
Voilà comme quelqu'une, entre tant de pucelles,
Laisse cueillir le fruit de ses pommes plus belles,
185 Plus par ravissement et par déception,
Que pour avoir en eux mis trop d'affection.
O trompeuse espérance! et bien heureuse celle
Qui n'a point engravé tels mots en sa cervelle!
Que vous êtes trompeurs et plein de vanité!
190 Bienheureuse qui n'oit votre importunité!
    Oncques je n'ai trouvé dans les vraies histoires
Ni dans les vieux écrits d'anciennes mémoires
Qu'une femme se soit donnée volontiers,
Sans l'importunité de ses plus familiers,
195 A nul homme vivant. Ains j'ai bien ouï dire
Qu'il fallait feindre avant un amoureux martyre,

We can never avoid the critical wound.
I feel it even now, for your perfections
Have so crushed my heart with passions
155 That I have no muscles, veins, or tendons
Which countless pains do not for you endure.
And yet for this I want to live and die
If only you will deign to ease my pain.''
 Another, more shameless still, says, ''Well, Madam!
160 Is there someone here who sullies your name?
Tell me, I pray you, and him I'll make feel
How dearly costs repentance by the yard.
I am too much your servant, too much I love your face
And the benign welcome of your fair grace.
165 Believe me surely that ever as I live,
On your beloved name, my life I'll stake.''
Yet another, well mouthed with words rhetorical,
Will even make white seem a libidinous hue,
And under cover of a powdered language
170 With mincing tropes will ornament his speech.
 ''If heaven, Madam, gave me life,'' says he,
''To be your servant, as I desire to be;
If that same heaven put you here below
To follow in the footsteps of its kindness,
175 If you have not a lioness' proud heart,
If you think not a crime that I do see you,
Why then delay my heart's relief,
And not find pleasure in our gentle loves?
And why let me cry out, with my last breath,
180 That I die for loving too much a lady proud?''
 Who would not be tricked by such honeyed words,
Haughty and proud, troublesome and tiresome?
That's how a maiden among so many
Allows the picking of her loveliest fruits;
185 It's more by deception and bedazzlement
Than placing in those words a faith too great.
O hope misleading! Happy is she
Whose mind with such words is not engraved!
How false you are, how full of vanity!
190 Happy is she who hearkens not your vexing pleas!
 I've never found in true histories
Nor in the aged texts of olden memoirs
That willingly a woman gave herself,
Without the meddling of her intimates,
195 To any living man. But oft I've heard it said
That man must feign love's martyrdom,

Etre passionné, ne dormir point la nuit,
Aller et revenir quand le soleil nous luit,
Un' oeillade adorer en secret élancée,
200 Rien, sinon, son objet, n'avoir en la pensée,
Feindre de n'aimer autre et faire rien sinon
Hausser jusques au ciel la gloire de son nom,
Inventer, composer, mille sonnets écrire,
Pour montrer vraiment que pour elle on soupire;
205 Guetter de ça, de là, ainsi que fait le loup
Quand il veut au troupeau faire quelque bon coup;
Tantôt dessus le front porter un bon visage,
Et tantôt ne montrer qu'un larmoyant image;
Aviser les moyens pour sûrement tenir
210 Ce joyau qu'on ne peut par armes soutenir,
User de braves mots, dresser mille ménades,
Apposter des servants, faire mille algarades.
    Que dirai plus? Voilà les grand's subtilités
Qu'on trouve en vos esprits de tels vents agités.
215 Aristote disait que l'humaine personne
Composée de chair plus délicate et bonne
Faisait par sympathie avoir l'espirit meilleur
A ceux-là qui étaient doués d'un tel bonheur.
Doncques, puisqu'ainsi est, qui est celui qui doute
220 Que le nôtre ne soit plus excellent sans doute,
Vu que tout notre corps est délicat et beau
Par dessus la beauté de votre belle peau?
On le peut voir assez selon l'expérience
Qui de ce tous les jours vous en donne assurance.
225 On le peut voir aussi par les inventions
Qui sortent tous les jours de nos perfections.
Qu'on lise seulement aux inventeurs des choses,
Mon Dieu, qu'on y verra de merveilles encloses!
Premier on y lira tant d'hommages parfaits,
230 On y lira encor tant de généreux faits;
On verra là-dedans leurs louanges hautaines
Jusques à inventer les sciences humaines,
Desquelles maintenant les hommes se font forts,
Comme d'un bastion contre cent mille morts;
235 Qui est pour vous montrer que, comme d'elles naissent
Les hommes, et encor par leur moyen accroissent,
Les sciences aussi qu'on dit d'humanité
Sont des inventions de leur divinité.
    Mais quoi! est-il pas vrai (afin que je ne mente)
240 Qu'elles ont commencé en la bonne Carmente:
Qu'une Leontia vainquit publiquement

Be ever passionate, never sleep the night,
Come and go at the break of day,
Adore a single glance covertly thrown,
200 Have nothing but a single object on his mind,
Pretend love for no other, and nothing do
But shout to heaven the glory of her name,
Invent, compose, a thousand sonnets write,
To prove that it's for her he sighs;
205 Spy here and there, as does the wolf
When he would deal the flock a mighty blow.
Sometimes he wears a cheerful face,
And sometimes only a tearful countenance;
He picks out the surest means at hand
210 To get the jewel that force of arms can't hold,
Uses bold words, trains a thousand furies, and
Posts his servants to launch attacks innumerable.
    What more is there to say? Those are the fine tricks
Your minds contain, driven by passion's winds.
215 The human person, Aristotle said,
Who's made of flesh more delicate and fine,
When blessed with such good fortune,
Would by contagion have the better mind.
Since this is so, who could then doubt
220 That ours is in truth the sex more excellent?
For our whole body is delicate and fine
Beyond the beauty of your beauteous skin.
This by experience you can clearly see,
Confirming each day its veracity.
225 But you can also see it in the inventions
That daily issue forth from our perfections.
Of inventors you need only read the works;
Heavens! What wonders therein you'll find!
You'll read at first so many perfect homages
230 And then again so many noble deeds;
Men's praises you'll see there haughtily sung,
Even as inventors of the human sciences,
Which now they proudly claim to be their own,
Their protection against a hundred thousand deaths.
235 But I can show you that since men are born
Of women, and by their means grow up,
So too the sciences that we call human
Are inventions of women's true divinity.
    Say then! Isn't it so (for I will not lie)
240 That learned women began in old Carmanta?
That a certain Leontia publicly vanquished

Théophraste le grand par maint bel argument?
Eustochion en fit autant à saint Hyérome,
Pour montrer aux Romains qu'elle était née à Rome.
245 Rome, mère des arts et des nobles esprits,
Où elle avait hébreu, grec et latin appris.
　　Une semaine, un mois, voire un'année encor,
Ne me suffirait pas pour vanter le trésor
De leurs subtils esprits; d'autre part l'univers
250 Ne les ignore pas. Saphe trouva les vers
Qui depuis, de son nom, furent nommés Saphiques,
Estimés hautement des hommes prohétiques.
Elle vainquit aussi par maint' docte raison
Tous les vantés savants de sa belle saison;
255 Autant en fait Corinne à leur grande louange,
Qui court bien empennée or' au More, or' au Gange;
Tantôt dessus Atlas guide ses pas légers,
Et tantôt vers le Nil annonce aux étrangers,
Puis deça, puis delà, va racontant au monde
260 Les vertus de ce sexe où tout honneur abonde.
Si l'Italie voulait les siennes étaler,
Si brave ne serait qui s'osât égaler
A la moindre de mill' et mill' en abondance,
Sans faire voir à tous bientôt son arrogance.
265 　　Tu m'en seras témoin docte Degambara:
Car qui sera celui si sot qui osera
Contredire à ton veuil et à cil de Pesquière,
Sans rapporter chez soi une douleur amère
D'avoir voulu en vain disputer contre vous,
270 De qui sort et le miel et le nectar tant doux?
Que dois-je dire encore d'Armill'Angosiole?
La terre des Germains et la terre espagnole
En ont des légions, qui tiendraient sûrement
Des sciences école à tous ouvertement,
275 Même aux mieux versés; mais par surtout la France
Aura le plus grand prix de toute la science.
　　Or je suis comme cell' qui entre en un jardin
Pour cueillir un bouquet quand ce vient au matin.
Là le thym hybléan, et là la rose belle,
280 Là l'oeillet, là le lis, là mainte fleur nouvelle,
S'offrent à qui mieux mieux, tellement qu'ell' ne sait
Comme doit de sa main entasser un bouquet;
Tout ainsi je ne sais laquelle je dois prendre
Première entre cent mill' qu'à moi se viennent rendre,
285 Tant la France est fertile en très nobles esprits,
Qui rendent tous mes sens extasement épris.

Great Theophrastus by many a fine argument?
Eustochion did the same to Saint Jerome,
To show the Romans she too was born in Rome,
245 Rome, mother of arts and noble minds,
Where Hebrew, Greek, and Latin she had learned.
   A week, a month, even perhaps a year
Would not suffice to laud the treasures
Of their subtle minds; indeed, the universe
250 Disdains them not. Sappho found verses
That have been labeled Sapphic after her,
And much esteemed by men prophetic.
She too triumphed through her learned reason
Over the vaunted sages of her celebrated time.
255 Likewise Corinne, by them much praised,
Who flies strong-winged to the More, the Ganges,
Sometimes o'er Atlas guiding her delicate step,
Sometimes near the Nile to strangers speaking,
Now here, now there, goes telling all the world
260 The virtues of this sex, wherein all honor does abound.
If Italy chose her women to make known,
No man however brave would dare to rival
The least of all those countless thousands,
Without to one and all his arrogance displaying.
265   You'll be my witness, learned Degambara,
For who would be so foolish as to dare
To contradict your will or that of Pesquière?
For he would gain but bitter sorrow,
Trying futilely with you to argue,
270 You, source of honey and sweetest nectar.
What should I say of Armille Angosiole?
The German land, the land of Spain have legions
Of such women; they could easily found
A school for learning, open to all,
275 Even the most learned; but above all it is France
Who'll win the prize for greatest knowledge.
   I am now like a woman who steps into a garden
When morning comes to pick some flowers.
Here's hyblean thyme, and there's a lovely rose,
280 A lily, a carnation, so many a fresh bloom,
All vying themselves to offer 'til she cannot tell
Just how her hands a bouquet will compose.
Likewise, I don't know which woman I should pick
First among the thousands who now appear to me,
285 So fertile is France in noble female minds,
Which drive my senses all to ecstasy.

Mais bien je ferai mieux: j'ensuivrai les avettes
Qui vont deça delà cueillant maintes fleurettes
Pour en faire du miel, ore dessus un mont
290 Et or' dans un beau pré vagabondes revont;
De même en ce discours l'une sera première,
L'autre mise au milieu, l'autre sera dernière,
Sans ordre ni sans art. Aussi ne faut-il pas
Donner, muse, le vert jusqu'après le trépas.
295 Viens donc, soeur des neuf soeurs et quatrième Charité,
Ma comtesse de Retz, viens, que tu sois écrite
La première en mes vers: le grec t'est familier,
De ta bouche ressort un parler singulier
Qui contente les rois et leur cour magnifique;
300 Le latin t'est commun et la langue italique;
Mais par surtout encor le français te connaît,
Pour son enfant t'avoue, honore, et te reçoit.
S'il faut feindre un soupir d'un amant misérable,
S'il faut chanter encore un hymne vénérable,
305 Tu ravis les esprits des hommes mieux disants,
Tant en prose et en vers tu sais charmer nos sens.
Venez après, Morel, Charamont, Hélisenne,
Des Roches de Poitiers, Grâces piériennes,
Vous aussi qui tenez le sceptre navarrois,
310 Et vous, ma générale, honneur des Piedmontois,
De qui l'illustre sang l'Italie environne,
Ayant régné longtemps sur Vincense et Veronne,
Et de qui les aïeux, des vertus amoureux,
Ont été de tout temps puissant et généreux.
315 Ore je ne dis rien de cette grand' princesse.
La perle de Valois, qui est au ciel déesse
Maintenant pour jamais. Toi qui régis ici
La France, qui se rend à ta douce merci,
Vois ce qu'en ta faveur, grand' Reine Catherine,
320 J'écris pour haut tonner la race féminine.
Ceux qui de notre temps ont couché par écrit
Les faits de tes grands rois viennent de ton esprit.
Tu es leur saint Parnasse et leur eau de Permesse;
Aussi chacun t'honor' et te tient pour déesse.
325   Mes dames, qui voudrait dignement vous vanter,
D'une Valeria il faudrait emprunter
Le savoir et la voix, ou d'une Cornélie
Le parler, ornement de l'ancienne Italie.
Trop peu forte est ma voix. Si quelqu'une de vous
330 Voulait ceci parfaire à la vue de tous,
Bientôt on jugerait sans appel que nous sommes,

But I'll do even better: I'll imitate the bees,
That go gathering flowerets here and there
To make their honey, now on a mountain,
290 Now in fields so fine; wandering, they return;
So too, in this my discourse, one will be first,
Another in the middle, and one must be last,
With neither art nor order; and so, my Muse,
You must not give the palm 'til after death.
295 Come, my Countess de Retz, sister of the Muses,
The fourth charity, come to be inscribed
First within my verse. Greek is known to you;
From your mouth comes a special parlance
That pleases kings and courts magnificent;
300 Latin to you is familiar, so too the Italian tongue;
But above all, French knows you well,
Welcomes, honors, and avows you as her child.
When you would feign a miserable lover's sigh,
Or sing another venerable hymn,
305 You ravish the minds of best-spoken men;
In prose and in verse our senses you charm.
Come next, Morel, Charamont, Elisene,
Des Roches de Poitiers, Graces of Pierie,
And you who hold the scepter of Navarre,
310 And you, too, my lady-general, pride of Piedmont,
Whose illustrious blood embraces all of Italy,
Having long ruled Vicenza and Verona,
And whose ancestors, loving virtue,
Have always been both powerful and noble.
315 But I'll say nothing of that princess great,
The pearl of Valois, goddess in the heavens
Now and forever. You who rule France,
Which surrenders to your sweet mercies,
See what I write of you, great Queen Catherine,
320 To shout the praises of the female race.
Those who, in our time, have put in writing
The exploits of your kings, from your own mind have learned,
You're their holy Parnassus and their Permessian waters;
Everyone honors and regards you as a goddess.
325   To praise you worthily, my ladies,
One would need borrow the knowledge and the voice
Of a Valeria, or the fine speech,
Ornament of ancient Italy, of a Cornelia,
Not strong enough is my own voice. But if one of you
330 Brought this to perfection, before the eyes of all,
Soon it would be judged, without appeal, that we,

Dès le commencement comme or', plus que les hommes.
　　Finis, Muse, finis mes plus chères amours;
Mignonne, c'est assez, finis-moi ce discours
335　Par l'amitié que Dieu a montré aux femelles,
Leur ayant départi ses grâces les plus belles.
On lit aux saints cahiers de l'Ancien Testament
Que celui qui tient tout fait un commandement
Au bon père Abraham de vouloir toujours faire
340　Ce que dirait Sarah, s'il lui voulait complaire.
Celui qui nous sauva, étant ressuscité,
Montra premièrement sa sainte humanité
Aux dames. Trismégiste et plusieurs autres sages
Nous en ont délaissé maints sérieux passages.
345　Tous disent que le lieu sans femmes habité
Est comme un vrai désert du tout inhabité,
Et qu'on doit grandement fuir l'humaine race
A qui ne plaît d'hanter la féminine grâce.
　　Où est l'honnêteté, où les chastes propos,
350　Où le plaisant ménage et où le doux repos,
Si ce n'est à la femme, à qui tout influence
De biens tombe du ciel en prodigue abondance?
Aussi voilà pourquoi toutes les vertus ont
Des femmes retenu le nom, vu qu'elles sont
355　D'honneur et de vertu beaucoup plus excellentes
Que des hommes ne sont les grand's troupes errantes.

(1581)

L'AGNODICE, OU L'IGNORANCE BANNIE DE CHEZ LES FEMMES

Il n'y a passion qui tourmente la vie
Avec plus de fureur que l'impiteuse envie:
De tous les autres maux on tire quelque bien;
L'avare enchaîné d'or se plaît en son lien;
5　Le superbe se fond d'une douce allégresse,
S'il voit un grand seigneur qui l'honore et caresse;
Le voleur, épiant sa proie par les champs,
Sourit à son espoir, attendant les marchands;
Le gourmand prend plaisir au manger qu'il dévore,

From dawn of time to now are more than men.
   So finish, Muse, finish my dearest loves.
Sweet one, enough, end this my discourse
335 With the friendship God always showed to women,
Since he has given them his qualities most fine.
In the holy books of the Old Testament we read
That he who holds all things did so command
Good father Abraham, always to do
340 What Sarah said, if he would please his Lord.
And He who saved us, rising from the dead,
First to women his sainted humanity revealed.
Trismegistus and several other sages
On this have left us many solemn texts.
345 All say that places uninhabited by women
Are, like the desert, inhabited by naught,
And that we'd better flee the human kind
That seeks not the presence of graces feminine.
   Where is virtue, where are chaste remarks,
350 Where is the happy home, where sweet serenity,
If not in women, to whom from heaven falls
An influx of good things in prodigal abundance?
And that is why the virtues, every one,
Have kept the name of women; for women are,
355 In virtue and honor, more excellent by far
Than are the great and wandering hordes of men.

—*Dorothy Backer*

CATHERINE DES ROCHES (1550–1587)

AGNODICIA, OR IGNORANCE BANISHED
FROM THE PRESENCE OF WOMEN

There is no passion that torments our life
With greater fury than does envy merciless.
From all the other ills we draw some good:
The miser wrapped in gold enjoys his chains;
5 The proud man melts with sweetest joy
When he's honored and caressed by noblemen;
The robber, spying in the fields his prey,
Smiles with hope as merchants he awaits;
The glutton who delights in the meal devoured

10 Et semble, par les yeux, le dévorer encore;
   Le jeune homme, surpris de lascives amours,
   Compose en son esprit mille plaisants discours;
   Le menteur se plaît fort s'il se peut faire croire;
   Le jureur, en bravant, croit augmenter sa gloire;
15 Mais ô cruelle Envie, on ne reçoit par toi
   Sinon le déplaisir, la douleur et l'émoi!
   A celui qui te loge, ingrate et fière hôtesse,
   Tu laisses, pour payement, le deuil et la tristesse.
   C'est par toi que tombé sous le bras fraternel,
20 Le pauvre Abel mourut, invoquant l'Eternel.
   Depuis, en te coulant aux autres parts du monde,
   Tu semas sur la terre une race féconde
   En ires et forfaits, fureurs et cruautés,
   Par qui les vertueux vivent persécutés;
25 Mais sur tous autres lieux c'est la contrée attique
   Qui témoigne le plus de ta puissance inique,
   Non point pour Théséus, de ses parents trahi;
   Pour le juste Aristide, injustement haï;
   Ni pour ce Thémistocle, allant chercher la terre
30 D'un roi que tant de fois il poursuivit en guerre;
   Ni pour voir Miltiade à tort emprisonné;
   Pour Socrate non plus, qui meurt empoisonné;
   Mais pour toi, Phocion, qui n'eus pas sépulture,
   Au pays tant aimé, où tu pris nourriture.
35 Une dame étrangère, ayant la larme à l'oeil,
   Reçut ta chère cendre et la mit au cercueil:
   Honorant tes vertus de louanges suprêmes,
   Elle cacha tes os dedans son foyer mêmes,
   Disant d'un triste coeur, humble et dévotieux:
40 Je vous appelle tous, ô domestiques dieux,
   Puisque de Phocion l'âme s'est retirée
   Pour aller prendre au ciel sa place préparée,
   Et que ses citoyens, auteurs de son trépas,
   L'ayant empoisonné, ores ne veulent pas
45 Qu'il soit enseveli dedans sa terre aimée,
   Se montrant envieux dessus sa renommée;
   Puisque mort il éprouve encor leur trahison,
   Aimons ce qui nous reste, honorons sa prison.
      L'Envie, regardant cette dame piteuse,
50 Dans soi-même sentit une ire venimeuse,
   Roulant ses deux grands yeux, pleins d'horreur et d'effroi,
   Ah! je me vengerai, ce dit-elle, de toi.
   Hé! tu veux donc aider, sotte, tu veux défendre
   Phocion, dont je hais encor la morte cendre:

10 With his eyes would devour it yet again;
The young man, wakened to lascivious loves,
Composes in his mind a thousand speeches;
The liar's most content when he's believed;
The swearer shocks and thinks his glory made.
15 But O cruel Envy, from you we receive
Nothing but displeasure, sorrow, and pain!
To him who harbors you, ungrateful haughty guest,
You leave, for payment, mourning and distress.
It's through you that, by arm fraternal fallen,
20 Poor Abel died, invoking the Eternal.
Since then, spreading your seed about the world,
You sowed upon the earth a fecund breed
Of angers and misdeeds, furors and cruelties,
By which the virtuous are ever persecuted
25 But more than any other, 'tis the Attic soil
That testifies to your malicious power.
I mean not Theseus by kin betrayed,
Nor just Aristides, unjustly hated,
Nor Themistocles, seeking out the land
30 Whose king so often he pursued in war;
Nor the sight of Miltiades, wrongfully in prison,
Nor even Socrates who died of poison.
But for you, Phocion, who had no burial,
In that most cherished land where you were nurtured,
35 A foreign lady, eyes all moist with tears,
Took your beloved ashes, and placed them in a coffin.
Honoring your virtues with highest praise,
She hid your bones inside your very house.
With sad, humble, and devoted heart, she said,
40 "I call upon you all, gods of the hearth,
Now that the soul of Phocion has departed
To go and take its rightful place on high;
Since his citizens, who caused his death
By poison, still do not want him buried here
45 Within the soil of his beloved land,
And show their envy of his fame;
Since even dead, he feels their treachery,
Let's love what's left, and honor yet his prison."
Envy, who observed this woeful lady,
50 Felt within the surge of venomous ire,
And rolling those huge eyes of fear and horror,
"Ah," she said, "on you I'll be revenged.
Foolish woman, who would defend and help
Phocion, whose funeral ashes I abhor,

55 Sache qu'en peu de temps je te ferai sentir
De ton hâtif secours un tardif repentir;
Car, en dépit de toi, j'animerai les âmes
Des maris, qui seront les tyrans de leurs femmes,
Et qui, de s'illustrer leur ôtant le pouvoir,
60 Leur défendront toujours l'étude et le savoir.
    Aussitôt qu'elle eut dit, aux hommes elle inspire
Le désir d'empêcher leurs femmes de s'instruire.
Ils veulent effacer de leur entendement
Les lettres, des beautés le plus digne ornement;
65 Et ne voulant laisser chose qui leur agrée,
Leur ôtent le plaisir où l'âme se recrée.
Que ce fut à l'Envie une grand'cruauté
De martirer ainsi cette douce beauté!
Les dames aussitôt se trouveront suivies
70 De fièvres, de langueurs et d'autres maladies;
Mais surtout la douleur de leurs enfantements
Leur faisait supporter d'incroyables tourments,
Aimant trop mieux mourir que d'être peu honteuses,
Contant aux médecins leurs peines langoureuses;
75 Les femmes, ô pitié! n'osaient plus se mêler
De s'aider l'une l'autre; on les faisait filer.
    En ce temps il y eu une dame gentille,
Que le ciel avait fait belle, sage et subtile,
Qui, piteuse de voir ces visages si beaux
80 Promptement engloutis des avares tombeaux,
Sous les habits d'un homme apprit la médecine;
Elle apprit la vertu des fleurs, feuille et racine;
Mais les dames, pensant que ce fut un garçon,
Refusaient son secours d'une étrange façon;
85 L'on connaissait assez, à leurs faces craintives,
Qu'elles craignaient ses mains comme des mains lascives.
    Agnodice, voyant leur grande chasteté,
Les estima beaucoup pour cette honnêteté:
Lors, découvrant du sein ses blanches pommes rondes,
90 Et de son chef doré les belles tresses blondes,
Montre qu'elle était fille, et que son gentil coeur
Les voulait délivrer de leur triste langueur.
Les dames, admirant cette bonté naïve,
Et de son teint douillet la blanche couleur vive,
95 Et de son sein poupin le petit mont jumeau,
Et de son chef sacré l'or crêpelu tant beau,
Et de ses yeux divins les flammes ravissantes,
Et de ses doux propos les grâces attirantes,
Baisèrent mille fois et sa robe et son sein,

55 Know that, before long, I'll make you feel
   A long repentance for your hasty deed.
   For to spite you, I will animate the souls
   Of husbands, who'll then tyrannize their wives,
   And take from them all source of high distinction,
60 Study and learning forever them deny."
      Once said, in men she then inspires
   An urge to stop their wives from learning.
   They yearn to take away their knowledge
   Of letters, most noble ornament of beauty,
65 And leave them naught which pleases them,
   But banish joy of spiritual renewal.
   What great cruelty was this for Envy
   Thus to martyrize such gentle beauty!
   Soon after, ladies were beset
70 With fevers, languors, other maladies;
   But most of all, the pain of giving birth
   Made them endure a torment past belief.
   For they preferred to die than bear that little shame
   Of telling doctors of their lingering pains.
75 Women, O Pity! no longer to each other
   Dared give help; forced they were to walk in single file.
      But in those days there was a noble lady
   Whom heaven had made lovely, wise, and knowing.
   Pitying the sight of lovely faces
80 So quickly shut within those meager tombs,
   She dressed up like a man, and mastered medicine,
   Learned the secret powers of flower, leaf, and root.
   And yet the ladies, thinking her a boy,
   In awkward manner did refuse her help;
85 Their timid glances made it ever clear
   They feared her hands like hands of ravishers.
      Agnodicia, who perceived the women's chasteness,
   Respected them for conduct past reproach;
   Baring the round white apples of her bosom,
90 The beauteous blond tresses of her golden head,
   She showed them she was woman, and that her noble heart
   Wanted but to free them of their woeful languor.
   The ladies, admiring then her simple goodness,
   The bright white hue of her soft complexion,
95 The small twin mountains of her rosy breast,
   The fine gold ringlets of her saintly head,
   The enchanting fire of her eyes divine,
   And the seductive grace of her dulcet speech,
   Kissed a thousand times her dress, her bosom,

100   Recevant le secours de son heureuse main.
     On voit en peu de temps les femmes et pucelles
     Reprendre leur teint frais et devenir plus belles;
     Mais l'Envie en frémit; un furieux serpent,
     Qu'elle tient en sa main, son noir venin répand:
105   Son autre main portait une branche épineuse;
     Son corps était plombé, sa face dépiteuse,
     Sa tête sans cheveux, où faisaient plusieurs tours
     Des vipères hideux, qui la mordaient toujours:
     Traînant autour de soi ses furieuses rages,
110   Elle s'en va troubler les chastes mariages;
     Car le repos d'autrui lui est propre malheur.
     Elle dit qu'Agnodice ôte aux maris l'honneur.
     Les maris furieux saisirent Agnodice
     Pour en faire à l'envi un piteux sacrifice.
115   Hélas! sans la trouver coupable d'aucun tort,
     Ils l'ont injustement condamnée à la mort!
     La pauvrette, voyant le malheur qui s'apprête,
     Découvrit promptement l'or de sa blonde tête;
     Et montrant son beau sein, agréable séjour
120   Des Muses, des Vertus, des Grâces, de l'Amour,
     Elle baissa les yeux, pleins d'honneur et de honte;
     Une vierge rougeur en la face lui monte,
     Disant que le désir qui la fait déguiser
     N'est point pour les tromper, mais pour autoriser
125   Les lettres, qu'elle apprit, voulant servir leurs dames;
     Montrant à les guérir, non à les rendre infames.
     Les hommes tous ravis, sans parler ni mouvoir,
     Attentifs seulement à l'ouïr et la voir,
     Comme l'on voit, parfois, après un long orage,
130   Rasserener les vents et calmer le rivage,
     Se trouvant tout ainsi vaincus par la pitié,
     Rapaisent la fureur de leur inimité;
     Faisant à la pucelle une humble révérence,
     Ils lui vont demander pardon de leur offense.
135   Elle, qui ressentit un plaisir singulier,
     Les supplia bien fort de faire étudier
     Les dames du pays, et leur laisser la gloire
     Que l'on trouve à servir les filles de Mémoire.
       L'Envie, connaissant ses efforts abattus
140   Par les faits d'Agnodice et ses rares vertus,
     A poursuivi depuis, d'une haine immortelle,
     Les dames qui étaient vertueuses comme elle.

(1578)

100 Receiving succor from her blessed hands.
      Girls and women soon after did appear
      To take on a glow again and more beautiful become,
      But this made Envy shudder; a hellish serpent
      In her hand, she cast its blackened venom wide.
105 With the other hand she clutched a thorned branch;
      Her body leaden and face filled with spite,
      Her hairless head was wrapped about
      With vipers that did hideously bite;
      Dragging along her furious rages,
110 She sallied forth to trouble faithful couples,
      For in the peace of others misery she found;
      Agnodicia, she claimed, robbed husbands of their honor.
      The men, in rage, then took captive Agnodicia
      To make of her a piteous sacrifice.
115 They found her guilty of no crime and yet, alas,
      Wrongly did they sentence her to die!
      The poor girl, seeing the end approach,
      At once revealed her golden mane;
      And showing them her lovely bosom,
120 Home of Muses, Virtue, Grace, and Love,
      She lowered her eyes in modesty and shame.
      Her face assumed a virgin blush,
      As she explained the cause of her disguise:
      Not to deceive husbands but to give
125 The learning she possessed in service to their wives,
      Showing them the path to cure and not to vice.
      The men, enraptured, neither spoke nor moved,
      But sat, attentive to her voice and sight,
      As sometimes one can see, after a storm,
130 The winds becalmed, the shores serene once more.
      Then by pity were they all o'erpowered,
      The fury of their enmity was calmed;
      Humbly making obeisance to the maiden,
      They asked her to forgive their erring ways.
135 And she, who derived from this especial pleasure,
      Pleaded with them to have the ladies study,
      To let them enjoy the glory that all find
      In serving the daughters of Memory renowned.
          And Envy, when she saw her efforts thwarted
140 By such acts, such merits truly rare,
      Has ever since pursued with endless rancor
      Women with Agnodicia's virtue.

—Dorothy Backer

À MA QUENOUILLE

Quenouille, mon souci, je vous promets et jure
De vous aimer toujours et jamais ne changer
Votre honneur domestiqu[e] pour un bien étranger
Qui erre inconstamment et fort peu de temps dure.

5 Vous ayant au côté, je suis beaucoup plus sûre
Que si encre et papier se venaient à ranger
Tout à l'entour de moi, car pour me revenger,
Vous pouvez bien plutôt repousser une injure.

Mais Quenouille, ma mie, il ne faut pas pourtant
10 Que, pour vous estimer et pour vous aimer tant,
Je délaisse du tout cette honnête coutume

D'écrire quelquefois; en écrivant ainsi
J'écris de vos valeurs, Quenouille, mon souci,
Ayant dedans la main le fuseau et la plume.

(1578)

SUR UNE DAME NOMMÉE AIMÉE

Belle, j'aurais un très grand tort
Si pour votre grâce estimée
J'avais reçu l'amoureux sort;
Pour autre que pour vous, ma chère Aimée,

5 Tous les olympiques flambeaux
De leur carrière enluminée
Ne sont point ornements plus beaux
Que les yeux de ma belle Aimée.

Amour, ravi de ses beaux yeux,
10 La main droite et de flèche armée
Darda dans mon coeur soucieux
L'ardent désir d'aimer Aimée.

TO MY DISTAFF

Distaff, my care, I promise thee and swear
To love thee always and never to exchange
Your homebound honor for an alien good
That wanders faithlessly and ceases to endure.

5 With you beside me I am safer far
Than if ink and paper were ranged
About me, for, as my avenger,
Far better will you fend off an injury.

But Distaff dear, it should not then be
10 That because I esteem and love thee so
I forsake completely this noble custom

Of writing at times; just as here,
Distaff, my care, of your merits I write,
Keeping in hand the spindle and the quill.

—Dorothy Backer

ANNE DE ROHAN (1584–1646)

ON A LADY NAMED BELOVED*

Beauty, it would be a great wrong,
If, for your worthy graces,
I had been dealt the lover's fate;
For anyone but you, my dear Beloved,

5 All the Olympic torches,
Illuminated in their course,
Are not lovelier ornaments
Than the eyes of my beautiful Beloved.

Cupid, delighted with those eyes,
10 His right hand armed with an arrow
Shot into my troubled heart
The ardent desire to love my Beloved.

*Translator's note—From the French Aimée.

Je ne sais s'ils sont cieux ou dieux
Dont la puissance m'est cachée,
15 Et qui me contraint en tous lieux
De mourir pour aimer Aimée.

A les voir ils me semblent cieux;
Ils sont de couleur azurée,
Par leur effet je les crois dieux,
20 Me forçant d'aimer cette Aimée.

Bref, je les tiens pour cieux et dieux,
Par cette force recelée
Et par leur aspect lumineux,
N'ayant rien plus cher que mon Aimée.

(1617)

À LA REINE DE SUÈDE, SUR LE MÉPRIS
QU'ELLE FAIT DE L'ESPRIT DES FEMMES

Vous avez bien raison, trésor de la science,
De croire qu'après vous nous ne possédons rien:
Il est vrai que le ciel vous partagea si bien,
Qu'en vous son moindre don va jusqu'à l'excellence.

5 Son extrême bonté vous mit dans l'abondance,
Pour vous donner moyen d'être notre soutien:
Cependant l'autre sexe a tout votre entretien,
Et vous nous refusez un peu de conférence.

Reine, dépouillez-vous de ces cruels mépris,
10 Peut-être qu'entre nous il est de beaux esprits,
Quoiqu'ils n'abondent pas en doctrine profonde.

Si tous ont mérité votre juste dédain,
Le ciel dût vous former d'un sexe masculin,
Ou faire qu'ici-bas vous suffisez sans seconde.

(1665)

I know not whether they be heavens or gods
Whose power from me is hidden
15 And compels me, both near and far,
To die so as to love my Beloved.

To see them, they seem like the heavens,
Of azure color are they,
But by their effects they're like gods,
20 Forcing me yet to love that Beloved.

For me, then, they're both heavens and gods,
Because of their hidden power
And luminous appearance,
For I hold nothing dearer than my Beloved.

—*Dorothy Backer*

MLLE CERTAIN (n.d.)

TO THE QUEEN OF SWEDEN, ON HER
CONTEMPT FOR WOMEN'S MINDS

You're perfectly right, O treasure of Knowledge,
To think that we possess naught compared to you:
'Tis true that heaven gave you such a share
That its humblest gift is excellence in you.

5 Heaven's great goodness blessed you in abundance
To give you means of being our support;
Yet the other sex has all your attention,
You refuse us even a bit of conversation.

O queen, cast aside this cruel contempt.
10 Perhaps among us there exist fine minds,
Though they may not abound in doctrine profound.

If all of them deserve your just disdain,
Then heaven should have made you masculine of sex,
Or else made sure that you, one of a kind, sufficed.

—*Dorothy Backer*

Pour le triomphe on s'apprête,
J'entends retentir les airs:
Mêlons nos voix aux concerts
Qui célèbrent cette fête.
5   Au prix qu'on donne en ce jour,
Essayons à notre tour
D'ajouter une couronne.
Je sais que c'est trop oser,
Et que pour SAPHO personne
10 Ne sait l'art d'en composer.

Mais pour vaincre cet obstacle
Faisons quelque effort au moins,
Le ciel peut-être à nos soins
A réservé ce miracle.
15 Le désir juste et pressant
D'un sexe reconnaissant
Pourrait-il être inutile?
Rien ne doit nous rebuter;
Moins l'entreprise est facile,
20 Plus elle est belle à tenter.

Venez filles de mémoire,
C'est pour SAPHO, doctes soeurs,
Venez nous fournir des fleurs
Pour honorer sa victoire.
25 Et vous, qu'on voit tout charmer,
Grâces, venez lui former
Une couronne immortelle.
Les Muses n'ont-elles pas
Beaucoup moins de savoir qu'elle
30 Et vous beaucoup moins d'appas?

Pleins d'une vaine espérance
Mille orateurs estimés
Par le beau prix animés
Etalaient leur éloquence,
35 Qui jamais se fût douté
Qu'aucune l'eût disputé
D'entre tout ce que nous sommes?
Mais chacun se méconta:
Ce que disputaient tant d'hommes,

ANNE DE LA VIGNE (1634–1684)

THE LADIES TO MADEMOISELLE DE SCUDÉRY: ODE

The triumph is at hand,
I hear the music resound;
Let's join our voices to the concerts
And celebrate this feast.
5   To the prize bestowed this day,
Let's try, in turn,
To add another crown.
I know my aim is too exalted:
Composing verses for SAPPHO
10 Is an art known to none.

But to overcome this obstacle
Let's at least make an effort;
Perhaps heaven for our trials
Has reserved a miracle.
15 The true and pressing desire
Of a most grateful sex—
How could that be useless?
Nothing must discourage us;
The harder the task,
20 The nobler the attempt.

Come, daughters of Memory,
This is for SAPPHO, learned sisters;
Come and provide us with flowers
To honor her victory.
25 And you, who charm one and all,
You graces, come make for her
One crown everlasting.
The Muses, haven't they
Far less knowledge than she,
30 And even fewer attractions?

A thousand respected orators,
Full of vain pretensions,
Spurred on by the noble prize,
All displayed their eloquence.
35 Who would have ever thought
That any of us women
Would dare to rival them?
Every man was discontented:
The prize so many disputed

40 Une fille l'emporta.

Ainsi l'on voit avec joie,
A des chasseurs emportés,
Qu'un vain espoir a flatté,
Souvent échapper la proie.
45 Après que de leurs efforts,
Des chiens et du son des cors
Le biche a su se défendre,
Le juste sort la conduit
A tel, qui joint pour la prendre
50 Plus d'adresse, à moins de bruit.

Vous, dont les doctes ouvrages
A cent autres préférés,
De tant d'esprits éclairés
Suspendirent les suffrages:
55 Rien ne vous peut consoler
Que dans l'art de bien parler
Une fille vous surmonte.
Mais pourquoi vous plaindre ainsi?
Quel homme peut avoir honte
60 De céder à celle-ci?

Comment à la seule vue
De son éloquent discours,
Tous ces Argus de nos jours
Ne l'ont-ils point reconnue
65 Sous quels charmes décevants,
Pour tromper tant d'yeux savants,
S'était-elle déguisée?
Ceux qui lui donnaient le prix
Eurent toujours en pensée
70 Quelqu'un de nos beaux esprits.

Telle en ces lieux où Bellone
Fit assembler tant de rois
Ilion vit autrefois
Une célèbre Amazone.
75 De tant de Grecs valeureux,
Qui dans ces champs malheureux
Finirent leur destinée,
Quiconque sentit ses coups,
Pensa d'Hector ou d'Enée
80 Avoir senti le courroux.

D'un succès si mémorable
Conservons le souvenir

40 Was captured by a maiden.

Thus it is with joy we see
The most impassioned hunters,
Flattered by vain hopes,
Often lose their prey.
45 When, despite their efforts,
Their dogs, the sounds of horns,
The doe defends herself,
A just fate leads her to the one
Who combines less fanfare
50 With more skill in capture.

You men whose learned works,
Preferred over a hundred others,
Failed to be selected
By so many enlightened minds:
55 Nothing can console you
That in the art of eloquence
A mere maid should surpass you.
But why do you complain?
What man can be ashamed
60 To yield to such a maid?

How is it that from the start
Of her discourse so eloquent
All these Arguses of our day
Failed utterly to realize
65 That under hidden charms
She'd been disguised
To beguile those learned eyes?
Those who gave her the prize
Had always intended it to be
70 For one of our fine male minds.

So too, in the lands where Bellonius
Had assembled many a king,
Ilion saw in olden times
An Amazon renowned.
75 Among so many valorous Greeks
Whose destinies were ended
In those unhappy fields,
Whoever felt her blows
Thought they bore the wrath
80 Of great Hector or Aeneas.

Of such a notable success
Let us preserve the memory.

Quel autre dans l'avenir
Nous fera plus honorable?
85 Que notre sexe à jamais
Voue à SAPHO désormais
Son encens et ses services:
Qu'il aime éternellement,
Et qu'elle en soit les délices,
90 Comme elle en est l'ornement.

Mais ta couronne achevée
T'invite à la recevoir,
Nymphe, qu'un rare savoir
A sur toute autre élevée:
95 Vois ces lauriers enlacés
Qui sous tes pas ramassés
Forment ici ta guirlande.
Moins verts les ont nos guerriers:
Et mépriser cette offrande,
100 C'est mépriser tes lauriers.

(1672)

RÉPONSE À L'OMBRE DE M. DESCARTES

Quoi vous m'apparaissez Ombre illustre et savante,
Que pour moi votre vue est douce et surprenante
Et que j'ai de bonheur et de joie en ce jour
De servir de prétexte à votre heureux retour!
5 Aux apparitions mon âme accoutumée,
Surprise de vous voir, n'en est point alarmée;
Et déjà le plaisir, par vos flatteurs discours,
S'en va de ma surprise interrompre le cours.
Si j'osais, grand Génie, en croire vos paroles;
10 Ombre, si vos serments n'étaient toujours frivoles;
Quel espoir flatterait mon esprit et mon coeur,
Que je me promettrais de science et d'honneur!
Je verrais par mes soins la vieille erreur détruite,
L'école avec la cour heureusement instruite;
15 Et tout le monde enfin par ma voix excité
Dans vos doctes écrits chercher la vérité.
En vain me flattez-vous d'une telle promesse,
J'y répondrai fort mal, je connais ma faiblesse
Je n'ai d'un vieux docteur ni l'air ni les façons

Who else in all the future
Will give us greater honor?
85 May our sex forevermore
Hereafter devote to SAPPHO
Its incense and its offices:
May it love her eternally,
And as she is now its ornament,
90 May she always be its joy.

But now your crown is finished
And invites you to receive it,
Nymph, whose rare knowledge
Raised you far above all women.
95 See these laurels entwined,
Gathered from beneath your feet,
That form your garland here.
Greener than those of warriors:
Thus to despise this offering
100 Is to despise your every laurel.

—*Dorothy Backer*

REPLY TO THE SHADE OF DESCARTES

Lo! you appear, illustrious and learned Shade;
How sweet and astonishing the sight of you!
What joy and happiness I feel this day
To be the reason for your glad return!
5 My soul is used to apparitions,
And though surprised to see you, is not alarmed;
But already your flattering speeches
With pleasure have interrupted my surprise.
If I but dared, great genius, to believe you,
10 If your promises were not vain, Shade,
What hope would fill my mind and heart,
What learning and honor would I gain!
I'd see by my efforts old errors destroyed,
School and court most happily enlightened,
15 And all the world, excited by my voice,
In your learned texts finally seek the truth.
In vain you flatter me with such a promise.
Badly would I fulfill it: my weakness I know;
Of an old doctor, I haven't the style or airs,

20 Et ne me sens point propre à donner des leçons.
   Aux grandes vérités je puis céder sans peine;
   Mais de les débiter je ne suis pas si vaine:
   Mon esprit par leur poids peut être assujetti,
   Sans, pour les soutenir, qu'il forme aucun parti.
25 Le coeur me manquerait s'il fallait l'entreprendre;
   Pour les bien établir, il faut mieux les entendre;
   Je laisse à nos savants l'art de les étaler,
   Et je ne les apprends que pour n'en point parler.
   Je sais que la plus belle et plus forte éloquence
30 Bien souvent ne vaut pas un modeste silence;
   Que pour nous la coutume a fait presque un devoir
   De parler rarement et de ne rien savoir;
   Et que si quelque dame a pris d'autres maximes
   Elle les doit cacher comme on cache les crimes.
35 Que ce soit un usage établi justement;
   Que ce soit du plus fort une loi seulement;
   Sans doute il est pour elle et plus sûr et plus sage
   De vouloir se soumettre à ce fâcheux usage.
   J'en excepte plus d'une en qui les justes cieux,
40 Ont joint heureusement tous leurs dons précieux;
   Que l'esprit ou le rang plus grand que l'ordinaire
   Dispense de ces lois qu'observe le vulgaire.
   Notre siècle fécond produit de toutes parts
   De savantes beautés qui n'ont point ces égards:
45 L'honneur de notre sexe et celui de l'empire,
   La sage Elisabeth que l'univers admire,
   S'est-elle assujettie à ces bizarres lois?
   Eût-elle en les suivant mérité votre voix?
   Son nom déjà fameux par sa naissance illustre,
50 De son rare savoir tirait un nouveau lustre;
   Et ton rare savoir augmentant son renom
   Tirait beaucoup d'éclat de son auguste nom.
   Ce n'est qu'à ce nom seul qu'on doit joindre le vôtre;
   On vous offenserait de le joindre à tout autre:
55 Moi-même j'y consens; car d'un homme aussi bien
   Je ne puis, sans rougir, voir le nom joint au mien:
   C'est une liberté qu'en vain on autorise,
   Chez moi l'amour d'un mort n'est pas même permise;
   Toute pure qu'elle est on pourrait la blâmer;
60 Enfin on a toujours quelque honte d'aimer,
   Et les entêtements les moins déraisonnables,
   Bien loin d'être approuvés ne sont pas excusables;
   Je vois votre mérite, et sans prévention
   Je m'en tiens sagement à l'admiration.

20 And don't think it right, lessons to give others.
    To great truths I submit with ease,
    But am not vain enough to pronounce them;
    My mind can be subdued by their weight
    Without resolving to defend them.
25 Courage would fail me in this undertaking;
    To lay down principles requires better understanding.
    I leave their artful exposition to our foremost sages,
    For I only learn, so as never to speak my learning.
    The best and strongest eloquence, I know,
30 Is often not as worthy as a modest silence.
    For us women, custom makes it almost duty
    To speak but rarely and to have no knowledge.
    And if a lady adopts some other maxims,
    She'd better hide them as one hides a crime.
35 Whether this custom is rightly established,
    Or merely the law of the mightiest,
    For her it's surely both safer and wiser
    Just to bow before this unpleasant custom.
    Yet there are exceptions, in whom heaven so just
40 Has happily joined all its precious gifts,
    Whose mind or rank, greater than the ordinary,
    Is dispensed from the laws observed by common man.
    Our bounteous century produces everywhere
    Learned beauties who have not these cares:
45 Wise Elizabeth, whom the universe admires,
    The honor of our sex and of the realm,
    Did she submit to these laws so strange?
    Had she submitted, would she have earned your praise?
    Her name, already famous by illustrious birth,
50 From her rare knowledge drew another luster;
    And your rare knowledge, Shade, extending her renown,
    Drew great brilliance from her august name.
    'Tis to her name only we can join yours;
    We would offend you, in joining it to another.
55 I myself agree, for I cannot without blushing
    See such a fine man's name joined to mine.
    That would be a liberty granted in vain:
    Even love for a dead man I'm not allowed.
    Pure as a woman might be, they'll blame her all the same.
60 In the end, there's always some shame in loving,
    And even the least unreasonable of passions,
    Far from condoned, are not to be excused.
    I see your merit, and without bias,
    Wisely I'm content you to admire.

65 Pour porter votre nom au temple de Mémoire,
   J'en laisse à vos amis le plaisir et la gloire:
   J'en connais quelques-uns dignes de cet emploi,
   Qui s'en font un honneur, qui s'en font une loi;
   Par eux bientôt la cour, le barreau, la Sorbonne
70 Croiront votre doctrine et la seule et la bonne;
   Par eux tous vos écrits, tous ces savants traités
   Seront lus hautement sans être contestés:
   Par eux mille succès dont le bonheur extrême
   Passera votre espoir, passera vos voeux même,
75 Rendront également célèbres parmi nous,
   Votre profond savoir, et leur amour pour vous.
      Alors sans faire bruit, sans me faire de fête,
   Je chanterai tout bas votre illustre conquête,
   Et je saurai d'un zèle ainsi grand que discret
80 A ce noble triomphe applaudir en secret.

   (1673)

du *SEXE VENGÉ PAR LE SEXE, OU NOUVELLE
SATIRE DES MARIS*

   Thalie, il vous souvient que j'ai fait depuis peu
   Sur votre mont sacré, le téméraire voeu,
   D'occuper mon loisir, sous vos divins auspices,
   Au dangereux métier de censurer les vices.
5 Vour savez qu'Apollon, qui ne dit rien de faux,
   Prédit que je serais la terreur des défauts;
   Que j'aurais dans mes vers, quoique fille timide,
   Pour combattre les sots un courage d'Alcide.
   Vous savez qu'il me fit un excellent discours,
10 Et qu'il m'offrit enfin son utile secours,
   Il ignorait alors, commençant ma carrière,
   Que je vous devais, Muse, attaquer la première,
   Vous ignoriez alors que ma sincérité,
   Vous oserait ici dire la vérité.
15 Tout mon sexe outragé me demande vengeance,
   Souffrez donc que je rompe un injuste silence.
      Vous êtes, il est vrai, fille du roi des dieux,

65 To bear your name to the temple of Mnemosyne,
   I leave to your friends the pleasure and the glory.
   I know a few of them worthy of this task,
   Who consider it an honor and make it their law.
   Through them, the court, the bar, and the Sorbonne
70 Will believe your doctrine best, the only one.
   Through them, your texts, your learned treatises
   Will be read far and wide, no more contested.
   Through them, a thousand triumphs whose great good fortune
   Will surpass your hopes, your wishes too,
75 And render celebrated among us all
   Your learning profound, and their love for you.
       And so, without great noise and fanfare for myself,
   I'll sing your illustrious conquest e'er so softly,
   And with a zeal as great as it's discreet,
80 To your noble triumph I'll give applause in secret.

—*Dorothy Backer*

MLLE DE *** (n.d.)

from *THE FAIR SEX AVENGED BY THE FAIR SEX,
OR A NEW SATIRE ON HUSBANDS*

Thalia, you will remember that recently I made
A reckless vow upon your sacred mountain,
To devote my leisure time, under your auspices divine,
To the dangerous craft of censuring vices.
5 You know Apollo, who never tells a lie,
Foretold I'd be the terror of all faults,
That I would show, in verse, though but a timid maid,
The courage of Alcides in combating fools.
You know that he made an excellent speech,
10 Offering me his beneficial aid;
He didn't know, when launching my career,
That I would first attack you, Muse;
Neither did you know that my sincerity
Would dare tell you the truth right here.
15 My outraged sex asks me for revenge;
Suffer that I break a silence so unjust.
    You are, 'tis true, the king of gods' own daughter,

Révérée en tout temps, invoquée en tous lieux:
Votre esprit est divin, votre beauté divine:
20 Tout sentirait en vous la céleste origine,
Si l'on ne vous trouvait, à notre occasion,
Coupable pour le moins d'une indiscrétion.
L'on est de votre sexe, on a cet avantage;
Il ne fallait donc pas inspirer en chaque âge
25 Cent critiques esprits, cent bilieux auteurs
Qui versent à grands flots leur encre sur nos moeurs.
Nos sincères vertus, par leurs plumes affreuses,
Sont toutes des vertus suspectes et douteuses.
Leur cerveau criminel, au gré de son désir,
30 A fait de notre coeur cent contes à plaisir.
Selon eux Pénélope, Artémise et Lucrèce
N'eurent que les dehors d'une haute sagesse,
L'une, nous disent-ils, s'est tuée après coup:
L'autre n'était point sage, il s'en fallait beaucoup.
35 Sénèque en ses écrits stoïquement nous montre,
Qu'il trouve d'Artémise et du pour et du contre.
Virgile tout divin, tout Virgile qu'il est,
Défend-il notre honneur, prend-il notre intérêt,
Lorsqu'il chante en faveur de son pieux Enée
40 De la chaste Didon le furtif hyménée?
Me direz-vous qu'ils ont, irrités contre nous,
Enfanté leurs écrits sans recourir à vous?
Leurs sublimes beautés, qui connaissent leur père,
Vous soutiennent ici que vous êtes leur mère.
45 Les vers du satirique aujourd'hui triomphants
N'auraient été sans vous que de grossiers enfants:
Jamais on n'aurait lu son odieux volume,
Si vous n'eussiez conduit son esprit et sa plume:
Non, il n'a que de vous cette immortalité
50 Qui nous va diffamer à la postérité.
   «Quand la verve le prend, faut-il pas que j'inspire,
Ces auteurs gros de fiel, ces faiseurs de satire;
De peur qu'en furieux se roulant dans nos bois,
Tous leurs ongles rongés, ils ne mangent leurs doigts;
55 Et de peur qu'à la fin, dans leur fureur extrême,
Ils ne mangent mes soeurs, Apollon et moi-même?
Comme chevaux fougueux je dois les caresser,
Les inspirer bien vite, et m'en débarasser,
Dans la crainte où je suis que, vomissant leur bile,
60 Notre fertile mont ne devienne infertile.
Puis a-t-on si grand tort, pour le dire entre nous,
De les avoir aidés, écrivant contre vous?

Revered forever, everywhere invoked:
Divine is your mind, divine your beauty too;
20 Everything would bespeak your heavenly origin,
If in our case you were not guilty
At the very least of indiscretion.
We are of your sex, we have that advantage;
You should not then have inspired in every age
25 Hundreds of critics, hundreds of bilious authors,
To spill floods of ink against our mores.
By their horrid pens, our genuine virtues
Suspect and dubious become.
Their criminal minds, by whimsical desire,
30 Invent about our hearts a hundred frivolous tales.
Penelope, Artemis, and Lucretia,
They say, had no more than the shell of wisdom.
One, they tell us, did kill herself too late;
The other was far from well behaved.
35 And Seneca in his writings stoically
Shows us both good and bad in Artemis.
Vergil divine, though Vergil he may be,
Does he defend our honor or our interests
When he sings the praises of his pious Aeneas,
40 The furtive marriage-bed of Dido chaste?
Do you claim that, angry with us,
They produced writings with no help from you?
Their beauties sublime, knowing their father,
Also claim you as their mother.
45 The verses of the satirist, triumphant today,
Would be mere vulgar urchins, but for you.
Never would we have read his odious volume
Had you not guided both his mind and pen.
No, from you alone he derives immortality
50 That defames us for posterity.
    "When the spirit moves them, must I not inspire
These poison pens, these writers of satire,
For fear that, roaming in the forest mad,
With nails chewed off, they'd go and bite their fingers;
55 And lest, indeed, in their extremest fury,
They devour me, my sisters, and Apollo?
Like high-strung horses, I must caress,
Inspire quickly, and dismiss them,
Since I fear the vomit of their bile
60 Will make our fertile mountain barren.
And, just between us, is it so very bad
To have helped them write 'gainst you?

Vous avez cent défauts, cent caprices étranges,
Cent faibles...l'on convient que l'on n'est pas des anges.»
65   Du moins vous fallait-il prendre le juste soin,
De brider leur fureur, qui les porte trop loin.
L'un du sexe ennemi, même dès sa jeunesse,
Dans trois femmes ici met toute la sagesse;
Encore se dit-il, lorsqu'il y songe un peu:
70   Moi? Je n'en voudrais pas mettre la main au feu.
L'autre écrit qu'on ne peut, sans être téméraire,
Faire une exception en faveur de sa mère:
Celui-ci ne veut pas, en son austère humeur,
Sur ce point délicat cautionner sa soeur:
75   L'autre en son cabinet, médisant à son aise,
Forme du sexe entier des matrones d'Ephèse,
Nos Lucrèces, dit-il, sans espoir de pardon,
De supplices affreux menacent Cupidon;
Ce dieu leur paraît-il? quelles métamorphoses!
80   Il est fouetté de lis et souffleté de roses.
Inutile récit! vous savez mieux que moi,
Les libelles nombreux, où la mauvaise foi,
A tracé de la femme un portrait effroyable
Tous sont lus et relus jusqu'au plus pitoyable.
85   Et c'est là que toujours et vieux et jeunes fous,
Prennent les traits aigus qu'ils lancent contre nous.
Ils puisent au plutôt dans ces noires fontaines,
D'injustes préjugés et d'indiscrètes haines:
Puis on lit dans leurs yeux, pendant leur entretien,
90   Qu'ils pensent mal de nous, lorsqu'ils en parlent bien,
Leurs dégoûts, leurs mépris n'ont que cette origine,
   «Je vais en rapporter d'autre que j'imagine.
Les mortels attirés par vos attraits vainqueurs,
Se jettent à vos pieds, vous présentent leurs coeurs,
95   Poussent de longs soupirs, versent de tendres larmes,
Estiment vos défauts, idolâtrent vos charmes,
Vous nomment leur déesse, et mille fois le jour;
Vous font mille serments d'un éternel amour;
Qu'au-delà du tombeau vous les verrez fidèles:
100   Tout cela pour vous rendre à leurs voeux moins rebelles,
Perdent-ils leurs soupirs? leur jargon est-il vain?
Votre divinité n'a plus rien de divin.
De leur dépit jaloux vous êtes les victimes.
Vos vertus sont défauts, et vos défauts sont crimes.
105   Votre visage perd ses plus vives couleurs,
Un vent de médisance en ravage les fleurs.
Le coeur, l'esprit, le corps, tout d'un coup tout se change,

You have faults by the hundreds, moods,
And weaknesses...We aren't angels, you know."
65   You should at least have taken proper care
To harness the furor that carries them too far.
One of the enemy sex, right from youth,
Finds wisdom in three women alone;
And even, says he, thinking it over:
70 I'd not put my hand in that fire.
Another writes that you cannot without audacity
Make an exception even of your mother.
This other refuses, in his humor austere,
To vouch for his sister on this delicate matter.
75 Another, from his safe desk, slandering us at will,
Regards the whole sex as tarts from Ephesus.
Our poor Lucretias, he says, without hope of pardon,
Threaten Cupid with hideous torture;
Let the god appear before them; what a change!
80 With lilies he's thrashed, pummeled with roses.
But it's a useless tale! You know better than I
The countless libels where bad faith
Has drawn of women horrible portraits;
They're all read and reread, even the most pitiful.
85 From these, fools young and old take
The sharp arrows they shoot against us;
So eagerly they draw from these black fountains
Unjust prejudices, blatant dislikes.
We read in their eyes, while in their company,
90 How ill they think of us when speaking fair;
Their contempt, disgust, comes from this source alone.
    "But there's another source I will describe:
Mortal men, drawn by your winning allure,
Throw themselves at your feet, offer you their hearts,
95 Heave lengthy sighs, shed tender tears,
Respect your faults, worship your charms,
Call you their goddess a thousand times a day,
Swear you a thousand oaths of love eternal
That they'll be faithful e'en beyond the tomb:
100 All to make you resist far less their desires.
But if they waste their sighs, if their chatter is in vain,
You become victims of their jealous rancour:
Your divinity no longer is divine;
Your virtues are faults, your faults are crimes;
105 Your face loses its lively colors,
And the wind of slander ravages its flowers.
Heart, mind, body, all are changed.

Vous êtes un démon et vous étiez un ange.
Ecoutez vos amants: soyez femmes de bien:
110 L'un et l'autre est égal, vous ne valez plus rien,
Leur esprit de travers, et toujours en débauche,
Met les folles à droite et les sages à gauche.
Vous, pour les en punir (retenez cet endroit)
Mettez les fous à gauche et les sages à droit.
115 «Les sales passions pour la beauté vénale,
Font que ce sexe encore vous hait et vous ravale.
Ils usent en maints lieux, sous un ciel effronté,
Leur amour, leur honneur, leur bien et leur santé;
Et conçoivent enfin, dans le fond de leur âme,
120 D'invincibles dégoûts pour ce qu'on nomme femme.»[...]

Quelque parfait bonheur qu'un doux hymen étale,
Le plus sûr est de vivre et de mourir vestale:
Car tantôt nos destins et le ciel en courroux
Punissent nos défauts par un avare époux,
125 Qui couche sur son or, qui rarement nous offre,
Un coeur indigne et bas qu'il dérobe à son coffre;
Dont il faut écouter le sermon toujours prêt,
Sur la sale lésine et le vil intérêt;
À qui le soir il faut, ayant nos poches nettes,
130 Rendre un compte odieux de toutes nos emplettes;
Que l'on ne peut tromper, si fine que l'on soit:
Il compte, pèse tout et de tout s'aperçoit;
Avec qui la vertu doit aller à la quête,
Ou pour s'orner le corps, ou se parer la tête,
135 N'osant pas engager ni vendre son honneur,
Mais cet arabe est-il digne de ce bonheur?
Tantôt nous devenons compagnes et victimes,
D'un joueur furieux, d'un magasin de crimes,
Dont il faut nuit et jour craindre le désespoir:
140 Chez qui riche au matin l'on est pauvre le soir;
Qui venu des forêts à cent fourbes ouvertes,
Violemment sur nous se venge de ses pertes;
Qui querelle le ciel; dont les affreux serments,
Font trembler la maison du faîte aux fondements.
145 Si ce blasphémateur, d'un juste coup de foudre,
A nos yeux effrayés, n'est pas réduit en poudre;
Si quelqu'un, épousant les intérêts des cieux,
Ne le dénonce pas aux magistrats des lieux;
Si revenant trop tard, une cohorte avide,
150 Lui dérobant son or, n'est pas son homicide
Du moins un coup de dés à tous ses biens fatal,
L'envoie obscurément mourir à l'hôpital,

You are a demon, you who were an angel.
Even if you listen to your lovers and are virtuous,
110 It's still the same; you're worth nothing anymore.
Their twisted minds always dissolute
Place foolish women on the right, wise ones on the left.
And you, to punish them (bear this in mind)
Put foolish men to left, wise ones to right.
115   Foul passions for venal beauty
Make their sex still hate and run you down.
Under the shameless sun in countless places,
They'll use their love, honor, health, and wealth,
And in the end, conceive, deep within their souls,
120 Unshakable disgust for all that's known as woman."[...]

Whatever perfect happiness a marriage may display,
The safest is to live and die a vestal.
For sometimes our fate and the wrathful heavens
To punish our faults wed us to a miser
125 Who sleeps on his gold and rarely offers
The base, unworthy heart he steals from his coffer;
Whose ever-ready sermons we must hear
On foul stinginess and vilest greed;
To whom nightly we must, though our pockets are clean,
130 Give of every penny an odious account;
Whom we can never fool, clever though we be,
For he counts and weighs everything, everything sees.
With him, virtue is reduced to beggary
When we want to adorn our body or head,
135 Since we dare not pawn or sell our honor,
Though this barbarian would deserve such fate.
Sometimes we become companions and victims
Of a mad gambler, a storehouse of crimes,
Whose desperation we fear both night and day;
140 For rich in the morning, poor we are at night.
Returning from the jungles full of swindlers,
Violently he wreaks on us his losses,
And even with heaven quarrels; his dreadful oaths
Make the whole house shake from pillar to post.
145 If this blasphemer's not reduced to cinders
By a just thunderbolt before our fearful eyes;
If someone, taking up the cause of heaven,
Doesn't denounce him to the local judge;
If, when returning home so late, a greedy mob,
150 Stealing his gold, doesn't murder him,
At least a throw of dice, fatal to his fortune,
Will send him to die ignobly in some hospital.

Voilà ses noirs destins, ou sa triste clôture.
　　Voici d'un froid jaloux les moeurs, ou la peinture,
155　Il nous aimera tant qu'il se fera haïr.
Il nous croira toujours prêtes à le trahir.
Il paraîtra sans nous incapable de vivre.
Il nous suivra partout, ou bien nous fera suivre.
Il aura pour suspects tous les temps, tous les lieux.
160　Il voudra que l'on soit et sans bouche et sans yeux.
Il rendra criminelle une oeillade innocente.
Il parlera toujours d'une voix menaçante.
Il nous étourdira d'inutiles leçons.
Il fera lit à part dans ses moindres soupçons.
165　Il deviendra pour nous aussi froid que décembre.
Il tiendra notre honneur sous la clef d'une chambre.
Il en bouchera tout: en clouera les volets.
Il en interdira l'entrée à nos valets.
Il n'y voudra bientôt plus admettre son ombre.
170　Il vera chaque jour croître son humeur sombre.
A la fin tout en proie à ses exhalaisons.
Il ira se guérir aux Petites-Maisons.[. . .]

Voilà de ce Thersite une légère ébauche,
Il vit par ses appâts et non par ses écus,
175　Les sens de sa Mélite et frappés et vaincus.
Toutefois il a peur, il lui parle sans cesse,
De livres, d'oraison, de prône, de confesse,
Il la prêche souvent, mais en forme; et voici
Un de ses longs discours que j'ai fort accourci.
180　　Il y montre d'abord que sans le tête-à-tête
L'amour ne serait pas une seule conquête;
Que son sexe toujours attaque fortement;
Que le nôtre toujours résiste faiblement;
Que les dames devraient ne hanter que des dames,
185　Point d'amitié, dit-il, d'hommes avec les femmes,
On ne la peut fixer. Elle prend droit son cours,
Vers le fleuve du tendre au pays des amours.
Là notre honneur souvent fait un triste naufrage,
L'on m'appellerait sot si vous n'étiez point sage,
190　N'admettez donc jamais en votre appartement,
De ces larrons d'honneur, dont je ne sais comment,
Le nombre est devenu si grand dans cette ville,
Qu'où l'on n'en pense qu'un, il en est plus de mille,
Que si quelques-uns d'eux se glissaient près de vous,
195　Il faudrait ma brebis, criant aux loups, aux loups,
Les obliger de faire une prompte retraite:

Such is his dark fate and his sad demise.
Here's the portrait and the habits of a jealous man:
155 He loves us so he makes us hate him.
He thinks we're always ready to betray him.
He seems without us quite unable to exist.
He follows us everywhere, or has us followed.
He views suspiciously all times, all places.
160 He wishes us to have no mouth, no eyes.
He deems guilty an innocent glance.
He always speaks in threatening tones.
He dizzies us with useless sermons.
He sleeps apart at the slightest irritation.
165 He is as cold to us as deep December.
He keeps our honor within a chamber locked.
He seals up every door, nails down the shutters.
He'll not even let the servants in.
He'd like to ban his very shadow.
170 He sees his gloomy mood grow daily worse.
And then, full prey to his exhalations,
He ends up in the madhouse seeking cure.[...]

Here's a light sketch of Thersites.
He lives by his charms, not his coins,
175 Dazzling the senses of his Melite.
Yet he's afraid, and talks incessantly
Of books and prayers, sermons and confessions.
He often lectures her by the book; and here's
One of his lengthy sermons much condensed:
180   He proves, first off, that without a tête-à-tête,
Love would not be true conquest.
That his sex always attacks most vigorously,
That ours always resists but feebly,
That women should only frequent other women.
185 "No friendship," he says,"'twixt the sexes,
For it cannot be checked; it takes its course
Straight toward the river of Tendre, in the land of love.
There our honor often shipwrecked becomes.
They'd call me a fool, were you not chaste.
190 Therefore, never admit to your apartment
Any of those thieves of honor whose number,
I know not how, has grown so great in town,
That where you think there's one, there are in fact a thousand,
If some of these made their slippery way toward you,
195 You should, my lamb, cry, Wolf! Oh, wolf!
And force them to beat a hasty retreat,

Puis venir vous ranger sous ma sûre houlette,
Qu'il en est parmi vous, qui se laissent manger,
Qui pourraient à leur aide appeler leur berger!
200   Mais ces loups bien souvent vous ôtent la parole.

Muse, que pensez-vous de ce discours frivole?
      «Mais il me paraît vague et fort injurieux,
      Il a de plus versé des pavots sur mes yeux,
      Je dors»;
                  Si vous dormez, je quitte la satire,
205   Et fais grâce aux maris que j'avais à décrire;
      Au prodigue guerrier, au ruineux plaideur,
      A celui près duquel on a besoin d'odeur,
      A l'impie odieux, au valétudinaire,
      A ceux que la pudeur me commande de taire,
210   A cent autres enfin, opprobre de l'hymen,
      Ciel, de tous ces fléaux préservez-nous, amen.

(1701)

CHANSON À BOIRE

Ami, c'est ton destin de suivre les Amours,
   Le mien est de boire toujours:
   Verse des pleurs auprès d'une inhumaine,
   Pour triompher de la fierté;
5   Je jouis de la liberté,
   Tandis que tu portes ta chaîne:
Ami, c'est ton destin de suivre les Amours,
   Le mien est de boire toujours.
   Ne perds jamais l'espoir de plaire,
10   Chéris tes soins et ton tourment;
Quand je m'enivrerai d'un breuvage charmant,
   Enivre-toi d'une chimère:
Ami, c'est ton destin de suivre les Amours,
   Le mien est de boire toujours.

(1714)

And then come hide under my crook secure,
For there are some of you who are devoured
When you could have called your shepherd to your aid!
200 But such wolves take your breath away."

O Muse, what think you of such frivolous talk?
  "It does seem vague and most injurious,
  Besides, it's cast some poppies on my eyes,
  I'm sleeping."
                        If you're sleeping, then I'll leave satire,
205 And spare the other husbands I wanted to chastise:
The prodigious warrior, the ruinous complainant,
The one whose presence gives us need of perfume,
The valetudinary, the odious free-thinker,
And others modesty forbids me name,
210 A hundred others, the scourge of marriage;
Heaven preserve us from all these plagues! Amen.

—*Dorothy Backer*

LOUISE-GENEVIÈVE DE SAINCTONGE (1650–1718)

DRINKING SONG

Friend, it's your fate to follow Love,
  'Tis mine to be always drinking.
  Go shed tears for a lady cruel
  To overcome her haughty pride.
5   I delight in liberty,
  While you still bear your chain.
Friend, it's your fate to follow Love,
  'Tis mine to be always drinking.
  Never lose hope of enticing,
10 Cherish your cares and torments;
While I get drunk on a charming draught,
  Be drunk on your illusions.
Friend, it's your fate to follow Love,
  'Tis mine to be always drinking.

—*Dorothy Backer*

EPÎTRE À MADAME LA MARQUISE DE C***

Veuve gracieuse et gentille,
Qui vaut bien une cointe fille,
Vous m'envoyez de vos muscats,
Fruit exquis, dont je fais grand cas;
5 Mais j'en fais encor davantage
De ce billet de votre main,
Lui seul enchante mon chagrin;
Certes c'est un grand avantage
Que d'avoir semblable faveur;
10 Tel est accablé de langueur,
Qui tiendrait un joyeux langage,
S'il recevait tant seulement,
De vous un petit compliment:
Mais vous n'êtes rien moins que tendre
15 Pour ce peuple d'amants soumis,
Vous les traitez en ennemis
Qui voudraient pouvoir vous surprendre,
Et ravir cette liberté
Dont votre coeur est enchanté.
20 Conservez, Dame cointe et gente,
Cette franchise si charmante,
Car onc n'est si touchant plaisir
Que vivre au gré de son désir;
Souvent l'hymen a fait connaître
25 Qu'un amant complaisant et doux
Devient un fort importun maître
Alors qu'on en fait un époux.
Vivez toujours en souveraine,
Sous vos lois on voit mille coeurs,
30 Ils seraient tous des déserteurs,
Si d'hymen vous preniez la chaîne.
L'époux ne déserterait pas,
Peut-être aurait-il l'humeur sombre,
Et peut-être, ainsi que votre ombre,
35 Ils s'attacherait à vos pas.
Je n'entreprendrai point de dire
Tout ce que l'hymen a de maux,
Certes, c'est par trop de travaux,
Ma plume n'y pourrait suffire;
40 Je compterais plutôt les fleurs
Qui parent les saisons nouvelles,
Plutôt de l'aurore les pleurs,
Et du ciel toutes les étoiles.

LETTER TO MADAME LA MARQUISE DE C***

Gracious and gentle widow,
More worthy than a modest maid,
You send me these grapes,
A fruit I find exquisite;
5 But more than fruit of any land,
I prize this letter from your hand;
Truly it is a boon
To receive so great a gift
To charm my sadness away;
10 Any man now languishing
Would begin to babble joyously
Were he only to receive
From you a written compliment.
But you are anything but tender
15 For that submissive horde of lovers;
You treat them like enemies
Trying to overtake you
And rob you of a freedom
That enthralls your heart.
20 Keep, gentle, modest lady,
A freedom so enticing.
Ne'er was there greater pleasure
Than to live at one's desire.
How often marriage teaches us
25 That the gentle and obliging lover,
When we make him a husband,
Becomes an importunate master.
Live then forever as a sovereign;
Under your rule we see a thousand hearts,
30 But soon deserters they'd become
If you took on the marriage chain.
If this husband did not desert you,
Perhaps he'd have a somber humor,
And perhaps like your shadow
35 He'd dog your every step.
I will not attempt to tell you
All the travails of Hymen,
Such effort it would require
My pen would not suffice;
40 I'd rather count the flowers
That adorn the new spring season,
And number the tears of dawn
Or the stars that dot the sky;

Point il ne vous chante de cela,
45 Le bon sens vous a dit, holà,
Vivez dans une paix profonde,
Assez d'autres peuplent le monde.
Moi je vous dis sincèrement,
Non comme un banal compliment,
50 Que vous avez, gentille Dame,
Un entier pouvoir sur mon âme.

(1714)

LETTRE À MADAME LA MARQUISE DE S[IMIANE] EN LUI ENVOYANT DU TABAC

Je n'ai point oublié que vous m'avez choisie
    Pour satisfaire un de vos sens,
    C'est un des plus indifférents
    Pour les plaisirs de cette vie.
5 Aussi, malgré les bruits que de vous on publie,
    Si vous eussiez formé l'envie
    De les rendre tous bien contents,
Je crois que votre coeur dans cette fantaisie
    Eût, sans balancer plus longtemps,
10   Envisagé d'autres talents
    Que ceux d'une chétive amie;
Mais vous n'avez que des petits besoins,
Et le seul odorat est chez vous en souffrance.
Vous imaginez-vous que mes yeux souffrent moins
15 Eloignés de votre présence?
Je ne puis cependant vous voir en pénitence,
Je vais vous soulager. Pour toute récompense
    De mon tabac et de mes soins,
J'exigerai de vous, trop aimable Corinne,
20 Que votre belle main quelquefois se destine
    A me marquer de tendres sentiments,
    Tous vos plaisirs, tous vos amusements.

He'll never sing to you of these.
45 Good sense has told you, yes indeed,
To live in peace profound:
Stop! There are enough who multiply.
I say to you sincerely
And not as mere banality
50 That over my soul, gentlest lady,
You have complete and utter power.

—*Dorothy Backer*

MME DE C*** (n.d.)

LETTER TO MADAME LA MARQUISE DE S[IMIANE],
ON SENDING HER TOBACCO

I've not forgotten you chose me
    To gratify one of the senses
    That's generally said to be
    Immaterial to life's pleasures.
5 Thus, despite the rumors spread abroad,
    If you truly had the longing
    To satisfy them one and all,
I think that in this fancy
    Your heart, without a pause,
10   Would not have chosen for the task
    A pitiful friend like me;
But you have needs of modest size;
In you, only the sense of smell is unfulfilled.
And yet do you imagine that my eyes
15 Away from you suffer any less?
Still, I cannot bear to see you penitent,
And will relieve your pain. As reward
    For my tobacco and my care,
    All I ask, my lovable Corinne,
20 Is that your hand sometimes choose
    To trace for me with tenderness
    All of your pleasures, all your fine times.

Dûssai-je y voir dépeints Satan et sa malice,
    Car dans l'oisiveté des champs
25 Il faut permettre un peu de vice.

(1715)

MADRIGAL

Vous me baisez comme une soeur:
Ces baisers sont pleins de douceur;
Mais souffrez que je les condamne.
Je ne suis qu'un mortel, ô nouvelle Diane,
5 Pourquoi me traitez-vous ainsi qu'un Apollon?
Je serai trop heureux du sort d'Endimion.

(1715)

Even if you painted Satan and his tricks,
    I say that in rustic idleness
25   One must tolerate a little vice.

—Dorothy Backer

PAULINE DE SIMIANE (1676–1737)

MADRIGAL

You kiss me like a sister,
Kisses filled with sweetness;
Yet you must allow me to condemn them,
For I'm only mortal, my Diane;
5 Why treat me like Apollo great?
I'd be so happy with Endymion's fate.

—Dorothy Backer

des *AMAZONES*

Thésée: De vos haines, Madame, interrompant le cours,
Ne pourrez-vous jamais nous voir sans défiance?
D'un homme désarmé craignez-vous la présence?
Ménalippe: Non; mon coeur aguerri par les travaux de Mars,
5 Des plus fameux héros ne craint point les regards.
Dès notre tendre enfance on nous destine aux armes;
Nos yeux farouches, durs et stériles aux larmes,
Ignorent l'art flatteur, inventé pour charmer;
Nous inspirons l'effroi, non le désir d'aimer.
10 Nos mains de nos attraits, négligeant la parure,
S'occupent sur le fer à forger notre armure.
Loin de régler nos pas sur des sons cadencés,
A la course, à la lutte, on les trouve exercés.
Les centaures, de nous apprirent à conduire
15 Les coursiers indomptés, que notre art sut réduire.
La hâche à deux tranchants secondant nos fureurs;
Des traits de l'ennemi rend nos efforts vainqueurs.
Fermes dans le danger, sans ruse et sans faiblesse,
A rompre vos projets, nous mettons notre adresse;
20 Et le fils de Vénus, dont tout fuit les attraits,
Sur les filles de Mars épuise en vain ses traits.
Si nous nous soumettons aux lois de la nature,
Ce n'est que pour régner dans la race future,
Et repeupler ces champs, des femmes dont le bras
25 Soit libre, généreux, et terrible aux combats.
Puissent-elles toujours, à nos vertus fidèles,
Voir nos tyrans détruits, et nos lois immortelles!
Thésée: J'admire, Ménalippe, et vos faits et vos lois,
Tout ce qu'en croit la terre, est moins que je n'en
vois;
30 Mais le sang des captifs qu'épargnant les batailles,
Devrait-il arroser le sein de vos murailles?
La cruauté ternit l'éclat de la valeur.
Ménalippe: Il fallait à la force opposer la rigueur,
Contre un sexe orgueilleux d'une injuste puissance,
35 Notre effort unanime emporta la balance;
Bientôt le désespoir, fils de l'adversité,
De la main tyrannique abat l'authorité.
Si chez vous, la vertu se montrait plus parfaite,
Notre fierté vaincue avouerait sa défaite;

MARIE-ANNE DU BOCCAGE (1710–1802)

from *THE AMAZONS*

Theseus: Will you never view us without distrust,
            Madame, and stop the flow of endless hate?
            Must you even fear the presence of a man disarmed?
Menalippa: No! My heart is inured by the labors of Mars,
5   And fears not the gaze of heroes most famed.
            From tenderest years we are destined for arms,
            Our wild eyes are hardened and barren of tears;
            We know not flattery, invented to please;
            It's fear we inspire, not love's desire.
10   Our hands disdain to adorn our charms,
            And turn to the steel that will forge us our armor.
            Far from fitting our steps to the beat of the dance,
            We exercise only for racing and battle.
            It's from us the centaurs learned how to ride
15   Untamed chargers bridled by our skill.
            The two-bladed axe supported our fury
            And helped us vanquish our enemy's arrows.
            Steadfast in danger, without guile or weakness,
            We devote our wits to destroying your plans.
20   And the son of Venus, whose wiles you all flee,
            On the daughters of Mars draws his shafts in vain.
            If we ever submit to the laws of nature
            It is only to reign over future generations,
            To repopulate these fields with women whose arms
25   Are free and noble, and terrible in the fray.
            May they ever, faithful to our virtues,
            See our tyrants destroyed, our laws immortal!
Theseus: I admire your deeds and your laws, Menelippa;
            What the world believes is not what I see here.
30   But the blood of captives whom battle has spared,
            Must it also wash over the heart of your ramparts?
            Cruelty tarnishes valor's renown.
Menelippa: We had to fight force with force of our own;
            'Gainst your sex overweening and power unjust,
35   Our united efforts tipped the scale in our favor;
            And soon dread despair, son of adversity,
            Brought down the weight of tyrannical rule.
            If virtue, in you, showed more perfection,
            Our conquered pride would admit to defeat.

40	Mais si vous l'emportez par plus d'exploits fameux,
	Vos vices sont plus grands, vos crimes plus
	nombreux:
	Vos droits, nés de la force, et non des dons de
	l'âme,
	Révoltent la raison, l'équité...

Thésée: Mais, Madame,

La crainte d'obéir détruit votre bonheur.

45   Sans cesse à nous braver, forçant votre valeur,

Au milieu des lauriers vous trouvez mille alarmes,

Dans les autres climats vous régnez par vos charmes:

Cet empire plus doux, ici n'est point connu;

Contre notre pouvoir, votre esprit prévenu,

50   A nous craindre, à nous fuir, épuise son adresse,

Se prive des plaisirs, ignore la tendresse,

De l'union des coeurs brise le doux lien.

Ménalippe: La liberté, Thésée, est le souverain bien.

La vaine soif de l'or, la discorde, l'envie,

55   Dans le sein des plaisirs germent et prennent vie.

Parmi nous, les travaux et la frugalité

Maintiennent la vertu, la paix, la vérité.

Sur l'empire des Rois, le nôtre a l'avantage;

Souvent dans vos états le pouvoir se partage;

60   Mille jeunes beautés soumettent leurs vainqueurs,

Au gré de leurs désirs dispensent vos faveurs.

Leur règne d'un instant dure assez pour vous nuire,

Pour usurper vos droits, qu'elles voudraient

détruire,

Et la vieillesse enfin les livre à vos mépris.

65   Loin de la craindre ici, le temps nous donne un prix;

Les rides sur le front y marquent la puissance:

Nul intérêt secret n'y porte à la vengeance,

Et le seul bien public y réunit les voix,

Les siècles à venir, surpris de nos exploits,

70   Si nos états détruits revivent dans l'histoire,

En admirant nos moeurs, auront peine à les croire.

Peut-être on doutera que jamais l'univers

Ait vu régner nos lois jusqu'au-delà des mers.

                                  (Act III, sc.5)

(1788)

40	But if you triumph by still more famous exploits,

40 But if you triumph by still more famous exploits,
Your vices are greater, more numerous your crimes;
Your rights, born of force and not gifts from the
    spirit,
Deeply offend our equity and reason...

Theseus: But Madame,
The fear of obeying destroys your good fortune.

45 Forcing your bravery endlessly to oppose us,
Among your laurels you find a thousand terrors.
In other climes you reign by charm alone;
That gentler empire is here unknown.
Against our power your mind, always on guard,

50 Fearing us, fleeing us, wastes all its talents,
Deprives you of pleasure, tenderness ignores,
And breaks the sweet bond of hearts united.

Menelippa: Freedom, Theseus, is the highest good.
The vain thirst for gold, discord, and envy

55 Takes root and life in the midst of these pleasures.
For us it is work and frugality
That keep virtue, peace, and truth alive.
Above the sway of Kings, ours has this advantage:
That often in your states power is divided;

60 A thousand pretty faces subject their victors
And dispense your favors by the whim of desire.
Their momentary reign lasts long enough to harm
    you,
Usurping all your rights, that they would fain
    destroy.
But age, in the end, to your contempt delivers them.

65 We do not fear it here; time makes us more precious.
Wrinkles upon the brow are the mark of our power.
No secret interest drives us to take our revenge,
And naught but public good unites us in one voice.
If our destroyed states should live again in history,

70 The centuries to come, amazed by our great deeds,
Admiring our mores, will wonder in disbelief.
Perhaps they'll even doubt that this universe of ours
Ever saw our laws rule far beyond the seas.

—*Dorothy Backer*

LA DÉLIVRANCE D'ARGOS

Une femme autrefois, émule de Tyrthée,
D'une héroïque ardeur comme lui transportée,
Vengea, la lyre en main, les citoyens d'Argos.
D'une jeune beauté leur salut fut l'ouvrage;
5   Et son noble courage
S'égala dans la Gréce à celui des héros.

Un bruit d'armes s'entend; des légions guerrières,
De la faible Mycène ont rompu les barrières.
L'Inachus s'est troublé; le sang rougit ses eaux:
10   Déja des assaillants les progrès sont rapides;
Et les vieux Pélopides
Gémissent sourdement au fond de leurs tombeaux.

Toi qu'enorgueillissait ta haute destinée,
Ville d'Agamemnon, ô ville infortunée!
15   Tes pâles combattants ont fui de toutes parts;
L'ombre du roi des rois, dont tu gardes la cendre,
Ne peut plus te défendre,
Et tes dieux protecteurs vont quitter tes remparts.

C'est Sparte qui t'assiège; où sera ton asile?
20   Mais le ciel tout-à-coup suscitant Télésille,
Elle accourt, et gémit de honte et de douleur.
La fille d'Apollon, tout au dieu qui l'inspire
Prend le glaive et la lyre,
Et d'Argos, par ses chants, ranime la valeur.

25   «Eh quoi! de leurs aïeux oubliant la vaillance,
Ces soldats effrayés abandonnent leur lance,
Et leur indigne fuite a trompé tous nos voeux!
Mes compagnes, venez, osez suivre ma trace,
Revêtir la cuirasse,
30   Et qu'un casque guerrier presse vos blonds cheveux.

«Vénus n'est pas toujours déesse par ses charmes;
A Sparte elle est guerrière: on lui donna des armes:
La compagne de Mars doit en suivre le sort.
Sexe timide et fier que souvent l'homme outrage,
35   Il te doit son courage;
Ton bras est moins nerveux, mais ton coeur est plus fort.

«Aux drapeaux étrangers renvoyons l'épouvante;
Du magnanime Hercule en vain Sparte se vante;

ADELAÏDE-GILLETTE DUFRESNOY (1765–1825)

THE DELIVERANCE OF ARGOS

In days of old, a woman emulating Tyrtheus,
And, like him, moved by a heroic ardor,
Avenged the citizens of Argos, lyre in hand.
They owed salvation to this young beauty
5   Whose noble courage
Rivaled the valor of Greece's heroes.

Sounds of arms resound; warring legions
Have broken the walls of weak Mycenae;
The troubled waters of Inachus run with blood,
10 And with speed the attackers forge ahead;
    The ancient breed
Of Pelops groans from deep within its grave.

You who were proud of your lofty destiny,
Whose pale warriors now scatter and flee,
15 City of Agamemnon, ill-starred city!
The ashen ghost of the king of kings
    Can defend you no longer,
And your protective gods now desert your ramparts.

Sparta besieges you; where is your refuge?
20 But suddenly heaven summons Telesilla;
She runs, shuddering with shame and pain.
Apollo's daughter she is; inspired by the god,
    She takes up sword and lyre,
And by her songs revives the Argoan valor.

25 "Alas! Forgetting the ancestral bravery,
These frightened soldiers throw away their lance,
Our hopes dashed by their shameless flight!
My comrades, come, dare to follow my path,
    Put on your armor,
30 And may a warrior's helmet bind your locks.

"Venus is not only a goddess by her charms;
In Sparta she's a warrior: she bore arms.
Mars' companion must follow his fate,
Proud and timid sex that man so often insults,
35   He owes you his courage;
Your arm's less sinewy, but stronger your heart.

"Let us send back fear to the foreign flags;
In vain does Sparta claim magnanimous Hercules;

Pélops de Jupiter est issu comme lui.
40 Quand les Grecs d'Ilion préparaient la conquête,
    Nous marchions à leur tête,
Et de Sparte elle-même Argos était l'appui.

«Argiens, que ma voix à l'honneur vous rappelle;
Serrez, pressez les rangs; que le glaive étincelle;
45 Que d'intrépides mains poussent les javelots.
Mon luth ne dira plus que l'hymne de la guerre
    Jusqu'au jour où la terre
Du sang des ennemis aura bu tous les flots.

«Les Muses que je sers n'ont point un coeur barbare.
50 Aux lieux où L'Inachus paisiblement s'égare,
Je modulais des vers aussi doux que ses bords.
Les maux de ma patrie ont soulevé mon âme;
    Et le dieu qui m'enflamme
D'un courroux inconnu vient remplir mes accords.

55 «O poétiques monts, remparts de ma patrie!
Fountaines! bois sacrés! chers à la rêverie;
Douce Argos! loin de toi dois-je fuir pour jamais?
Les dieux souffriront-ils qu'un vainqueur vous profane!
    Apollon et Diane,
60 Armés de traits vengeurs, veillent sur vos sommets.

«Je le vois, ma prière est vers eux parvenue,
Et leur arc redoutable a brillé dans la nue:
Ils donnent le signal, ils marchent devant nous.
Marchons, ne craignons plus les descendants d'Hercule:
65   Déjà Sparte recule,
Et ses fils effrayés expirent sous nos coups.

«Non, jamais L'Eurotas ne me verra captive;
Il ne m'entendra point, sur ma lyre plaintive,
Réjouir ses échos du bruit de nos revers.
70 Non; qu'aux champs de l'honneur Télésille succombe!
    Qu'on grave sur sa tombe:
Elle aima mieux la mort que l'opprobre des fers.»

C'est ainsi que chantait la prêtresse inspirée.
Elle triomphe; Argos est bientôt délivrée.
75 Sa voix bénit des dieux le secours immortel.
Son sexe eut dans ce jour l'honneur de la victoire;
    Et pour garder sa gloire
A Vénus triomphante on bâtit un autel.

(1813)

Pelops is also Jupiter's progeny.
40 When the Greeks readied the conquest of Ilion,
    We headed the march;
Argos herself was Sparta's main support.

''People of Argos, my voice recalls you to honor;
Close ranks, press on, raise your glittering swords!
45 Drive the javelins home with intrepid hands.
My lute will sing no more but hymns of war
    Until the day our land
Has soaked up the waves of enemy blood.

''The Muses I serve do not have savage hearts.
50 There where Inachus peacefully flows,
I sang verses as gentle as its shores.
But then my country's woes aroused my soul;
    And my inflaming god
Fills my chords with fierceness yet unknown.

55 ''O lyric mountains, ramparts of my native land!
Fountains! sacred woods! dear to my revery;
Sweet Argos! Must I forsake you now forever?
Will the gods suffer that a conqueror profane you?
    May Apollo and Diana,
60 Armed with avenging darts, protect your summits.

''I see that my prayer has finally reached them;
A formidable rainbow glitters in the clouds above:
They give the signal, they march before us.
March on, let's fear no more the sons of Hercules:
65   Now Sparta retreats,
And her affrighted sons fall beneath our blows.

''Never will Eurotas see me captive;
Never will he hear me, on my plaintive lyre,
Fill the echoing plains with our misfortunes.
70 No; let Telesilla fall in the field of honor,
    Let her gravestone say:
'Death she preferred to the shame of chains.' ''

It was thus the inspired priestess sang.
She triumphs; Argos is soon delivered from her foes.
75 For their immortal help her voice blessed the gods.
That day her sex had the honor of the victory;
    And to preserve her glory,
There they built an altar to Venus triumphant.

—Dorothy Backer

EPÎTRE AUX FEMMES

La colère suffit, et vaut un Apollon.
        Boileau, Satire I

O femmes, c'est pour vous que j'accorde ma lyre!
O femmes, c'est pour vous qu'en mon brûlant délire,
D'un usage orgueilleux bravant les vains efforts,
Je laisse enfin ma voix exprimer mes transports.
5 Assez et trop longtemps la honteuse ignorance
A jusqu'en vos vieux jours prolongé votre enfance;
Assez et trop longtemps les hommes égarés
Ont craint de voir en vous des censeurs éclairés:
Un siècle de justice à nos yeux vient de naître;
10 Femmes, soyez aussi ce que vous devez être.

Si la nature a fait deux sexes différents,
Elle a changé la forme, et non les éléments.
Même loi, même erreur, même ivresse les guide;
L'un et l'autre propose, exécute, ou décide;
15 Les charges, les pouvoirs, entre eux deux compensés,
Par un ordre immuable y restent balancés;
Tous deux pensent régner, et tous deux obéissent;
Ensemble ils sont heureux, séparés ils languissent;
Tour à tour l'un de l'autre enfin guide et soutien,
20 Même en se donnant tout ils ne se doivent rien.

L'homme injuste pourtant, oubliant sa faiblesse,
Outrageant à la fois l'amour et la sagesse,
L'homme injuste, jaloux de tout assujettir,
Sous la loi du plus fort prétend nous asservir:
25 Il feint, dans sa compagne et sa consolatrice,
De ne voir qu'un objet créé pour son caprice;
Il trouve dans nos bras le bonheur qui le fuit:
Son orgueil s'en étonne, et son front en rougit.
Esclave révolté des lois de la nature,
30 Ses clameurs, il est vrai, ne sont qu'un vain murmure:
Mais que, par les mépris dont il veut nous couvrir,
Il nous vend cher les droits qu'il ne peut nous ravir!
Nos talents, nos vertus, nos grâces séduisantes,
Deviennent à ses yeux des armes dégradantes
35 Dont nous devons chercher à nous faire un appui
Pour mériter l'honneur d'arriver jusqu'à lui.
Il étouffe en nos coeurs la fierté, le courage;

CONSTANCE-MARIE DE SALM-DYCK (1767–1845)

LETTER TO WOMEN

Anger is enough, and worthy of Apollo.
Boileau, Satire I

O women, for you I tune my lyre!
O women, it's for you that in my passion,
Braving the vain efforts of self-proud habit,
At last I let my voice express my transport.
5   Enough, too long has shameful ignorance
Prolonged our childhood into old age.
Enough, too long, men gone astray
Have feared to find in you enlightened critics.
A century of justice dawns before us;
10   Women! be, then, what you should be.

If nature made two sexes different,
She changed the form, but not the elements.
The same laws, errors, frenzy guides them both;
One and the other propose, decide, dispose.
15   Duties and powers 'twixt the two are shared
And by immutable order stay in balance.
Both claim to rule, and both obey.
Together they are joyful, apart they languish.
By turns, one guides and supports the other;
20   Even giving their all, nothing is owed.

But unjust man, forgetting he is weak,
Grievously injures both wisdom and love;
Yes, unjust man, craving to conquer all,
Claims to subject us to the law of might,
25   Pretends to see his partner and consoler
As nothing but the object of his caprice.
He finds elusive happiness in our arms;
And so his brow blushes, his pride is hurt.
A slave rebelling 'gainst the laws of nature,
30   His shouts are nothing but a vain complaint.
But oh, how dear he sells the rights he cannot ravish
By the contempt he tries to shower upon us.
Our talents, virtues, our seductive graces
Become the basest weapons in his eyes;
35   We stoop to use them as a kind of crutch
To merit the honor of reaching his station.
He smothers pride and courage in our hearts

Il nous fait une loi de supporter l'outrage,
Pour exercer en paix un empire absolu,
40 Il fait de la douceur notre seule vertu...
Qu'ai-je dit, la douceur? Ah! nos âmes sensibles
Ne lui refusent pas ces triomphes paisibles;
Mais ce n'est pas assez pour son esprit jaloux:
C'est la soumission qu'il exige de nous...
45 Ingrat! Méconnais-tu la sagesse profonde
Qui dirige en secret tous les êtres du monde?
Méconnais-tu la main qui traça dans ton coeur
De ton amour pour nous le principe vengeur?
Voyons-nous, dan nos bois, nos vallons, nos montagnes,
50 Les lions furieux outrager leurs compagnes?
Voyons-nous dans les airs l'aigle dominateur
De l'aigle qu'il chérit réprimer la grandeur?
Non; tous suivent en paix l'instinct de la nature:
L'homme seul à ses lois est rebelle et parjure.

55 Cependant le réveil des sens impérieux
Rétablit un instant l'équilibre à ses yeux;
Le désir, le besoin, triomphent du système:
L'homme redevient homme aussitôt qu'il nous aime;
Défenseur généreux, être sensible et bon,
60 Il retrouve à la fois son coeur et sa raison,
Et, laissant à nos pieds le vain titre de maître,
Il obéit aux lois qu'il vient de méconnaître.
C'est là, dans les transports d'un amoureux lien,
Qu'il voit que sur nos coeurs sa force ne peut rien;
65 Que notre volonté seulement nous commande;
Que l'on n'obtient de nous qu'alors qu'on nous demande;
Et que la liberté dont nous nous honorons
N'est point remise aux mains que nous-même enchaînons.

Femmes, ne croyez point que ce soit tout encore:
70 Trop souvent ce bonheur s'éclipse à son aurore;
Et l'espoir que l'amour va vous rendre aujourd'hui,
Demain, malgré vos soins, disparaît avec lui.
C'est par des traits plus sûrs qu'il faut montrer aux hommes
Tout ce que nous pouvons et tout ce que nous sommes:
75 C'est à les admirer qu'on veut nous obliger;
C'est en les imitant qu'il faut nous en venger.
Science, poésie, arts, qu'ils nous interdisent,
Sources de voluptés qui les immortalisent,
Venez, et faites voir à la postérité.
80 Qu'il est aussi pour nous une immortalité!
Déjà plus d'une femme, osant braver l'envie,
Aux dangers de la gloire a consacré sa vie;

And forces us to bear the outrage;
That he may hold his utter rule in peace
40 He gives us but one virtue: gentleness...
Did I say, gentleness? Ah! our sensitive souls
Do not refuse him his quiet triumphs;
But this suffices not his jealous mind:
From us he demands an absolute submission...
45 Ungrateful one! Don't you know the wisdom
That secretly directs all earthly beings?
And know you not the hand that etched your heart
With the revenging principle of your love?
Do we see in the forests, mountains, valleys,
50 The furious lion abuse his companion?
Or in the air the dominating eagle
Deny the grandeur of his mate?
No! All creatures quietly follow nature's instinct;
Rebellious man alone forswears her laws.

55 And yet, the wakening of the imperious senses
Briefly restores balance in his eyes.
Desire and need triumph over his system:
When he loves us man becomes man again.
Generous, sensitive, and fair defender,
60 He rediscovers both his heart and reason,
And leaving at our feet his master's title
He now obeys the laws he once ignored.
'Tis there, in transports of an amorous bond,
He sees over our hearts his power has no sway;
65 That will alone rules and commands us,
That he must ask for what he would obtain
And that the freedom which so honors us
Is not in his hands, which we can always bind.

Women, do not believe that this is all:
70 Too often, joy is eclipsed at the very dawn,
And hope, which love revives in you today,
Try as you might, may depart with him tomorrow.
It is by surer signs to men that we must show
All that we are, all that we can do.
75 The world demands that we admire them:
Imitate them we must to gain revenge.
Oh, poetry, arts, and science, they forbid us,
Sources of delight that immortalize them;
Come and show the world as yet unborn
80 That immortality exists for us as well.
Already many a woman, braving envy,
Has sacrificed her life to perilous fame.

Déjà plus d'une femme, en sa fière vertu,
Pour l'honneur de son sexe, ardente, a combattu.
85 Eh! d'où naîtrait en nous une crainte servile!
Ce feu qui nous dévore est-il donc inutile?
Le dieu qui dans nos coeurs a daigné l'allumer,
Dit-il que sans paraître il doit nous consumer?
Portons-nous sur nos fronts, écrit en traits de flamme:
90 *l'homme doit régner seul et soumettre la femme?*
Un ascendant secret vient-il nous avertir
Quand il faut admirer, quand il faut obéir?
La nature pourtant aux êtres qu'elle opprime
Donne de leur malheur le sentiment intime:
95 L'agneau sent que le loup veut lui ravir le jour;
L'oiseau tombe sans force à l'aspect du vautour...
Disons-le: L'homme, enflé d'un orgueil sacrilège,
Rougit d'être égalé par celle qu'il protège;
Pour ne trouver en nous qu'un être admirateur,
100 Sa voix dès le berceau nous condamne à l'erreur;
Moins fort de ce qu'il sait que de notre ignorance,
Il croit qu'il s'agrandit de notre insuffisance,
Et, sous les vains dehors d'un respect affecté,
Il ne vénère en nous que notre nullité.

105 Ecoutons cependant ce que nous dit le sage:
«Femmes, est-ce bien vous qui parlez d'esclavage?
Vous, dont le seul regard peut nous subjuguer tous!
Vous, qui nous enchaînez tremblants à vos genoux!
Vos attraits, vos pleurs feints, vos perfides caresses,
110 Ne suffisent-ils pas pour vous rendre maîtresses?
Eh! qu'avez-vous besoin de moyens superflus?
Vous nous tyrannisez; que vous faut-il de plus?»
Ce qu'il nous faut de plus! un pouvoir légitime.
La ruse est le recours d'un être qu'on opprime.
115 Cessez de nous forcer à ces indignes soins;
Laissez-nous plus de droits, et vous en perdrez moins.
Oui, sans doute, à nos pieds notre fierté vous brave:
Un tyran qu'on soumet doit devenir esclave.
Mais ce cruel moyen de nous venger, hélas!
120 Nous coûte bien des pleurs que vous ne voyez pas.
Il est temps que la paix à nos coeurs soit offerte:
De l'étude, des arts, la carrière est ouverte;
Osons y pénétrer. Eh! qui pourrait ravir
Le droit de les connaître à qui peut les sentir?

125 Mais déjà mille voix ont blâmé notre audace;
On s'étonne, on murmure, on s'agite, on menace;
On veut nous arracher la plume et les pinceaux;

Already more than one with proud virtue
Has ardently defended the honor of her sex.
85 Ah! Whence was born in us a servile fear?
This fire that burns within us, is it useless?
The god who deigned to light it in our hearts,
Does he insist that secretly it consume us?
And do our brows bear letters, writ in flame,
90 *Man must rule alone, subjugate the female?*
Is there a secret power come to warn us
When we should flatter and when obey?
Yet nature gives to beings she oppresses
A secret sense to warn them of disaster.
95 The lamb knows that the wolf would take his life.
The bird falls unprompted at the vulture's sight...
Let's say it: Puffed with sacrilegious pride,
Man blushes to be equaled by a woman
In his charge. To keep us wholly his admirer
100 His voice condemns us to errors from the cradle,
Less strong by his knowledge than our ignorance,
He sees himself enlarged by our shortcomings,
And under vain signs of false respect
He venerates us only for our nothingness.

105 But listen now to what the wise man says:
"Women, do you dare to speak of slavery?
You whose mere glance can subjugate us all!
You who enchain us, trembling, at your knee!
Your beauties, feigned tears, perfidious caresses,
110 Do they not suffice to make you mistress?
Then what need have you of further means?
You tyrannize us! What more do you want?"
What more do we want! Legitimate power.
Trickery is the resource of a being oppressed.
115 Stop forcing us to these unworthy ruses.
Give us more rights, you will lose fewer.
No doubt, our pride defies you at our feet;
A tyrant humbled must become a slave.
But what a cruel revenge this is, alas!
120 The tears it cost us you never witness.
It's time that peace were offered to our hearts.
The road is open to the arts and learning.
Let us dare take it! Who could ever steal
The right to know the arts from those who can feel?

125 But now a thousand voices blame our daring.
Complaining, disturbed, astonished, they menace.
They try to tear from us the pen and brush,

Chacun a contre nous sa chanson, ses bons mots.
L'un, ignorant et sot, vient, avec ironie,
130 Nous citer de Molière un vers qu'il estropie;
L'autre, vain par système, et jaloux par métier,
Dit d'un air dédaigneux: *Elle a son teinturier.*
Des jeunes gens, à peine échappés du collège,
Discutent hardiment nos droits, leur privilège;
135 Et leurs arrêts, dictés par la frivolité,
La mode, l'ignorance, ou la fatuité,
Répétés en échos par ces juges imberbes,
Après deux ou trois jours sont passés en proverbes.
En vain, l'homme de bien, qui toujours nous défend,
140 Contre eux, dans sa justice, éclate hautement,
Leur prouve de nos coeurs la force, le courage,
Leur montre nos lauriers conservés d'âge en âge;
Leur dit qu'on peut unir grâces, talents, vertus;
Que Minerve était femme aussi bien que Vénus:
145 Rien ne peut ramener cette foule en délire;
L'honnête homme se tait, nous regarde, et soupire.
Mais, ô dieux! qu'il soupire et qu'il gémit bien plus
Quand il voit les effets de ce cruel abus!
Quand il voit le besoin de distraire nos âmes
150 Se porter, malgré nous, sur de coupables flammes;
Quand il voit ces transports que réclamaient les arts
Dans un monde pervers offenser ses regards,
Et sur un front terni la licence funeste
Remplacer les lauriers du mérite modeste!
155 Ah! détournons les yeux de cet affreux tableau.
O femmes! reprenez la plume et le pinceau.
Laissez le moraliste, en sa folle colère,
Restreindre nos talents au talent de lui plaire;
Laissez-le, tourmentant des mots insidieux,
160 Dégrader notre sexe et vanter nos beaux yeux;
Laissons l'anatomiste, aveugle en sa science,
D'une fibre avec art calculer la puissance,
Et du plus ou du moins inférer, sans appel,
Que sa femme lui doit un respect éternel.
165 La nature a des droits qu'il ignore lui-même:
On ne la courbe pas sous le poids d'un système;
Aux mains de la faiblesse elle met la valeur;
Sur le front du superbe elle écrit la terreur;
Et, dédaignant les mots de sexe et d'apparence,
170 Pèse sa grandeur les dons qu'elle dispense.

Mais quel nouveau transport! quel soudain changement!
L'homme paraît enfin armé du sentiment;

Each armed against us with his songs and jokes.
Here's one, an ignorant fool, who thinks to cite
130 A line in Molière mangled with irony.
Another, vain by habit, jealous by trade,
Says with disdainful air, "She dyes her hair."
And younglings, barely out of college,
Boldly debate our rights, their prerogatives.
135 Their decrees, dictated by frivolity,
By fashion, ignorance, and fatuity,
Echoed by these beardless magistrates,
After two or three days become adages.
In vain the good man, always our defender,
140 With justice explodes against one and all,
Proves the force, the courage of our hearts,
Shows our laurels, saved from age to age,
Tells how we combine talent, virtue, and grace;
That Minerva was a woman no less than Venus:
145 But nothing brings this mad mob to its senses.
The man of culture, muted, looks at us and sighs.
But, O gods! let him groan and sigh far more
When he sees the effects of such brutal abuse,
And sees the distracted needs of our soul
150 Driven, against our will, toward shameful flames.
Those passions that offend his gaze
In this perverted world, art should have claimed;
And the laurels of modest merit are replaced
By deadly license on a tarnished brow.
155 Oh, let us turn our eyes from this dread sight
Women, take up your pen and brush again.
Let the moralist, in his rage and madness,
Restrict our talents to seductive ploys.
Let him, twisting his insidious words,
160 Degrade our sex and laud our lovely eyes.
Let the anatomist, blinded by his science,
Artfully calculate the power of a muscle,
Infer, without appeal, 'twixt the more and the less,
That his wife owes him eternal respect.
165 Nature has rights that he himself knows not:
You cannot bend her to a man-made system;
She places values in the hands of weakness,
And the brow of haughty men she brands with terror.
Disdaining words like sex and appearance,
170 She weighs the gifts she bestows by grandeur.

But what new transport! Oh, what sudden change!
Man comes at last, armed with feeling;

Il nous crie: «Arrêtez, femmes, vous êtes mères!
A tout autre plaisir rendez-vous étrangères;
175 De l'étude et des arts la douce volupté
Deviendrait un larcin à la maternité.»
O nature, ô devoir, que c'est mal vous connaître!
L'ingrat est-il aveugle, ou bien feint-il de l'être?
Feint-il de ne pas voir qu'en ces premiers instants
180 Où le ciel à nos voeux accorde des enfants,
Tout entières aux soins que leur âge réclame,
Tout ce qui n'est pas eux ne peut rien sur notre âme?
Feint-il de ne pas voir que de nouveaux besoins
Nous imposent bientôt de plus glorieux soins,
185 Et que pour diriger une enfance timide
Il faut être à la fois son modèle et son guide?
Oublieront-ils toujours, ces vains déclamateurs,
Qu'en éclairant nos yeux nous éclairons les leurs?
Eh! quel maître jamais vaut une mère instruite?
190 Sera-ce un pédagogue enflé de son mérite,
Un mercenaire avide, un triste précepteur?
Ils auront ses talents, mais auront-ils son coeur?
Disons tout. En criant: *Femmes, vous êtes mères!*
Cruels, vous oubliez que les hommes sont pères;
195 Que les charges, les soins, sont partagés entre eux;
Que le fils qui vous naît appartient à tous deux;
Et qu'après les moments de sa première enfance
Vous devez, plus que nous, soigner son existence.
Ah! s'il était possible (et le fut-il jamais?)
200 Qu'une mère un instant suspendît ses bienfaits,
Un cri de son enfant, dans son âme attendrie,
Réveillerait bientôt la nature assoupie.
Mais l'homme, tourmenté par tant de passions,
Accablé sous le poids de ses dissensions,
205 Malgré lui, malgré nous, à chaque instant oublie
Qu'il doit plus que son coeur à qui lui doit la vie,
Et que d'un vain sermon les stériles éclats
Des devoirs paternels ne l'acquitteront pas.

Insensés! vous voulez une femme ignorante;
210 Eh bien, soit; confondez l'épouse et la servante:
Voyez-la, mesurant ses leçons sur ses goûts,
Elever ses enfants pour elle, et non pour vous;
Voyez-les, dans un monde à les juger habile,
De leur mère porter la tache indélébile;
215 Au sage, à l'étranger, à vos meilleurs amis,
Rougissez de montrer votre femme et vos fils;
Dans les épanchements d'un coeur sensible et tendre,

He cries out: "Stop, women! You are our mothers!
To all other joys become you strangers.
175 The pleasures of sweet study and the arts
Would rob and plunder your maternity."
They understand you ill, O nature, O duty!
Is this ingrate blind or just pretending?
Does he claim not to know in those instants
180 When heaven grants us wished-for children,
That we, devoted to their tender needs,
Care in our souls for naught but them?
Does he claim not to know that later needs
Impose on us more glorious attentions,
185 That the direction of timid infancy
Requires us to be both guide and model?
Do they always forget, these vain declaimers,
That our enlightenment will enlighten them?
What tutor is ever worth an educated mother?
190 A pedagogue blown up with pride?
An avid mercenary, gloomy pedant?
Her talents they may have; what of her heart?
Let's say it, shouting: "Women, you are mothers!"
Cruel men who have forgotten you are fathers,
195 That tasks and cares are shared between the two;
The son born to you belongs to both.
After the first moments of infancy,
You, more than we, should care for his existence.
Ah! If it happened (but did it ever?)
200 That a mother withheld kindness for an instant,
The child's cry in her tender heart
Would soon awaken dormant nature.
But man, tormented by so many passions,
Burdened as well with the weight of dissension,
205 Despite himself, in spite of us, always forgets
He owes more than his heart to her who gave him life,
And that the sterile glitter of an empty sermon
Does not acquit him of paternal duty.

Madmen! You want your women ignorant.
210 So be it. Confuse the wife with the servant.
Look at her, giving lessons by her sights,
Raising the children for herself, not you.
Look at them, in a world able to judge,
Bearing their mother's indelible mark.
215 To the wise man, the stranger, your best friend,
Blush to display your wife and sons.
May no one in your household comprehend

Que personne chez vous ne puisse vous comprendre;
Traînez ailleurs vos jours et votre obscurité;
220 On ne vous plaindra pas, vous l'aurez mérité.

Regardons maintenant celui dont l'âme grande
Cherche dans sa compagne un être qui l'entende;
Regardons-les tous deux ajouter tour à tour
Le charme des talents au charme de l'amour.
225 Qu'un tel homme est heureux au sein de sa famille!
Il voit croître aux beaux-arts et son fils et sa fille;
Ecoutant la nature avant de la juger,
Il cherche à l'ennoblir, et non à l'outrager.
Chez lui l'humanité ne connaît point d'entrave;
230 L'homme n'est point tyran, la femme point esclave,
Et le génie en paix, planant sur tous les deux,
De l'inégalité décide seul entre eux.
O jours trop tôt passés de mon heureuse enfance!
C'est ainsi que mon coeur sentit votre existence;
235 C'est ainsi qu'en mon sein vous sûtes imprimer
Ces immuables droits que j'ose réclamer.
Un père généreux, agrandissant mon être,
M'apprit dès le berceau ce que je pouvais être;
Et du titre de femme en décorant mon front,
240 Il m'en fit un honneur et non pas un affront.
O toi qui m'animas de cette pure flamme,
De ce séjour de paix où repose ton âme,
Jette sur mes travaux un regard bienfaisant,
Et bénis ces transports d'un coeur reconnaissant.

245 Ne croyez pas pourtant, épouses, méres, filles,
Que je veuille jeter le trouble en vos familles,
D'une ardeur de révolte embraser vos esprits,
Et renverser des lois que moi-même je suis.
Il est des noeuds sacrés et d'honorables chaînes;
250 Il est de doux plaisirs et de plus douces peines;
Et cet échange heureux des soins de deux époux
Fait leur bien mutuel et le charme de tous.
C'est l'ordre qui m'irrite, et non pas la prière;
C'est l'ordre que repousse une âme haute et fière;
255 Mais céder à la voix d'un généreux ami,
C'est s'obliger soi-même et jouir plus que lui.
Ne croyez pas non plus qu'en ma verve indiscrète
J'aille crier partout: *Soyez peintre ou poète.*
Je sais que la nature, avare en ses bienfaits,
260 Nous donne rarement des talents purs et vrais;
Mais telle, que retient la critique ou l'envie,

The unrestrained outburst of your feeling heart;
Drag elsewhere your long-benighted days:
220 No one will pity the fate you deserve.

And now see one whose soul is great and good,
He seeks a mate who understands him;
Look at them, adding each by turns,
The pleasures of talent to the charms of love.
225 How happy such a man in his family's bosom!
He sees his son and daughter grow in culture,
Listens to nature before he judges her,
Seeks to ennoble, not to offend her.
There is no obstacle to his humaneness;
230 The man's no tyrant, the woman no slave.
And over them both, the mind at peace
Alone decides the inequality between them.
Oh, days too soon gone by, my happy childhood!
'Tis thus in my heart I felt your being,
235 'Tis thus in my breast you etched forever
These changeless rights that now I dare to claim.
A generous father, raising up my being,
Taught me from infancy what I could become,
And sealing my brow with the name of woman
240 Made not an insult of it but an honor.
Oh, you who fired me with this pure flame,
From that most peaceful haven where you rest,
Cast down upon my labors a beneficent gaze
And bless these transports of a grateful heart.

245 Think not, however, wives, mothers, daughters,
That I would sow dissension in your homes,
Fire your minds with the ardor of revolt,
Or overturn the laws that I too follow.
For there are sacred bonds and chains of honor,
250 There are sweet pleasures and still sweeter pains.
The sharing of cares between two happy spouses
Is their mutual good, everyone's delight.
No, it is commands that anger me, not prayers.
It's orders that repel a lofty mind that's proud.
255 But yielding to the voice of a giving friend
Is to give oneself more joy than to him.
And do not think, in my enthusiasm,
That everywhere I shout, "A painter or poet be!"
I know that nature is stingy with her bounty
260 And rarely gives us talents pure and true.
But a woman held back by envy or reproach

Sent au fond de son coeur le germe du génie;
Et c'est là que mon vers, armé d'un trait vainqueur,
Veut porter malgré tout un transport créateur.
265 Et quand il se pourrait qu'à ma voix enflammée
Quelque autre femme en vain cherchât la renommée,
Lui doit-on pour cela d'injurieux discours?
L'homme dans ses travaux réussit-il toujours?
Ne vaut-il donc pas mieux d'une ardente jeunesse
270 Charmer par les talents la dangereuse ivresse,
Que de la condamner au plaisir dégradant
D'inventer ou proscrire un vain adjustment?
Oui, l'étude est pour tous un bonheur nécessaire:
On apprend à juger, si l'on n'apprend à faire;
275 L'esprit en s'éclairant ne peut que s'ennoblir,
Et c'est sur l'ignorance enfin qu'il faut gémir.
Moi-même, osant braver les dangers de la scène,
J'ai marché vers le but où ma main vous entraîne;
Moi-même, sur Sapho rappelant quelques pleurs,
280 J'ai suivi ses leçons et chanté ses douleurs;
Moi-même à mes côtés j'ai vu la sombre envie
Sur mes tranquilles jours porter sa main impie...
Eh! que font à mon sort ces êtres orgueilleux?
Mon bonheur est à moi, leurs travers sont pour eux.
285 Que dis-je? ils m'ont servie; et plus que des louanges,
Ces ris, ces mots piquants, ces critiques étranges,
En éclairant mes yeux sur mes propres défauts,
Retranchaient à mes torts bien plus qu'à mon repos.

O femmes, qui brûlez de l'ardeur qui m'anime,
290 Cessez donc d'étouffer un transport légitime;
Les hommes vainement raisonnent sur nos goûts:
Ils ne peuvent juger ce qui se passe en nous.
Qu'ils dirigent l'état, que leur bras le protège;
Nous leur abandonnons ce noble privilège;
295 Nous leur abandonnons le prix de la valeur;
Mais les arts sont à tous ainsi que le bonheur.

(1797)

Feels within her heart the spark of genius.
There, my verses, armed with a winning shaft,
Aim to fire a creative urge against all odds.
265 And if some other woman heard my voice,
And, taking fire, then sought fame in vain,
Should she, for all that, suffer insulting words?
Do men in their labors always succeed?
Isn't it better to let talents charm away
270 The dangerous fevers of an ardent youth
Than to condemn her to degrading pleasure
Inventing or defending vapid ornament?
Yes, study is for all a necessary joy:
If we don't learn to do, we still learn to judge.
275 The mind enlightened can but be more noble;
Ignorance alone should make us groan.
I myself, defying the perils of the stage,
Marched toward the goal where my hand would draw you.
Remembering tears shed over Sappho, I myself
280 Sang her sorrow and followed her rule.
I have seen grim envy at my side
Place its impious hand upon my tranquil days...
Ah! How can these haughty beings do harm to my fate?
Their faults are theirs, my happiness my own.
285 I'd even say they served me; more than praises,
Their laughter, glib jokes, strange critiques,
By opening my eyes to my own shortcomings
Diminished them more than my peace of mind.

O women, burning with the fire that burns me,
290 Stifle no longer your legitimate rapture.
Men reason all in vain upon our tastes.
They cannot judge what's happening within us.
Let them direct the State, their arms protect it;
We leave to them this noble privilege,
295 Abandon to them the prize of valor.
But art, like happiness, belongs to all.

—*Dorothy Backer*

À M***

Eh quoi! Dorval, tu m'applaudis,
Lorsque je vante les écrits
De la jeune Chloé que déjà l'on renomme!
Moi, d'une femme envier les succès,
5   Craindre d'encourager ses timides essais!....
O dieux! me prends-tu pour un homme?

EPÎTRE À L'EMPEREUR NAPOLÉON (EN 1810), LE LENDEMAIN DU JOUR OÙ LES ARTICLES 324 ET 339 DU CODE PÉNAL ONT ÉTÉ ARRÊTÉS DANS LE CONSEIL D'ÉTAT

C'est pour le faible aussi que sont faites les lois.

Du bonheur des Français sage dépositaire,
Toi qui grand, à la fois dans la paix, dans la guerre,
Sur le trône, des lois affermis le pouvoir,
Souffriras-tu qu'au nom de l'honneur, du devoir,
5   Un code, effroi du crime, en devienne complice;
Que l'époux meurtrier échappe à sa justice;
Qu'il donne à sa fureur le droit d'ôter le jour
A deux faibles amants égarés par l'amour?...

Deux amants! qu'ai-je dit! Quand ils seront victimes,
10   Quelles preuves rendront leurs trépas légitimes?
Qui dira que l'erreur, qu'un coupable dessein,
N'a pas guidé, poussé le bras de l'assassin?
Quand ils ne pourront plus se défendre, répondre,
Qui les accusera, qui pourra les confondre?
15   Sera-ce cet époux dans ses emportements,
Coupable et condamné, s'ils étaient innocents?
Sera-ce des valets dont son or le rend maître?
Des amis indignés, mais craignant de paraître?
Sera-ce des témoins par lui-même apostés?
20   Des témoins!... s'il en a, ses coups sont médités.
Ce n'est plus cet époux qu'a transporté l'outrage,
C'est un être cruel, sans honneur, sans courage,
De celle dont la loi le rend le protecteur,
Calculant le trépas en permettant l'erreur.

TO M***

> What? Dorval, me you applaud
> When the writings I do laud
> Of young Chloe, who's making her name!
>   Me, I'd envy a woman's fame?
> Fail to cheer her timid pen!...
>   Good Lord! you take me for a man?

—*Dorothy Backer*

EPISTLE TO THE EMPEROR NAPOLEON (1810) THE DAY AFTER ARTICLES 324 AND 339 OF THE PENAL CODE WERE SET FORTH IN THE COUNCIL OF STATE

It is also for the weak that laws are made.

You who are great both in peace and in war,
Wise guardian of France's happiness,
You whose throne affirms the power of law,
Will you suffer, in honor and duty's name,
5 That a Code, terror of crime, become crime's accomplice?
And let a murdering husband justice escape
And allow his fury to take the lives
Of two weak lovers whom love led astray?...

Two lovers! what! Since they are the victims,
10 What proofs will make their deaths legitimate?
Who says it wasn't error or an evil plot
That guided, drove the arm of the assassin?
When they can nevermore defend themselves,
Who can accuse them, who can confound them?
15 If this pair were innocent, will it be
The husband, guilty and condemned in all his rage?
The servants whom he masters with his gold?
Indignant friends who fear a court appearance?
Witnesses chosen expressly by himself?
20 Witnesses!...if he has them, then his blows were planned.
And he's no wronged husband driven mad by outrage,
But a cruel man with no honor or courage
Who allowed the error and calculated the death
Of the woman whom by law he is made to protect.

25   Je veux que, cependant, on souffre sans murmure
    Cet excès de rigueur dont frémit la nature;
    Que l'hymen offensé, la passion, l'honneur,
    Puissent de la vengeance autoriser l'horreur;
    Comment, ce qui de l'un rend la mort légitime,
30   Pour l'autre, aux yeux des lois, cesse-t-il d'être un crime?
    De quel droit un époux, notre premier appui,
    Veut-il punir en nous ce qu'il excuse en lui?
    Quelle main a tracé cet article barbare,
    Qui des lois, par les lois, tout à coup nous sépare,
35   Consacre l'arbitraire, et pour le même tort,
    Accable le plus faible, excuse le plus fort?

    «Il se peut, nous dit-on, qu'une flamme étrangère
    Fasse naître de vous un enfant adultère.»
    Oui; mais si cette erreur mérite le trépas,
40   Un infidèle époux ne la commet-il pas?
    Ne prodigue-t-il point son or et sa tendresse
    Au fils né de l'amour qu'il porte à sa maîtresse?
    Si dans un autre hymen on la vit s'engager,
    N'aura-t-il pas un fils sous un nom étranger?
45   Aux yeux de la raison également coupables,
    Deux époux seront-ils autrement punissables?
    Par un léger tribut sans honte s'acquittant,
    L'un pourra-t-il lever un front de crainte exempt,
    Quand, pour la même faute, avec ignominie,
50   L'autre va perdre ensemble et l'honneur et la vie?

    Au moins, si la justice en armant un époux,
    Pouvait guider aussi ses transports et ses coups;
    Si l'épouse victime était toujours coupable;
    Mais, sire, ton génie aussi grand qu'admirable
55   En vain des nations réglera le destin,
    Aux passions de l'homme il ne peut mettre un frein!
    Un frénétique époux, aveuglé par sa rage,
    Dans chaque homme verra le rival qui l'outrage.
    Sûr de l'impunité, ses soupçons, ses discours,
60   De son épouse en pleurs désoleront les jours:
    En elle du trépas la légitime crainte
    Fera naître l'effroi, le désordre, la plainte,
    Et par les lois enfin l'hymen ensanglanté
    Verra fuir à jamais l'amour épouvanté.

65   Sire, ne permets pas que de la noble France
    On livre aux passions la moitié sans défense!
    Si jadis ont régné ces terribles excès,

25   Yet I want us now to bear without a murmur
This excessive rigor that makes nature shudder:
That passion, honor, or Hymen offended
Should tolerate the horror of such a vengeance.
How can a crime legitimize death for one,
30 Which for the other is legally no crime at all?
By what right can a husband, our main support,
Punish in us what in him is forgiven?
What hand has drawn this barbarous article,
Which, in one blow, cuts us from the law by law,
35 Sanctions the arbitrary and, for the same wrong,
Crushes the weakest and excuses the strong?

"A flame out of wedlock," they tell us,
"Could well bring forth an adulterous child."
Yes, but if such an error death does deserve,
40 Doesn't a faithless husband commit the same?
Doesn't he give his gold and affection
To the son born of love to his mistress?
If she joins herself in another marriage,
Will his son not live under that man's name?
45 When in the eyes of reason both are guilty,
Should the spouses unequally be punished?
By paying a slight tribute, with no shame,
Shall the one raise his head free from fear,
While, for the same mistake, the other shall lose
50 Her honor and life in utter disgrace?

At least, if justice, when she arms the husband,
Could also guide his outbursts and his blows
If the victim wife were always guilty;
But, Sire, your genius, great and admirable,
55 In vain will determine the fate of all nations
If the passions of men it cannot contain!
A maddened husband, blinded by rage,
Sees in every man his offending rival.
Certain of impunity, his suspicious harangues
60 Will desolate his spouse in her tearful days.
And the legitimate fear of death will cause
Moans, terror, and anarchy within her soul,
And by these laws, the bloodied married state
Will see love flee in horror evermore.

65 Sire, let not noble France's defenseless half
Be delivered as a prey to passions!
If such excesses were once the order of the day,

La sagesse des temps modéra leurs effets:
Ils sont passés ces jours de grossière ignorance,
70 Où l'usage excusait, ordonnait la vengeance;
Ce n'est plus dans ce siècle, au sein de la clarté,
Que l'on verse le sang avec impunité.
Oui, c'est le voeu de tous que je te fais entendre;
Que toujours le Français soit généreux et tendre;
75 Que l'homme ait son pouvoir, que la femme ait ses droits,
C'est pour le faible aussi que sont faites les lois!
Qu'elles soient la terreur de l'affreuse licence,
Qu'elles forcent le vice à gémir en silence;
Mais que, pour nous frapper, leur glaive défenseur,
80 Sire, ne soit pas mis aux mains de la fureur!

Que si l'époux vengeur te paraît excusable,
Réserve en ta sagesse une grâce au coupable;
Mais qu'il ne soit pas dit, qu'en ce siècle si grand,
L'assassin d'une femme a droit d'être innocent.

(1810)

Note de l'auteur—Je citerai ici les deux articles du Code pénal qui sonte le sujet de cet épître.
Art 324. «Le meurtre commis par l'époux sur l'épouse, ou par celle-ci sur son époux, n'est pas excusable, si la vie de l'époux ou de l'épouse qui a commis le meurtre n'a pas été mise en péril dans le moment même où le meurtre a eu lieu. Néanmoins, dans le cas d'adultère, prévu par l'art. 336, *le meurtre commis par l'époux sur son épouse, ainsi que sur le complice, à l'instant où il les surprend en flagrant délit dans la maison conjugale, est excusable.*»
Art. 339. «*Le mari qui aura entretenu une concubine dans la maison conjugale,* et qui aura été convaincu sur la plainte de la femme, *sera puni d'une amende de cent francs à deux milles francs.*»
Lorsque ces deux articles furent adoptés, ils devinrent, dans la société, le sujet de beaucoup de discussions, ce qui m'inspira cette épître à l'Empereur, que je fis en peu d'heures, et que je lui adressai à l'instant. Il trouva mes réclamations justes; car, quelques jours après, dans un de ces cercles qui avaient lieu deux fois par semaine aux Tuileries, il vint à moi, et me dit: «*J'ai lu vos vers; vous avez raison; c'est bien, très-bien.*» Je sus aussi que, dans le même temps, il avait dit à plusieurs reprises, dans une des séances du conseil d'État, en parlant de ces articles, que les femmes s'en plaignaient, et qu'elles avaient raison.
Cette petite satisfaction fut la seule que me valut mon épître; mais je ne pouvais en espérer davantage.

The wisdom of our times has softened their effects:
Those days of grossest ignorance are past,
70 Wherein custom excused or demanded vengeance.
No longer in this enlightened century
Can blood be shed, and with impunity.
Yes, 'tis the wish of all I make you hear:
May the French always be generous and tender,
75 And man have his power, woman her rights.
'Tis for the weak as well that laws are made!
And may they ever be the terror of dreaded license,
And force all vices to groan in silence.
But, Sire, do not let swords for defense
80 Be placed in fury's hands to strike us down!

And if the avenging husband is excusable,
Save, in your wisdom, grace for the guilty.
But let it not be said that in a century so great,
A woman's murderer is lawfully innocent.

—Dorothy Backer

Author's note—Here are the two articles of the Penal Code that are the subject of
this epistle:
   Art. 324. "Murder of the wife committed by the husband, or of the husband by
his wife, is not excusable if the life of the spouse who committed the murder was
not in danger at the time the murder occurred. However, in case of adultery, as
provided in article 336, murder of a wife and her accomplice *committed by her
husband*, at the moment he finds them *flagrante delicto* in the conjugal house, is
excusable."
   Art. 339. "*The husband who shall have maintained a concubine in the conjugal house*,
and who is convicted on the complaint of his wife, *shall be punished with a fine of
100 francs to 2000 francs*."
   When these two articles were adopted, they became the subject of much
discussion in society, which inspired me to write this Epistle to the Emperor,
which I did in a few hours, and sent him immediately. He found my claims
justified, for, some days later, in one of those groups that met twice a week in the
Tuileries, he came to me and said, "*I have read your verses; you are right; it's good,
very good.*" I also learned that, in the same period, he said several times, in
speaking of these articles during one of the sessions of the Council of State, that
women were complaining of them, and that they were right to do so.
   This small satisfaction was the only one my Epistle gave me, but I could not
hope for more.

RÉPONSE AUX VERS DE M. LEBRUN INTITULÉS:
«MON DERNIER MOT SUR LES FEMMES POÈTES»

Quand Lebrun dans ses vers heureux,
De toute femme auteur condamnant la manie,
   Déplora la triste folie
Qui faisait d'une belle, un poète ennuyeux;
5   Dans l'antique mythologie
Cherchant quelques appuis à son droit incertain,
   A côté de Psyché, des grâces,
Aux femmes désormais il désigna leurs places.
   Mais dans l'Olympe féminin,
10   Je vois les neuf soeurs qu'il oublie;
La beauté, les talents, mêlant leurs attributs,
   Et la ceinture de Vénus
   Près de la lyre d'Uranie.

Au Pinde comme ailleurs, les hommes sont jaloux:
15 Il faut partout céder, et borner tous nos goûts,
A briguer de leur choix la gloire passagère;
Ils savent que l'esprit peut défendre le coeur...
   Ainsi d'un adroit adversaire
   La langage toujours menteur
20 Ne vante en nous que l'art et d'aimer et de plaire;
   Et ce serait une ruse de guerre,
   Si ce n'était une ruse d'auteur.
   O Muses, des talents aimables
   Versez le charme sur nos jours:
25 Bannissez loin de nous des dieux plus redoutables:
J'implore vos présents bien moins que vos secours!
Dérobez à l'Amour la douce rêverie
Qui remplit des beaux ans les dangereux loisirs;
D'un coeur né pour aimer soyez les seuls plaisirs,
30 Et trompez-le du moins sur l'emploi de la vie.

Ah! lorsque de leurs dons nous comblant à la fois,
   La beauté, l'heureuse jeunesse,
Appellent des plaisirs la dangereuse ivresse;
Souvent de la raison nous négligeons la voix.
35 Ne parlez pas alors et d'étude et de gloire;
Elle offrirait en vain ses brillantes faveurs:
Songe-t-on au moyen d'occuper la mémoire,
Si l'on peut, d'un regard, occuper tous les coeurs?
A de si vains succès quand l'âge enfin s'oppose,

PHILIPPINE DE VANNOZ (1775–1851)

REPLY TO THE VERSES OF M. LEBRUN ENTITLED: "MY LAST WORD ON WOMEN POETS"

When Lebrun in his felicitous lines
Denouncing the mania in every woman writer
  Deplored the piteous derangement
That turns a beauty into a tiresome poet;
5   He sought in mythology of old
Some basis for his doubtful judgment;
  Alongside Psyche and the Graces
He assigned women to their places.
  But on the feminine Olympus
10   I see he overlooked nine sisters:
Beauty blending its attributes with talent,
  And Venus's sash
  Beside Urania's lyre.

On Pindus as elsewhere, men are jealous:
15 In all things we must yield and limit our desires
To courting, through their favor, fleeting glory.
The mind they know can protect the heart...
  Like a clever adversary,
  Language, always the liar,
20 Lauds us only for the art of pleasing love;
  This would merely be a ruse of war
  Were it not also the writer's tactic.
  O Muses, bestow upon our lives
  The charms of your delightful talents;
25 Banish far from us more fearful gods:
I implore your gifts even less than your aid!
Take from love the sweet revery
That fills the finest years with shameful leisure,
And be instead, for a loving heart, the only pleasure,
30 Or fool it, at least, on the way life is spent.

Ah! When showering us with their gifts all at once,
  Beauty and blissful youth
Promote the risky headiness of pleasure,
Making us neglect the voice of reason.
35 Speak not, then, of learning or of glory;
It would offer for naught its sparkling favors;
Who dreams of capturing immortality
When with a glance one captures every heart?
When age at last precludes such empty triumphs,

40 Quand la gloire à nos yeux offre un nouvel attrait,
Toute femme en soupire, et place avec regret
Les lauriers sur un front où se fane la rose.
    Par l'ordre d'un destin jaloux,
La beauté détrônée a perdu sa puissance;
45 Mais l'esprit peut encor, d'un espoir aussi doux,
    Lui rendre l'heureuse espérance;
    Et l'Hippocrêne alors pour nous
    Est la fontaine de Jouvence.
    Toujours humbles dans nos projets,
50 N'allons point, en muses hardies,
    Disputer aux mâles génies
Les chants de gloire et les vastes sujets;
    Mais du moins mon sexe réclame
    Les sujets simples et touchants:
55 Qui peut mieux parler qu'une femme
    Le langage des sentiments?
Leur plume tour à tour et sensible et légère
Sut immortaliser Corinne et Deshoulières:
Du Pinde, leur domaine, osez les rappeler:
60 Semblables à ces peuples barbares
    Qui de leurs paradis bizarres
    Voulaient, dit-on, nous exiler,
    Le zèle ardent qui vous enflamme
    Au même sort nous asservit:
65 On peut bien contester une âme
    A qui l'on refuse l'esprit.

    O siècles de chevalerie,
    Siècles d'amour et de vertus,
    Que toute femme un peu jolie
70 Regrette en son âme attendrie,
    Et qu'en France on ne verra plus,
    Qui de Mars soumis à Vénus
    Nous retraçaient l'allégorie!
    Alors, inspirant les héros
75 De leurs combats, de leurs travaux,
    Nos regards étaient le salaire:
A ceux qui commandaient par le droit de la guerre,
    Nous commandions par droit d'amour.
Règne admirable, heureux temps disparus sans retour!
80 Mon sexe est soumis à son tour
    Mais contre un arrêt tyrannique
De l'empire lettré nous invoquons les lois;
Et l'on sait que toujours l'égalité des droits
    Fut celle de sa république.

40 When glory in our eyes takes on new appeal,
Every woman sighs and regretfully places
A laurel wreath on the brow whose blush is fading.
By order of a vengeful destiny
Beauty dethroned loses her power;
45 But the mind, with a hope as sweet,
Can make her happy with expectation;
And Hippocrene then becomes for us
Youth's enduring fountain.
Always humble in our goals,
50 Let us not, as brazen muses,
Ever battle masculine genius
For songs of glory and epic subjects;
My sex at least lays claim to
Simple and moving themes:
55 Who better than a woman can
Speak the tongue of feelings?
Their pens now sensitive, now deft,
Were able to immortalize Corinne and Deshoulières;
From Pindus, their domain, make bold to summon them:
60 Like those barbarous nations
That sought to banish us, it is told,
From their fantastic Edens,
The burning zeal that enflames you
Binds us to a similar fate.
65 One may well question the presence of a soul
In anyone who is denied a mind.

O ages of chivalry
Never to be seen again in France,
Ages of love and virtue
70 That every seemly woman
Regrets in her tender heart,
Ages whose allegory is retraced
In Mars subdued by Venus!
It was then that heroes were inspired
75 In their combats and their trials,
And our glance was the only prize.
Over those who ruled by right of war,
We ruled by right of love.
Splendid reign, happy times gone forever!
80 My sex in turn is now subdued.
But against a tyrannical decree
We invoke the laws of an empire of letters,
For we know that equality of rights
Has always been the rule of its republic.

85   Auteurs vous ne permettrez pas
     Qu'un réformateur monarchique
De ce gouvernement changeant la forme antique,
     Introduise dans nos états
     Les abus de la loi Salique.

(1808)

L'ANGE GARDIEN

Dieu a ordonné à ses anges de vous garder
pendant tout le temps de votre vie.
                Psalm 91

Oh! qu'il est beau cet esprit immortel,
Gardien sacré de notre destinée!
Des fleurs d'Eden sa tête est couronnée,
Il resplendit de l'éclat éternel.
5 Dès le berceau sa voix mystérieuse
Des voeux confus d'une âme ambitieuse
Sait réprimer l'impétueuse ardeur,
Et d'âge en âge il nous guide au bonheur.

L'ENFANT
Dans cette vie obscure à mes regards voilée,
10 Quel destin m'est promis? à quoi suis-je appelée?
Avide d'un espoir qu'à peine j'entrevois,
Mon coeur voudrait franchir plus de jours à la fois!
Si la nuit règne aux cieux, une ardente insomnie
A ce coeur inquiet révèle son génie;
15 Mes compagnes en vain m'appellent, et ma main
De la main qui l'attend s'éloigne avec dédain.

L'ANGE
Crains, jeune enfant, la tristesse sauvage
Dont ton orgueil subit la vaine loi.
Loin de les fuir, cours aux jeux de ton âge,

Authors, you will not accept
       That a royalist reformer,
    Changing the ancient form of that regime,
       Should introduce into our estates
       The abuses of the Salic law.

—*Beth Archer*

AMABLE TASTU (1798–1885)

THE GUARDIAN ANGEL

For he shall give his angels charge over thee,
to keep thee in all thy ways.
                              Psalm 91

How beautiful this immortal spirit,
Holy guardian of our destiny!
The flowers of Eden crown his head;
He shines with eternal radiance.
5 Already at birth, his mysterious voice
Restrains the impetuous ardor
Of an ambitious soul's troubled desires,
And from age to age he's the way to happiness.

THE CHILD
In this obscure life, concealed from my sight,
10 What destiny awaits me? What is my calling?
Hungering for a goal I barely perceive,
My heart would span many days at a time!
If night reigns over the skies, a burning sleeplessness
Reveals to this restless heart its genius;
15 My comrades call me in vain, and my hand
With disdain leaves the hand that awaits it.

THE ANGEL
Child, beware the untamed sadness
That subjects your pride to its vain law.
Rather than flee them, run to the game of your years,

20 Jouis des biens que le ciel fit pour toi:
   Aux doux ébats de l'innocente joie
   N'oppose plus un front triste et rêveur;
   Sous l'oeil de Dieu suis ta riante voie,
   Enfant, crois-moi, je conduis au bonheur.

LA JEUNE FILLE

25 Quel immense horizon devant moi se révèle!
   A mes regards ravis que la nature est belle!
   Tout ce que sent mon âme, ou qu'embrassent mes yeux
   S'exhale de ma bouche en sons mélodieux!
   Où courent ces rivaux armés du luth sonore?
30 Dans cette arène il est quelques places encore,
   Ne puis-je à leurs côtés me frayer un chemin,
   M'élancer seule, libre, et ma lyre à la main?

L'ANGE

   Seule couronne à ton front destinée,
   Déjà blanchit la fleur de l'oranger;
35 D'un saint devoir doucement enchaînée,
   Que ferais-tu d'un espoir mensonger?
   Loin des sentiers dont ma main te repousse,
   Ne pleure pas un dangereux honneur:
   Suis une route et plus humble et plus douce:
40 Vierge, crois-moi, je conduis au bonheur.

LA FEMME

   Oh! laissez-moi charmer les heures solitaires;
   Sur ce luth ignoré laissez errer mes doigts;
   Laissez naître et mourir ses notes passagéres
   Comme les sons plaintifs d'un écho dans les bois.
45 Je ne demande rien aux brillantes demeures,
   Des plaisirs fastueux inconstant univers;
   Loin du monde et bruit du laissez couler mes heures
   Avec ces doux accords à mon repos si chers.

L'ANGE

   As-tu réglé dans ton modeste empire
50 Tous les travaux, les repas, les loisirs?
   Tu peux alors accorder à ta lyre
   Quelques instants ravis à tes plaisirs.
   Le rossignol élève sa voix pure,
   Mais dans le nid du nocturne chanteur
55 Est le repos, l'abri, la nourriture...
   Femme, crois-moi, je conduis au bonheur.

20 Enjoy the gifts that heaven has bestowed on you:
    To the sweet play of innocent joy
    Do not turn your sad and pensive brow;
    Under the eye of God, follow your smiling path.
    Child, trust me, I am the way to happiness.

THE YOUNG GIRL
25 How vast a horizon stretches before me!
    To my ravished eyes how beautiful is nature!
    All that my soul feels, that my eyes encompass
    Exhales from my mouth in melodious sounds!
    Where are they running, those rivals with sonorous lutes?
30 In that arena there are still some places,
    Can't I make a way for myself at their side,
    Go off alone, free, with my lyre in hand?

THE ANGEL
    The only crown destined for your brow
    Is the orange flower already blooming,
35 By a holy bond gently chained;
    What would you do with a treacherous hope?
    My hand drives you far from those paths.
    Do not lament a dangerous honor:
    Follow a road more humble and pleasant.
40 Virgin, trust me, I am the way to happiness.

THE WOMAN
    Let me while away the lonely hours,
    Let my fingers wander over forgotten lute strings;
    Let its fleeting notes come to life and die
    Like the plaintive sounds of an echo in the woods.
45 I ask naught from lordly manses,
    Fickle world of sumptuous pleasures;
    Far from the clamor and the crowd, let my days elapse
    With sweet harmonies dear to peace of mind.

THE ANGEL
    In your modest domain have you seen to
50 All the chores, the meals, the pastimes?
    Then you may grant your lyre
    A few moments stolen from your pleasures.
    The nightingale raises its pure voice,
    But in the nest of the nocturnal warbler
55 Are repose, shelter, nourishment...
    Woman, trust me, I am the way to happiness.

LA MERE

Revenez, revenez, songes de ma jeunesse,
Eclatez nobles chants, lyre, réveillez-vous!
Je puis forcer la gloire à tenir sa promesse;
60 Recueillis pour mon fils, ses lauriers seront doux.
Oui, je veux à ses pas aplanir la carrière,
A son nom, jeune encore, offrir l'appui du mien,
Pour te conduire au but y toucher la première,
Et tenter l'avenir pour assurer le sien.

L'ANGE

65 Vois ce berceau, ton enfant y repose;
Tes chants hardis vont troubler son sommeil;
T'éloignes-tu? ton absence l'expose
A te chercher en vain à son réveil.
Si tu frémis pour son naissant voyage,
70 De sa jeune âme exerce la vigueur;
Voilà ton but, ton espoir, ton ouvrage;
Mère, crois-moi, je conduis au bonheur.

LA VIEILLE FEMME

L'hiver sur mes cheveux étend sa main glacée;
Il est donc vrai! mes voeux n'ont pu vous arrêter,
75 Jours rapides! et vous, pourquoi donc me quitter
Rêves harmonieux qu'enfantait ma pensée?
Hélas! sans la toucher, j'ai laissé se flétrir
La palme qui m'offrait un verdoyant feuillage,
Et ce feu, qu'attendait le phare du rivage,
80 Dans un foyer obscur je l'ai laissé mourir.

L'ANGE

Ce feu sacré renfermé dans ton âme
S'y consumait loin des profanes yeux;
Comme l'encens offert dans les saints lieux,
Quelques parfums ont seuls trahi sa flamme.
85 D'un art heureux tu connus la douceur,
Sans t'égarer sur les pas de la gloire;
Jouis en paix d'une telle mémoire;
Femme, crois-moi, je conduis au bonheur.

LA MOURANTE

Je sens pâlir mon front, et ma voix presqu'éteinte
90 Salue en expirant l'approche du trépas.
D'une innocente vie on peut sortir sans crainte;
Et mon céleste ami ne m'abandonne pas.

THE MOTHER

Come back, come back, dreams of my youth,
Awake, my lyre; noble songs, burst forth!
I can force glory to keep her word;
60 Gathered for my son, her laurels will be sweet.
Yes, I want to smooth the way for him,
To his name, still so young, offer mine in aid,
For to lead him to the end, I must reach it first,
And try my fortune to assure his own.

THE ANGEL

65 See this cradle, your child slumbers there;
Your daring songs will disturb his sleep.
You wander off? Your absence leaves him
To seek you in vain on awakening.
If you tremble for his future voyage,
70 Then test the mettle of his young soul;
This is your goal, your hope, your life's work.
Mother, trust me, I am the way to happiness.

THE OLD WOMAN

Winter lays its icy hand upon my head.
Is it true then? My pleas could not stay you,
75 Fleeting days! And you, why must you leave me,
Harmonious dreams my mind engendered?
Alas, without grasping it, I allowed to wither
The palm that a verdant fullness offered me,
And that flame, awaited by the beacon on the banks,
80 In a darkened hearth I let die out.

THE ANGEL

That sacred fire that burned in your soul
Consumed itself far from vulgar eyes;
Like incense offered in hallowed places,
Only a few fragrances betrayed its flame.
85 You knew the sweetness of a blissful art;
Without straying on the paths of glory,
You can relish in peace your memories.
Woman, trust me, I am the way to happiness.

THE DYING WOMAN

I feel my brow grow pale, my voice almost stilled
90 Welcomes, as I expire, the approach of death.
An innocent life can be left without fear;
And my celestial companion stays by my side.

Mais, quoi! ne rien laisser après moi de moi-même?
Briller, trembler, mourir comme un triste flambeau!
95 Ne pas léguer du moins mes chants à ceux que j'aime
Un souvenir au monde, un nom à mon tombeau!

L'ANGE

Il luit pour toi le jour de la promesse,
Au port sacré je te dépose enfin,
Et près des cieux ta coupable faiblesse
100 Pleure un vain nom dans un monde plus vain.
La tombe attend tes dépouilles mortelles,
L'oubli tes chants, mais l'âme est au Seigneur;
L'heure est venue, entends frémir mes ailes,
Viens, suis mon vol, je conduis au bonheur!

(1835)

LA FEMME DU PEUPLE

Songez que d'un baiser pourrait éclore une âme;
Songez en vous penchant sur le sein de la femme,
Au mystère divin de la maternité;
Adorez sa beauté, gardez sereine et pure
Cette source sacrée où toute créature
Puise un souffle de vie et d'immortalité.

Un tribun haranguait, sur la place publique,
La foule radieuse au mot de République.
Ce mot, qui renfermait des promesses pour tous,
Illuminait les fronts, rendait les coeurs plus doux.
5 Par l'espoir apaisé, ce grand flot populaire,
En qui le dénouement fait monter la colère,
Murmurait confiant au mot fascinateur:
«—La République vient, c'est notre rédempteur!
Plus de corps torturés où meurt l'intelligence!
10 Plus de cris de la faim, plus d'appels de vengeance!»
Et le magique mot, de ces coeurs pleins de foi
Sortait, Vivat bruyant d'une nouvelle loi!
L'orateur qui parlait à cette foule émue
Avait l'accent vibrant, le geste qui remue,

But how! leave behind nothing of myself?
To have glimmered, flickered, and died like a sad flame!
95 Not even to bequeath my songs to those I love,
A remembrance to the world, a name for my tomb!

THE ANGEL
The day of promise glows for you,
I bring you at last to the sacred harbor,
And near the heavens your sinful frailty
100 Weeps for a vain name in a vainer world.
The grave awaits your mortal remains,
Oblivion your songs, but your soul is the Lord's.
The hour has come; hear my beating wings.
Come, follow my flight, I am the way to happiness!

—Beth Archer

LOUISE COLET (1810–1876)

A WORKING-CLASS WOMAN

Remember that a soul can flower from a kiss;
Remember when bending over a woman's breast
The divine mystery of motherhood;
Worship her beauty, keep tranquil and pure
This sacred fount from which all beings
Draw living breath and immortality.

A tribune on the public square harangued
The crowd radiant with the word Republic.
This word, filled with promises for all,
Made faces glow and hearts more tender.
5 Appeased by hope, this great tide of people
In whom deprivation kindles anger,
Murmured, trusting in the seductive word:
"The Republic is coming, our redeemer!
No more tortured bodies, whose spirit is killed,
10 No more moans of hunger, nor cries of vengeance!"
And the magic word, from these hope-filled hearts
Issued forth acclaiming the new covenant!
The orator who addressed the impassioned crowd,
Spoke in vibrant tones, his gestures eloquent,

15 La forme qui du fond cache l'inanité,
Et pour thème ce sphinx: la solidarité!
«Oui! le bonheur pour tous! et par tous dès ce monde,»
Répétait-il, penché sur la cité profonde
Où tout un peuple, ardent à saluer ce jour,
20 N'avait plus qu'un seul coeur dilaté par l'amour!

Cependant une femme, à l'écart immobile,
Dans ses haillons soyeux se drapant en sibylle,
Le sourire ironique et le regard aigri,
Pressant sur son sein maigre un enfant amaigri,
25 S'écria: «Le bonheur! c'est un sarcasme, ô femmes!
Elle n'est pas pour nous, cette fête des âmes!
Fût-elle pour nos fils, nos frères, nos amants,
Elle n'est pas pour nous, femmes: tribun, tu mens!...
Ne promets pas si tôt la fin de nos misères...
30 Car, s'il est vrai que Dieu nous ait faits solidaires,
Tant que nous, dont les flancs portent l'humanité,
Nous, plus grandes que vous par la maternité,
Tant que nous resterons une chair avilie,
De honte et de douleur, double et profonde lie
35 Qui fermente et gémit au fond de vos cités,
Ne parlez pas d'amour et de félicités!
Ne parlez pas d'amour, hommes! dont l'âme impure
Trouve la volupté dans notre flétrissure;
Violateurs de Dieu qui jetez au hasard
40 Votre paternité dans quelque lupanar,
Où, comme un vil bétail, la faim et l'ignorance
Parquent pour vos plaisirs des femmes sans défense:
Esclavage hideux qu'en leur impiété
Votre église et vos lois nomment nécessité!
45 Ne parlez pas d'amour, jusqu'au jour où le monde
Rougira du contact de cette plaie immonde,
Où tout homme craindra d'en approcher son sein
Plus que d'être voleur, plus que d'être assassin!
Car le crime est plus grand par les maux qu'il entraîne;
50 Le sang prostitué brûle de veine en veine,
Etouffant l'idéal, tarissant la beauté,
Disputant jusqu'à l'âme à la Divinité,
Lui transmettant du corps la honte et la souillure,
Et versant de sa fange à toute créature.
55 Ce stigmate a flétri, dans chaque adolescent
La jeunesse de l'âme et la fraîcheur du sang.
Où sont les beaux hymens des races primitives?
Étreintes de corps purs! transports d'âmes naïves!
Chaste amour qu'ont détruit d'impudiques amours;

15 The form masking the absence of content,
And his theme—that Sphinx, solidarity!
"Yes, happiness for all! And for all in *this* life,"
He repeated, leaning toward the teeming city
Whose entire population, eager to greet that day,
20 Had but a single heart swollen with love!

A woman, however, standing still to one side,
Draped like a sibyl in her silken rags,
Her smile ironic and her glance embittered,
Clutching to her scrawny breast a scrawny child,
25 Cried out, "Happiness! What a joke, O women!
It is not for us, this festival of souls!
It might be for our sons, our brothers, our lovers;
It is not for us, women: Tribune, you lie!...
Do not promise so soon the end of our miseries,
30 For, if it is true that God made us solidary,
So long as we, whose loins bear humanity,
We, greater than you by virtue of maternity,
So long as we remain flesh vilified
By shame and pain, the deep and double dreg
35 That festers and groans in the heart of your cities,
Do not speak of love and happiness!
Do not speak of love, you men! whose tainted souls
Find lustful pleasure in our blight;
Violators of God who carelessly fling
40 Your fatherhood into sundry brothels,
Where, like lowly cattle, hunger and ignorance
Stable for your delights defenseless women:
Horrid slavery that in their impiety
You church and your laws call necessity!
45 Speak not of love, until the day when the world
Blushes on contact with that ignoble wound,
When men are more afraid to touch her body
Than to become thieves or even murderers!
The crime is greater for the evils that ensue;
50 Prostituted blood burns from vein to vein,
Stifling the ideal and desiccating beauty,
Even robbing the Godhead of the soul's purity,
Transmitting the shame and mire of the body
To every creature, and pouring out its filth.
55 This stigma, in every adolescent, withers
The youth of the soul, the freshness of the blood.
Where are the beautiful weddings of ancient races?
Embraces of pure bodies! Transports of innocent souls!
Chaste love that was destroyed by shameless loves,

60 Source de voluptés dont Dieu traça le cours,
   Mais dont le flot souillé par les flots de la terre
   Grossit fatalement l'océan adultère.
   L'homme au cloaque impur se plonge sans dégoût:
   Le pourceau vit joyeux aux bourbes de l'égout!
65 Rayonnement d'en-haut, amour, senteur divine!
   Tu ne dilates plus son immonde poitrine!

   «Et nous qui l'aspirons, ce parfum immortel,
   Croyants désespérés d'un culte sans autel,
   Esclaves tout meurtris d'inextricables chaînes,
70 Athlètes ignorés, vaincus aux luttes vaines,
   Martyrs de siècle en siècle engloutis ici-bas,
   Femmes, filles de Dieu, nous ne protestons pas!
   Nous sommes un débris de l'antique esclavage:
   L'homme a toujours gardé sur nous le droit d'outrage,
75 Du joug qu'il nous impose il se fait l'insulteur,
   Comme il traitait l'esclave avant le Rédempteur.
   Sacrilège, il corrompt et change en flétrissure
   Les aspirations de la sainte nature:
   Cette vierge, qui cache un coeur sous sa beauté,
80 Pour lui n'est qu'une nuit d'infâme volupté.
   C'eût été du bonheur pour une vie entière!
   Mais l'aveugle insensé souffle sur la lumière;
   L'être qu'il déposa dans ce sein profané,
   Meurt ou vit renié du sang dont il est né.
85 Plus de droits à l'amour pour la femme flétrie;
   Paria sans foyer, ilote sans patrie,
   Du plaisir vagabond alimentant les jeux,
   Rebut du fantaisiste et du voluptueux,
   Narguant la mort, riant du malheur qui la tue,
90 Le soir, aux carrefours, elle se prostitue!

   «Et l'homme? il fait ce mal avec impunité!
   Il ment, il trompe, il rit de sa paternité;
   Lâche, il renie, absous de sa part d'homicide,
   Celle que l'abandon pousse à l'infanticide;
95 Son crime est innocent, car son crime est caché,
   Et ce qu'il nomme honneur n'en est pas entaché!

   «O bateleurs pompeux de clubs et d'assemblées,
   Tartufes de pitié, consciences troublées
   Prêchant les droits de l'homme, et proclamant bien haut
100 Que tout meurtre est maudit, qu'infâme est l'échafaud!
   Qui de vous, qui de vous, descendez dans vos âmes,
   A respecté la vie éclose aux flancs des femmes?
   Qui de vous, qui de vous, ne devra compte à Dieu
   Du mystère sacré dont il se fit un jeu?

60 Wellspring of pleasures whose course was traced by God,
But whose flow soiled by the tides of the earth
Fatally swells the adulterous seas.
Man into this cesspool plunges without disgust:
The swine live happily in the muck of sewers!
65 Radiance from on high, love, divine aroma,
You no longer penetrate his foul heart!

"And we who inhale this immortal scent,
Despairing believers of an altarless cult,
Slaves bruised by inextricable chains,
70 Neglected athletes, vanquished in empty agons,
Martyrs from age to age engulfed here below,
Women, daughters of God, we never even protest!
We are the vestige of ancient slavery:
Man has held over us the right of abuse,
75 Insulting the yoke he forces upon us,
As he insulted slaves before the Redeemer came.
Sacrilegious, he corrupts and turns to blight
The aspirations of sacrosanct nature:
This virgin, hiding a heart beneath her beauty,
80 Is for him no more than a night of lechery;
It might have been the happiness of a lifetime!
But the blind fool snuffs out the flame;
The creature he implanted in that defiled womb
Dies or lives denied by the blood that bore him.
85 No more rights to love for the tarnished woman;
Homeless pariah, helot without a land,
Feeding the games of vagrant pleasure,
Despised object of the pervert and the rake,
Taunting death and mocking the misery that kills her,
90 At night, on the avenues, she sells herself!

"And the man? He commits this crime with impunity!
He lies, he cheats, he scoffs at his paternity;
Coward absolved of his share in the murder, he denies
The one driven to infanticide by his abandon.
95 His crime is guiltless, because it is concealed,
And what he calls honor remains untainted.

"O pompous mountebanks in clubs and assemblies,
Pretenders of compassion, murky consciences
Preaching the rights of man, and loudly proclaiming
100 That every murder is accursed, the scaffold evil!
Who among you, which one of you—search your hearts!—
Respected the life flowering in the wombs of women?
Who among you, which of you, will not be judged
By God, for the sacred mystery he toyed with?

105 «Peuple, ne raille pas, car c'est dans tes familles
   Que l'opprobre descend; il décime tes filles,
   Hommes qui m'entourez d'un murmure offensant,
   Quoi! n'avez-vous jamais pleuré sur votre sang?
   Et vous femmes, mes soeurs en douleurs, vous que j'aime,
110 Oh! plaignez-moi! Voyez cette enfant triste et blême,
   Ce sont des jours pareils que lui garde le sort:
   Cette enfant serait femme, il lui vaut mieux la mort!»

   Elle fendit la foule, et, courant au rivage,
   S'élança dans le fleuve. Un cri joyeux, sauvage,
115 Un cri de délivrance aux flots échappa seul:
   La Seine la couvrit de son calme linceul,
   Et la foule bruyante, en s'éloignant distraite,
   Disait: «Elle était folle; elle a troublé la fête.»

   (1850)

MON LIVRE

   Je ne vous offre plus pour toutes mélodies
   Que des cris de révolte et des rimes hardies.
   Oui! Mais en m'écoutant si vous alliez pâlir?
   Si, surpris des éclats de ma verve imprudente,
 5 Vous maudissiez la voix énergique et stridente
     Qui vous aura fait tressaillir?

   Pourtant, quand je m'élève à des notes pareilles,
   Je ne prétends blesser les coeurs ni les oreilles.
   Même les plus craintifs n'ont point à s'alarmer:
10 L'accent désespéré sans doute ici domine,
   Mais je n'irai pas tirer ces sons de ma poitrine
     Pour le plaisir de blasphémer.

   Comment? la Liberté déchaîne ses colères;
   Partout, contre l'effort des erreurs séculaires,
15 La Vérité combat pour s'ouvrir un chemin;
   Et je ne prendrais pas parti dans ce grand drame?
   Quoi! ce coeur qui bat là, pour être un coeur de femme
     En est-il moins un coeur humain?

105 "People, do not laugh: it is on your families
That falls the disgrace; it decimates your daughters.
Men who surround me with insulting whispers,
What! have you never wept over your own blood?
And you, women, my sisters in pain, you whom I love
110 Oh! pity me! You see this child, sad and pale?
Such a life has fate reserved for her:
This child would be a woman! She is better dead!"

She broke through the crowd, and running to the bank,
Flung herself in the river. A wild, joyous shriek,
115 A cry of deliverance was all that escaped from the waters;
The Seine covered her with its unrippled shroud.
And the noisy crowd, wandering off listlessly,
Said: "That madwoman, she spoiled the festivities."

—*Beth Archer*

LOUISE ACKERMANN (1813–1890)

MY BOOK

In place of melodies, I offer you nothing
But cries of revolt and emboldened rhymes.
Yes! But what if, hearing me, you paled? What if,
Surprised by the outbursts of my impudent speech,
5 You cursed the strong and strident voice
    That made you shudder?

And yet when I reach such tones,
I have no thought of offending hearts or ears.
Even the most fearful have no cause for alarm:
10 A note of despair no doubt here prevails,
But I'd not wrench such sounds from my breast
    For the mere pleasure of blasphemy.

What? Liberty unleashes its wrath;
Everywhere, against the weight of centenary wrongs,
15 Truth struggles to clear a path;
And I should not take part in that great drama?
How! This heart that beats, though a woman's heart,
    Is it any less a human heart?

Est-ce ma faute à moi si dans ces jours de fièvre
20 D'ardentes questions se pressent sur ma lèvre?
Si votre Dieu surtout m'inspire des soupçons?
Si la Nature aussi prend des teintes funèbres,
Et si j'ai de mon temps, le long de mes vertèbres,
    Senti courir tous les frissons?

25 Jouet depuis longtemps des vents et de la houle,
Mon bâtiment fait eau de toutes parts; il coule.
La foudre seule encore à ses signaux répond.
Le voyant en péril et loin de toute escale,
Au lieu de m'enfermer tremblante à fond de cale
30   J'ai voulu monter sur le pont.

A l'écart, mais debout, là, dans leur lit immense
Je contemple le jeu des vagues en démence.
Puis prévoyant bientôt le naufrage et la mort,
Au risque d'encourir l'anathème ou le blâme,
35 A deux mains j'ai saisi ce livre de mon âme,
    Et l'ai lancé par-dessus bord.

C'est mon trésor unique, amassé page à page.
A le laisser au fond d'une mer sans rivage
Disparaître avec moi je n'ai pu consentir.
40 Le dépit du courant qui l'emporte ou l'entrave,
Qu'il se soutienne donc et surnage en épave
    Sur ces flots qui vont m'engloutir!

(1874)

RÉVOLTE

Vous entendrez, Seigneur, la plainte de la femme.
Si vraiment dans son corps vous avez mis une âme,
Pourquoi laissez-vous l'homme, à chaque heure du jour,
Opprimer sa faiblesse, avilir son amour,
5 L'enchaîner, l'asservir, qu'elle avance ou recule,
Dire: Va sous la tente, ou rentre en ta cellule!
Tu n'iras pas plus loin, tu n'as rien ici-bas!
L'air, l'onde, le soleil, ne te connaissent pas;
Baisse ton voile obscur, passe inerte et glacée:

Is it my fault if in these feverish days
20 Burning questions press upon my lips?
If, above all, your God arouses my distrust?
If nature also assumes funereal shades,
And if in my life, all along my spine,
    I felt every possible shudder?

25 Long the plaything of winds and waves,
My ship takes in water from everywhere; it's sinking.
Lightning alone still answers its signals.
Seeing it imperiled, far from any harbor,
Instead of shutting myself trembling in the hold,
30   I chose to climb up to the bridge.

At a distance, but upright, there, in their vast bed
I survey the frenzied play of the waves.
Then, seeing imminent shipwreck and death,
At the risk of incurring curse or blame,
35 I seized the book of my soul with both hands
    And cast it over the rail.

It is my only treasure, compiled page by page.
To let it disappear with me in the depths
Of a shoreless sea, I could not allow.
40 The spiteless current carries it off or blocks its way;
May it stay up and like wreckage float
    On the waves that will engulf me.

—*Beth Archer*

ADINE BRABART RIOM (1818–1899)

REVOLT

You would hear, O Lord, woman's lament
If in her body you had truly placed a soul.
Why do you allow man, at every hour of the day,
To tyrannize her weakness, debase her love,
5 Fetter and subject her movements forward and back,
Saying: ''Go into the tent, or back to your cell!
Go no farther, you have nothing on earth!
The air does not know you, nor the sea or sun!
Lower your somber veil, live inert and frozen!

10 Je t'interdis d'abord l'élan de la pensée,
Les dignités, les arts, les charges et l'emploi,
Car le sol, le travail, l'honneur, tout est à moi!

Oui, je ne te comprends qu'à mes genoux sans cesse,
Sers-moi comme une esclave, ou comme une maîtresse:
15 Choisis entre ces noms...c'est l'unique faveur
Que je daigne accorder!...—Mille fois non, Seigneur!
Lorsqu'il me parle ainsi, ma colère s'allume,
Daignez mettre en mes mains la faucille ou la plume,
Ce qu'il rejette enfin; mais n'allez pas encor
20 Me charger de son nom et de son anneau d'or!

Ou bien, puisque partout la terre est son empire,
Laissez-moi m'exiler sur les flots!...Le navire
Se balance et répond en s'éloignant de moi:
Sur la mer, après Dieu, l'homme est l'unique roi;
25 A lui les mâts, les ponts, le drapeau, l'équipage.
Que son autorité soit inique ou sauvage,
Qu'importe! il est l'arbitre et le maître du sort,
Il a le droit de vie, il a le droit de mort!

A vaincre sans combat sa puissance exercée
30 Vient encore opprimer jusque à ma pensée.
Quoi! la terre, et la mer et le ciel! Oui, mon Dieu,
Il semble à mon malheur que même du saint lieu
Les portes à son gré sont ouvertes ou closes!
O Christ, Verbe éternel, avez-vous dit ces choses?
35 Ne m'a-t-il pas trompée, oh! parlez-moi, Seigneur,
Confondez son orgueil et levez-vous vainqueur.
Venez, protégez-moi, n'avez-vous pas d'entraille?
Ne m'entendez-vous pas? Où voulez-vous que j'aille?
Lui partout, lui toujours, qui me dit: Sois à moi!
40 Qui me pousse à l'abîme en me glaçant d'effroi.
L'entendez-vous encore: Allons, sois mon esclave,
Ma volonté n'admet nul retard, nulle entrave!
Seule, où donc irais-tu? Que peux-tu devenir?
Tu n'as qu'un but, c'est moi, qui suis ton avenir!

45 Venez à mon secours, ou donnez-moi des armes!
Il a vu ma faiblesse, il a ri de mes larmes!
Car, il n'est que trop vrai, j'avais cru le charmer
Et j'avais commencé, Dieu puissant, par l'aimer,
Par l'aimer d'un amour immense, inextinguible!
50 O mon Dieu! j'étais folle en ce rêve impossible!
Il était plus que vous ma vie et mon soleil...
Quand vous fûtes vengé par un affreux réveil!

10 I forbid you, first, any flight of thought,
Honors and arts, duties and labor,
For soil, work, and glory all are mine!

"Only on your knees before me do I see you,
You may serve me as slave or mistress:
15 Choose between these names...this is the sole favor
I deign to grant you!..." —A thousand times no, O Lord!
When he speaks to me so, my anger flares;
Place in my hands a scythe or a pen,
Anything he disdains; but burden me
20 No longer with his golden band and his name!

Or yet, since all the earth is his domain,
Let me go into exile upon the waves!...
The ship rocks and replies as it moves away:
On the sea, after God, man is the only king;
25 To him the masts, the decks, the pennant, and the crew.
If his rule be brutal or unjust,
No matter! He is judge and master of its fate.
He holds the right to life, the right to death.

Accustomed to vanquish without a struggle,
30 His power seeks to oppress even my thoughts.
What! Earth and sea and sky as well? Dear God,
For my misfortune, even the gates of heaven
Seem to close and open at his bidding!
Did you say these things, O Christ, eternal Word?
35 Did he not deceive me? Oh, speak to me, Lord,
Humble his pride and arise victorious.
Come and protect me; have you no mercy?
Do you not hear me? Where would you have me go?
He, everywhere, always he, saying, Be mine!
40 Who pushes me to the abyss as I stiffen with terror.
Do you not hear him still: Come, be my slave,
My will brooks no hindrance, no delay!
Alone, where would you go? What would you become?
I am your only aim, I am your future!

45 Come to my rescue, or give me arms!
He has seen my weakness, laughed at my tears!
And yet, it is true, I tried to charm him!
At first I loved him, all-powerful God,
Loved him with an immense, unquenchable love!
50 O my God, that impossible dream was madness!
He was, more than you, my life, my sun...
And then you were avenged by a dreadful awakening!

Il a brisé mon coeur, il a tué mon âme,
J'ai vu tomber mon ciel sur mon idole infâme!
55 Et vous croyez, Seigneur, quand vous fermez vos bras,
Que l'excès de mes maux ne vous accuse pas?...

Un jour, lorsque Esaü transporté de colère
S'arrachait les cheveux et se tordait à terre,
60 Son père lui disait en sa morne stupeur:
«Fils, ne m'accuse pas: une fatale erreur
Donne tout à ton frère, et ces troupeaux superbes,
Et ces vignes en fleurs, et ces pesantes gerbes,
L'huile des oliviers, les soyeuses toisons,
65 Les récoltes de fruits de toutes les saisons.
Mon fils, j'ai tout donné du couchant à l'aurore,
Les puits et leur fraîcheur, l'ombre du sycomore,
Les prés, les champs, les bois où croit le palmier vert,
Et tout ce qui s'étend d'ici jusqu'au désert.
70 C'est en vain que vers toi s'ouvrent mes mains tremblantes,
En vain que je tressaille à tes larmes brûlantes,
Sous le toit paternel tu deviens un banni,
Et n'as droit qu'à ce mot: Mon enfant, sois béni!»

Seriez-vous impuissant comme le patriarche?
75 Créateur éternel, n'avez-vous donc plus d'arche
Pour bercer sur les flots vos enfants malheureux,
Quand tous les éléments se déchaînent contre eux?
Mais où donc êtes-vous? Quand mes cris vous appellent,
L'oiseau tombe des cieux, les pierres étincellent
80 Comme au choc de l'acier! plus aigus, plus stridents,
Ils vous cherchent en vain dans tous vos firmaments.
Que leur répondez-vous?...
                    ...L'homme est roi sur la terre,
N'appelle à ton secours ni le bras de ton père,
85 Ni la Haine, l'Amour, la Justice ou le Sort,
Ni l'Enfer, ni le Ciel!...
                    ...Viens, j'oubliais la Mort!

(1864)

He broke my heart, he killed my soul,
I saw the heavens fall on my infamous idol!
55 But when you cross your arms, O Lord, do you believe
That my extreme affliction does not indict you?...

One day, when Esau, beside himself with fury,
Tore out his hair and writhed upon the ground,
His father said to his pained amazement,
60 "Son, do not blame me; one fatal error
Bestows all on your brother: these fine flocks,
Flowering vines and fat sheaves of wheat,
The oil of the olive trees, the silken fleeces,
The harvest of fruits in every season.
65 My son, I gave everything from sunset to dawn,
The wells with their freshness, the shade of the sycamore,
The pastures, the fields, the green grove of palms,
And all that lies from here to the desert.
In vain do my trembling hands open out to you,
70 In vain do I wince at your burning tears.
Under your father's roof you are now an exile,
Entitled only to these words: Blessed be, my son!"

Would you be as powerless as this patriarch?
Eternal creator, have you no longer an ark
75 To rock your wretched children on the waves
When all the elements explode against them?
Where, then, are you? When my cries call out for you
The bird falls from the skies, the stones spark
As though struck by steel: sharper, harsher,
80 Vainly do they seek you in the vaulted heavens.
And what is your reply?...
                              ...Man is king on earth.
Ask not your father's arm to help you,
Or Hatred, Love, Justice, or Destiny,
Hell or Heaven...
                              ...And yet, there is always Death!

—Beth Archer

de *LA FILLE-MÈRE*

LE JUGEMENT*

«Entendu la défense et le réquisitoire,
Attendu qu'il résulte un fait acquis, notoire,
Que la prévenue a mis au monde un enfant
Né vivant et viable et qu'elle se défend
5 D'avoir fait ou commis aucune violence,
Mais qu'il est avéré qu'en cette circonstance
En n'appelant personne à lui porter secours
En cette solitude, elle a, par un concours
De faits délictueux, commis un homicide
10 Par imprudence et non l'infanticide;
Mais attendu qu'avant d'absoudre ou de punir
Le juge a la devoir, le droit de définir
Le mobile réel, la véritable cause
Qui, dans le cas présent, comme en toute autre chose,
15 Ont pu déterminer la grave infraction
Dont l'organe public veut la répression;
Attendu qu'en effet, notre société même
Ainsi organisée, a créé le problème
Qui se pose aujourd'hui, problème original
20 Qui mène l'accusée au pied du tribunal.
Attendu que la fille en cachant sa grossesse
Et son accouchement ainsi que sa détresse
Redoutait la cruelle et sourde hostilité
De toute sa famille et que la société,
25 Si prodigue souvent de railleries amères,
Accable de mépris les pauvres filles-mères,
Quand la maternité, bien comprise d'ailleurs,
Devrait nous désarmer et nous rendre meilleurs;
Que c'est, en résumé, la société, si tendre
30 Pour tous les séducteurs, qui doit enfin comprendre
Qu'elle est bien responsable, en ses décrets hautains,
De tant d'accouchements forcément clandestins;
Qu'il existe, en faveur de cette prévenue
Au sujet de sa faute un fait qui l'atténue
35 Et que le juge doit, à défaut du pardon
Qui n'est pas dans nos lois, lui faire un juste don

*Note de l'auteur—Le jugement reproduit aussi fidèlement que possible les considérations d'un arrêt rendu par le Président Magnaud en l'année 1900..

CAMILLE BÉLOT (n.d.)

from THE UNWED MOTHER

THE DECISION*

"Having heard the defense and the prosecution,
Considering the one established, notable fact,
That the defendant gave birth to a child,
Living and healthy, and that she denies
5 Having committed any act of violence;
But that in this circumstance it is proved that
By calling no one to lend assistance
In her solitude, she has, by concurrence
Of punishable acts, committed accidental
10 Homicide and not infanticide;
But considering that before absolving or punishing,
The judge has the duty and the right
To determine the real motive, the true cause
Which, in the present case, as in all things
15 May have led to the serious infraction
That the people's voice wishes punished;
Considering that our society itself,
As it is organized, has created the problem
Before us today, the original problem
20 That led the accused before the bar;
Considering that the girl concealed the pregnancy
And the birth, as well as her wretchedness,
Fearing the cruel and blind hostility
Of her entire family, and that society,
25 So often generous with its bitter mockery,
Hurls contempt at those poor unwed mothers,
Whereas motherhood, rightly understood, in fact
Ought to disarm us and make us better;
That, in sum, it is society, so forgiving
30 Toward all seducers, that should finally understand
The responsibility it bears, by its arrogant decrees,
For so many births perforce clandestine;
That there exists, on behalf of this defendant
An attenuating factor with regard to her crime,
35 And that the judge, in place of a pardon,
Which is not within our laws, must offer her

*Author's note—This text reproduces as faithfully as possible the court's
reasoning for the judgment handed down by Judge Magnaud in 1900.

Des dispositions bienveillantes du Code.
Mais qu'il est très fâcheux que, dans son triste exode
La prévenue ait fait créance aux préjugés
40 Qui causent des délits cruellement vengés;
Attendu qu'une fille, en réparant sa faute
Et montrant comme mère une vertu si haute
Mérite d'autant plus le respect du prochain
Qu'elle est seule à nourrir son enfant orphelin;
45 Que plus condamnable est la femme mariée
Dont la coquetterie est trop contrariée
Par la maternité qu'elle évite à dessein
En laissant savamment stériliser son sein;
Attendu qu'au surplus, tant qu'ici-bas la femme
50 Est tenue en tutelle et que son droit réclame
Elle a beaucoup moins de responsabilité
Que celui qui maintient son infériorité;
Enfin, par ces motifs et comme réprimande
Le tribunal condamne à seize francs d'amende
55 El puisqu'à la rigueur il ne peut déroger
Fait application de la loi Bérenger.»

Des applaudissements éclatent dans la foule
Qui se sent tout émue et lentement s'écoule
En approuvant tout haut et répétant le nom
60 D'un juge qui mérite un éternel renom.

(1901)

NOCTURNE

J'adore la langueur de ta lèvre charnelle
Où persiste le pli des baisers d'autrefois.
   Ta démarche ensorcelle,
Et la perversité calme de ta prunelle
5 A pris au ciel du nord ses bleus traîtres et froids.   ╲

Tes cheveux, répandus ainsi qu'une fumée,
Clairement vaporeux, presque immatériels,

The benevolent provisions of the legal code.
It is most unfortunate, however, that in her pitiful flight
The defendant gave credence to the prejudices
40 That cause the crimes so cruelly avenged;
Considering that a girl, by expiating her misdeed
And demonstrating such high virtue as a mother,
Merits all the more respect from others
Since she alone must care for her orphan child;
45 More reprehensible is the married woman
Whose coquetry is so hindered
By motherhood she willfully avoids it,
Knowingly letting herself be sterilized;
Considering furthermore that so long as woman
50 Is kept in tutelage and must beg her rights,
She has far less responsibility
Than he who perpetuates her inferiority;
In conclusion, for these reasons and as a reprimand,
The court sentences her to a fine of sixteen francs,
55 And since it cannot depart from the letter of the law,
Invokes upon the woman the Bérenger law.''**

Applause explodes in the audience,
Which is deeply moved and files slowly out,
Loudly commending and repeating the name of
60 A judge who deserves eternal renown.

—Beth Archer

**Editor's note—The law, proposed by René Bérenger (1830-1915) and passed in 1891, provided that first-time offenders would receive a suspended sentence. A lawyer and senator, Bérenger also headed an organization for the rehabilitation of convicts.

RENÉE VIVIEN (1877–1909)

NOCTURNE

I love the languor of your sensual lips
Bearing still the fold of yesterday's kisses.
    Your gait is bewitching;
And the calm perversity of your eyes
5 Stole from northern skies their treacherous, icy blue.

Your hair, wafting like smoke,
Vaporously pale, as though not material,

Semblent, ô Bien-Aimée,
Recéler les rayons d'une lune embrumée,
10   D'une lune d'hiver dans le cristal des ciels.

Le soir voluptueux a des moiteurs d'alcôve;
Les astres sont comme des regards sensuels
    Dans l'éther d'un gris mauve,
Et je vois s'allonger, inquiétant et fauve,
15   Le lumineux reflet de tes ongles cruels.

Sous la robe, qui glisse en un frôlement d'aile,
Je devine ton corps,—les lys ardents des seins,
    L'or blême de l'aisselle,
Les flancs doux et fleuris, les jambes d'Immortelle,
20   Le velouté du ventre et la rondeur des reins.

La terre s'alanguit, énervée, et la brise,
Chaude encore des lits lointains, vient assouplir
    La mer enfin soumise...
Voici la nuit d'amour depuis longtemps promise...
25   Dans l'ombre je te vois divinement pâlir.

(1901)

LITANIE DE LA HAINE

La Haine nous unit, plus forte que l'Amour.
Nous haïssons le rire et le rythme du jour,
Le regard du printemps au néfaste retour.

Nous haïssons la face agressive des mâles.
5   Nos coeurs ont recueilli les regrets et les râles
Des Femmes aux fronts lourds, des Femmes aux fronts pâles.

Nous haïssons le rut qui souille le désir.
Nous jetons l'anathème à l'immonde soupir
D'où naîtront les douleurs des êtres à venir.

10   Nous haïssons la Foule et les Lois et le Monde.
Comme une voix de fauve à la rumeur profonde,
Notre rébellion se répercute et gronde.

Amantes sans amant, épouses sans époux,
Le souffle ténébreux de Lilith est en nous,
15   Et le baiser d'Eblis nous fut terrible et doux.

Seems O dearest love,
To cast the rays of a veiled moon,
10 A winter moon in a crystal-cold heaven.

The sensuous evening is moist with love;
The stars glance seductively
    In the mauve-gray sky,
And I see reaching out, frightening and wild,
15 The luminous gleam of your cruel nails.

Under your gown, which glides with the rustle of a wing,
I discern your body—the glowing lilies of your breasts,
    The delicate gold of the underarm,
The soft ample thighs, the legs of a goddess,
20 The velvet belly and rounded loins.

The earth, now weak, grows languorous, and a breeze,
Still warm from distant beds, comes to smooth
    The sea at long last daunted...
Here, finally, the long-awaited night of love...
25 In the shadows I see you grow divinely pale.

—*Beth Archer*

A LITANY OF HATE

Hatred, more powerful than Love, unites us.
We hate laughter and the rhythm of life,
The glance of spring with its baleful return.

We hate the violence of men.
5 Our hearts have stored the chagrins and gasps
Of Women with furrowed brows, Women with pale faces.

We hate the lust that sullies desire.
We execrate that obscene sigh
That engenders the agonies of beings to come.

10 We hate the Crowd and the Laws of the World.
Like the deep roar of a beast in the wild
Our rebellion rumbles and resounds.

Loving women without lovers, wives without husbands,
The sinister breath of Lilith resides in us,
15 And Elbis' kiss was both ghastly and sweet to us.

Plus belle que l'Amour, la Haine est ma maîtresse,
Et je convoite en toi la cruelle prêtresse
Dont mes lividités aiguiseront l'ivresse.

Mêlant l'or des genêts à la nuit des iris,
20 Nous renierons les pleurs mystiques de jadis
Et l'expiation des cierges et des lys.

Je ne frapperai plus aux somnolentes portes.
Les odeurs monteront vers moi, sombres et fortes,
Avec le souvenir diaphane des Mortes.

(1904)

PSAPPHA REVIT

La lune se levait autrefois à Lesbos
Sur le verger nocturne où veillaient les amantes.
L'amour rassasié montait des eaux dormantes
Et sanglotait au coeur profond du sarbitos.

5 Psappha ceignait son front d'augustes violettes
Et célébrait l'Erôs qui s'abat comme un vent
Sur les chênes...Atthis l'écoutait en rêvant,
Et la torche avivait l'éclat des bandelettes.

Les rives flamboyaient, blondes sous les pois d'or...
10 Les vierges enseignaient aux belles étrangères
Combien l'ombre est propice aux caresses légères,
Et le ciel et la mer déployaient leur décor.

...Certaines d'entre nous ont conservé les rites
De ce brûlant Lesbos doré comme un autel.
15 Nous savons que l'amour est puissant et cruel,
Et nos amantes ont les pieds blancs des Kharites.

Nos corps sont pour leurs corps un fraternel miroir.
Nos compagnes, aux seins de neige printanière,
Savent de quelle étrange et suave manière
20 Psappha pliait naguère Atthis à son vouloir.

Lovelier than Love, Hate is my mistress,
And in you I yearn for the cruel priestess
Whose rapture is quickened by my pallor.

Blending the gold of broombrush with the night of iris,
20 We renounce the mystical tears of old
And the expiation of tapers and lilies.

No longer will I beat on sleeping doors.
Odors heavy and pungent will waft up to me
With the gossamer memory of dead women.

—*Beth Archer*

SAPPHO LIVES AGAIN

In Lesbos long ago the moon would rise
Over the orchard where lovers held their nightly vigil.
Sated passion rose from those sleeping waters
And sobbed deep in the heart of the lyre.*

5 Sappho circled her brow with imperial violets
And celebrated Eros, who swoops down like a wind
Upon the oak trees...Attis listened to her pensively
And the torch made her circlets shine brighter still.

The shores were flaming, blond under spots of gold...
10 The virgins taught the lovely foreign maidens.
How propitious the shadows are for delicate caresses,
And the sky and sea spread out their decoration.

...Some of us have kept the rites
Of that burning Lesbos gilded like an altar.
15 We know that love is strong and cruel
And our lovers have the white feet of Graces.

Our bodies are for theirs a sisterly mirror,
Our friends, with breasts white as springtime snow,
Know in what strange and suave manner
20 Sappho used to bend Attis to her will.

*Translator's note—A misprint is presumed, since the word as spelled, *sarbitos,* does not exist in Greek, whereas the word *barbitos* means a stringed instrument or lyre.

Nous adorons avec des candeurs infinies,
En l'émerveillement d'un enfant étonné
A qui l'or éternel des mondes fut donné...
Psappha revit, par la vertu des harmonies.

25 Nous savons effleurer d'un baiser de velours,
Et nous savons étreindre avec des fougues blêmes;
Nos caresses sont nos mélodieux poèmes...
Notre amour est plus grand que toutes les amours.

Nous redisons ces mots de Psappha, quand nous sommes
30 Rêveuses sous un ciel illuminé d'argent:
«O belles, envers vous mon coeur n'est point changeant...»
Celles que nous aimons ont méprisé les hommes.

Nos lunaires baisers ont de pâles douceurs,
Nos doigts ne froissent point le duvet d'une joue,
35 Et nous pouvons, quand la ceinture se dénoue,
Être tout à la fois des amants et des soeurs.

Le désir est en nous moins fort que la tendresse.
Et cependant l'amour d'une enfant nous dompta
Selon la volonté de l'âpre Aphrodita,
40 Et chacune de nous demeure sa prêtresse.

Psappha revit et règne en nos corps frémissants;
Comme elle, nous avons écouté la sirène,
Comme elle encore, nous avons l'âme sereine,
Nous qui n'entendons point l'insulte des passants.

45 Ferventes, nous prions: «Que la nuit soit doublée
Pour nous dont le baiser craint l'aurore, pour nous
Dont l'Erôs mortel a délié les genoux,
Qui sommes une chair éblouie et troublée...»

Et nos maîtresses ne sauraient nous décevoir,
50 Puisque c'est l'infini que nous aimons en elles...
Et, puisque leurs baisers nous rendent éternelles,
Nous ne redoutons point l'oubli dans l'Hadès noir.

Ainsi, nous les chantons, l'âme sonore et pleine.
Nos jours sans impudeur, sans crainte ni remords,
55 Se déroulent, ainsi que de larges accords,
Et nous aimons, comme on aimait à Mytilène.

(1906)

We worship with infinite innocence,
Marveling like a wide-eyed child
Given the endless gold of spheres...
Sappho lives again, through the grace of harmonies.

25 We know how to plant a kiss of velvet
And how to embrace with languid ardor;
Our caresses are our lyric poems...
Our love is greater than any love.

We repeat those words of Sappho when we lie
30 Dreaming under a sky shot with silver:
"Oh, lovely ones, toward you my heart remains unchanged..."
Those we love have looked with scorn on men.

Our moonlit kisses have a pale gentleness,
Our fingers never crumple the down of a cheek,
35 And when the sash comes unfastened, we can be
Lovers and sisters all in one.

Desire in us is not as strong as tenderness,
And yet our love for a young girl conquered us
By the will of scathing Aphrodite,
40 Whose priestess each of us remains.

Sappho lives and reigns in our trembling bodies;
Like her, we have heard the siren,
Like her as well, we have peaceful hearts,
We who never heed insults of passersby.

45 With fervor we pray: "May night be twice as long
For us whose kisses shun the dawn, for us
Whose knees were parted by mortal Eros,
For us whose flesh is dazzling and unquiet..."

And our mistresses cannot disappoint us,
50 For it is the infinite in them that we adore...
And since their kisses make us eternal,
We do not fear the oblivion of Hades' darkness.

Thus we laud them, our hearts overflowing and resounding.
Our days without immodesty, fear, or remorse,
55 Unfold like vast harmonies,
And we love, as they once loved in Mytilene.

—Beth Archer

À UNE FIANCÉE

Donc, vous vous mariez, immolant vos vingt ans
En hostie à la loi des anciennes méprises,
Vous allez consacrer votre amour aux églises,
Pour offrir l'esclavage à vos futurs enfants.

5 Vous légitimerez aux regards des passants
Votre union de vierge à la terre promise,
Joignant votre bêtise à tant d'autres bêtises
Pour donner à notre âge un neuf gémissement!

Vous voulez enfanter, devenir une mère,
10 Donner au monde un homme, une âme à la matière,
Bétail reproduisant le mal de vos aïeux.

Vautrée en le passé pour taire vos alarmes
N'entendez-vous ces cris qui montent jusqu'aux cieux,
Demandant le non-être au Créateur des larmes?

(1900)

FEMME

Femme à la souple charpente,
Au poitrail courbe, arqué pour
Les gémissements d'amour,
Mon désir suivra tes pentes—
5 Tes veines, branchages nains—
Où la courbe rejoint l'angle;
Jambes fermant le triangle
Du cher coffret féminin.

—O femme, source et brûlure—

10 Je renverse dans ma main
Ta tête—sommet humain,
Cascade ta chevelure!

(1920)

NATALIE CLIFFORD BARNEY (1877–1972)

TO A BRIDE-TO-BE

And so you marry, offering your youth
In sacrifice to ancient lawful error;
You dedicate your love to sacred truth
To bless your child with slavery and terror.

5 The world will consecrate the public vows
That bind you virgin to the promised land,
Joining your blindness to the blinded crowds,
Adding a new moan to their long demand.

You want to grow and swell and to give birth,
10 To give a life to man, a soul to earth,
And once more bear the brute pain of the years.

Hugging the past to stifle your own cry,
Do you not hear those voices fill the sky
Asking for Nothing from the Source of tears?

— *Barbara Johnson*

WOMAN

Woman, supple frame,
Curving archway, bent for moans
Of love,
My desire will follow your slopes—
5 The tiny branches of your veins
Where angles join with curves;
Legs enclosing the delta
Of the cherished womanly safe.

—O woman, water and fire—

10 I pull your head back
In my hand—the human crest,
Cascade of hair!

—*Barbara Johnson*

DISTIQUES

Tu veux que je te fasse un amoureux poème.
Ecoute donc plutôt si mon silence t'aime!

Je ne saurais donner au sage alexandrin
Les plaintes du plaisir, le rhythme de nos reins!

5 Quand, sous mon corps élu, je sens battre ta joie,
Exprimer mon désir qui t'effleure et te broie?

Sois ma maîtresse douce et folle; au lieu de mots
Accepte sur ta chair d'extatiques sanglots!

Et lorsque je retombe avec toi—si ma bouche,
10 Eloquence muette, est celle qui te touche,

Laisse-moi parcourir ton être harmonieux
De tes pieds recourbés à tes courbes cheveux.

Nerfs d'accord, bien tendus: musique, sortilège,
Harpe dont je détiens le secret des arpèges—

15 Pour toi, l'art de mes mains, orgueilleux instrument,
Fait l'amour en poète, et les vers en amant!

(1920)

L'INJUSTICE

Pendant que notre corps et notre âme se donnent
   Librement à notre seul homme,
     Que pures, fraîches, libres,
   Riches du trésor d'être honnêtes,
5 Nous contentons aussi le rêve de nos têtes
     Et de nos fibres,

   Je pense, avec un coeur serré,
A vous qui, malgré vous, faites l'amour, les filles!
A votre pauvre corps de louage qu'on pille,
10 Et mon être est meurtri des maux que vous souffrez.

COUPLETS

You asked me for a love poem.
Listen, rather, to the love my silence speaks!

I cannot say in steady, docile iambs
The moans of pleasure, the rhythm of our loins.

5 When beneath my body I feel your beating joy,
Will I say my desire brushing and crushing you?

Come be my love sweet and wild; instead of words
Upon your flesh accept my enraptured sobs.

And when we fall back, spent—if my mouth,
10 Mute eloquence, still touches you,

Let me explore your body's harmony
From the arch of your foot to your flowing hair.

Senses finely tuned; music, charm,
Harp whose secret chords I hold,

15 For you, my artful hands, proud instrument,
Make love as a poet, verse as a lover!

—*Barbara Johnson*

LUCIE DELARUE-MARDRUS (1880?–1945)

INJUSTICE

All the while we give our body and our soul
   Freely to a single man,
     And rich with our respectability,
   Pure, unfettered, fresh,
5 We fulfill the dream in our heads
      And in our flesh,

   I think, with anxious heart, O prostitutes,
Of you who must make love against your will,
Of your poor bodies for hire, for plunder,
10 And my being is battered by the ills you suffer.

Les instincts ont croisé leurs lames de duel:
Le mâle que tourmente une bête cachée
S'approche. On lui vendra le geste naturel.
L'un cherche son plaisir, l'autre cherche son pain,
15   Chacun sa faim!
   C'est la quotidienne bouchée.

Or les épouses sont, dans leur lit bienheureux,
Avec l'homme choisi roulé dans leurs cheveux,
Celles qu'on respecte et qu'on berce et qu'on soigne...
20 Les filles! Vous aussi êtes celles qu'on soigne,
      Mais c'est au fond des lupanars!
      Pour que tout homme de hasard
Puisse en sécurité vous broyer dans ses poignes.

Ainsi l'amour public déferle sur vos corps
25   Sans que jamais personne vous aime.
      Et vous ne savez plus vous-mêmes
La profondeur d'horreur de votre sort.

—Très précieuse chair dont on a perdu l'âme,
Ah! combien dans mon coeur s'amasse de rancune
30 Contre votre fatale et mauvaise fortune,
Filles qui malgré tout, êtes ma soeur, la femme!

(1904)

REFUS

De l'ombre; des coussins; la vitre où se dégrade
Le jardin; un repos incapable d'efforts.
Ainsi semble dormir la femme «enfant malade»
Qui souffre aux profondeurs fécondes de son corps.

5 Ainsi je songe...Un jour, un homme pourrait naître
De ce corps mensuel, et vivre par delà
Ma vie, et longuement recommencer mon être
Que je sens tant de fois séculaire déjà;

Je songe qu'il aurait mon visage sans doute,
10 Mes yeux épouvantés, noirs et silencieux,
Et que peut-être, errant et seul avec ces yeux,
Nul ne prendrait sa main pour marcher sur la route.

The instincts have unsheathed and crossed their blades·
The male tormented by the hidden beast
Comes near. A natural act is sold.
He wants his pleasure; you, your bread;
15   Each is hungry;
  Both are fed.

The wives in their happy beds
The chosen man rolled in their hair
Receive respect and comfort and care...
20 Prostitutes! You too are cared for,
      But in the depths of brothels!
      So that each passing man
      Can safely crush you in his hands.

And so a public love unfurls across your breast
25   And you are loved by no one.
      Even the horror of your fate
You have forgotten.

—Precious flesh whose soul is barely human,
What deep resentment fills my heart
30 Against your sad, unenviable lot,
Prostitutes, my sisters despite all, O Woman!

—*Barbara Johnson*

REFUSAL

Shadows; pillows; the garden sloping down
Behind the window; a slackness unfit for effort.
So woman seems to sleep like a "sick child"
Pained by the body's fertile depths.

5 I dream...Some day, a man could spring
From this monthly body, and live beyond
My life, lengthening anew my being
That feels already centuries old.

I dream he no doubt would have my face,
10 My frightened eyes, dark and silent;
And if he wandered alone with eyes like these,
No one would take his hand along the road.

Ayant trop écouté le hurlement humain,
J'approuve dans mon coeur l'oeuvre libératrice
15 De ne pas m'ajouter moi-même un lendemain

Pour l'orgueil et l'horreur d'être une génitrice...
—Et parmi mes coussins pleins d'ombre, je m'enivre
De ma stérilité qui saigne lentement.

(1904)

SI TU VIENS

Si tu viens, je prendrai tes lèvres dès la porte,
Nous irons sans parler dans l'ombre et les coussins,
Je t'y ferai tomber, longue comme une morte,
Et, passionnément, je chercherai tes seins.

5 A travers ton bouquet de corsage, ma bouche
Prendra leur pointe nue et rose entre deux fleurs,
Et, t'écoutant gémir du baiser qui les touche,
Je te désirerai, jusqu'aux pleurs, jusqu'aux pleurs!

—Or, les lèvres au sein, je veux que ma main droite
10 Fasse vibrer ton corps—instrument sans défaut—
Que tout l'art de l'Amour inspiré de Sapho
Exalte cette chair sensible intime et moite.

Mais quand le difficile et terrible plaisir
Te cambrera, livrée, éperdûment ouverte,
15 Puissé-je retenir l'élan fou du désir
Qui crispera mes doigts contre ton col inerte!

The human howl rings loudly in my ears,
And so my heart approves the liberating act
15 Of refusing another future for myself

Just for the pride and horror of begetting...
—Deep in the shadows of my bed, I drink
The slowly bleeding wine of my sterility.

—Barbara Johnson

IF YOU COME

If you come, I will meet your lips at the door;
Without a word we will move to shadowy pillows
Where I will lay you out, long as a corpse,
And search, passionately, for your breasts.

5 Between the flowers at your throat, my mouth
Will take their naked, blushing tips;
Feeling you moan at the touch of every kiss,
I will desire you to the edge of tears!

My lips on your breast, my right hand will arouse
10 Your quivering body—flawless instrument—
And may all the artistry of sapphic love
Exalt its moist responsive inner flesh.

But when with difficult and painful pleasure
You arch, abandoned, opened wildly,
15 Can I restrain the mad desiring surge
That clasps my fingers at your lifeless throat!

—Barbara Johnson

HISTOIRE EN FORME DE POÉSIE

L'ANDROGYNE

Ce n'est pas entre Lui et Moi. C'est entre Moi et Moi que se poursuit la controverse.—Car toute chose était alors obscurcie par le soleil.—Si les femmes aiment tant les robes, c'est que les hommes les ont déçues.—Le jour où chacune transformera le Bonheur—cet hôte extérieur—en parasite de son sang, la grande couture fera faillite.— Et j'étais là en bleu de travail, dès six heures au matin, heureuse comme Louise dans son grand air, heureuse de ce bonheur trop sûr du travail qui part, les machines allaient m'assourdir, les dactylos me harceler, ô tranquillité d'être au coeur de la Force!

Paix armée. On disait:—Quand revient le Patron? Il était parti pour six mois; demain deux ans l'anniversaire. Et sur son bureau, une revue oubliée montrait des visages de chefs d'orchestre, tous couverts par leur talent. Mais à la page suivante étaient les cantatrices et nulle n'était couverte par son talent. On disait: «Oh, je l'aurais crue plus jolie.»

Femme, ton nom est Beauté puis il devient Utilité. J'étais encore dans le premier secteur, poursuivie par les souvenirs des années de rodage.—O ma poupée; O mon oiseau, répétait le mari-amant qui m'aurait voulue loin de son habitat, passant le soir pour l'enlever dans le cabriolet bleu devenu nacelle qui décolle. Et pas un mot de ses occupations. Pas de rapport avec le personnel.—Les fleurs n'auront pas d'enfants.—Mettre l'esprit en état d'hibernage.—Un oeuf ne se casse jamais sans dégât: tout amour qui débute est fragile.—Et nous riions avec des amis, en des dîners somptueux, l'esprit de société annule l'extérieur, point n'existaient l'usine et les prolos.—Pas d'asile pour les âmes.—L'enjôleuse qui perd.—Et je crevais de jalousie devant sa dactylo. Elle savait les noms de ses correspondants, elle avait le droit d'effacer des virgules, de faire observer une erreur. Et son comptable pouvait écrire d'une belle calligraphie appliquée: à reporter, folio six, folio quinze.—C'est en tenant la gomme oblique qu'on efface le mieux les taches, sans trouer le papier, ainsi pour atténuer des brouilles et des malentendus.—Mais toute incursion dans son territoire trouait le mur d'entente, l'homme se dressait pour garder les portes. Et toute allusion pour passer la gomme en oblique laissait des trainées grises.

Mais un jour, il est revenu. Et j'étais si fière de lui montrer l'usine bourdonnante, les comptes prospères et les figures allantes que son

MARGUERITE GRÉPON (c. 1890–)

STORY IN POETIC FORM

THE ANDROGYNE

It isn't between Him and Me. It's between Me and Me that the controversy continues.—For everything was then obscured by the sun.—If women like dresses so much, it's because men have let them down.—The day each woman can change Happiness—that exterior host—into a parasite in her blood, high fashion will go bankrupt.— There I was in my blue work clothes, at six o'clock in the morning, as happy as Louise with her grand airs, happy with that all-too-certain happiness of starting out for work, with the machines ready to deafen me, the typists to assail me, but oh, what peace to be at the heart of Force!

Armed peace. They said: When's the boss coming back? He'd left for six months; he's been away two years. And on his desk an old magazine showed the faces of orchestra conductors, each covered with talent. On the next page were the divas, and none was covered by her talent. They said: "Oh, I thought she'd be prettier."

Woman, thy name is Beauty, and then it becomes Utility. I was still in the first sector, haunted by memories of my training years.—Doll Baby, Little Bird, the husband-lover would say, wanting me far from his habitat, me coming by at night to pick him up in the blue cab that would take off like a balloon. Not a word about his job. No relations with the staff.—The flowers will have no children.—Putting the mind in hibernation.—Eggs don't ever break without damage; all young love is fragile.—And we laughed with friends at sumptuous dinners; small talk annuls the outside world; factory and workers ceased to exist.—No rest for the weary.—The flatterer is foiled.—And I was jealous of his secretary. She knew the names of his correspondents; she had the right to erase a comma, point out an error. And his accountant could write in fine, meticulous script: "carry over to book six, book fifteen." If you hold the eraser at an angle you remove spots best, without tearing through the paper; the same goes for softening quarrels and misunderstandings.—But any foray into his territory tore through the wall of understanding; and he would rise to guard the doors. Any allusion for erasing at an angle left a trail of grayish stains.

But one day he came back. And I was so proud to show him the factory humming, the accounts prospering, people bustling, that his

silence m'est parvenu, monstrueux, suspect, contrit. Un silence d'homme hostile, car j'avais perdu les clés d'or en présentant les clés d'airain. Et il admirait d'un ton persifleur, et il félicitait d'un air consterné.—Et nous avancions dans un or meurtrier.—Parfait, parfait, disait le rival à son concurrent. Ma robe de travail m'avait changée de monde, du lit aux barricades. Il se souvenait des chiffons froissés, de la douce soie des culottes bleues, il se souvenait: la nuit, il resta sans pouvoir.

Est-ce qu'on peut faire l'amour avec un homme? songeait sa chair rêtive. L'androgyne longtemps pleura, disant: «De quoi faut-il se mutiler? De l'une ou de l'autre nature?» Sacrifice d'Abraham, quelle part fut donc la plus féconde? Transporta sur les cimes?—Il fait froid sur les cimes.—De quel péché coupable?—Et passent les slogans, la vérité renaît.—Est-ce qu'on peut redevenir moitié? argumentait la prétentieuse. Mais l'autre répondait:—Comprenez-vous, gens de partout, que la plus grande chose à faire, c'est de rester petites?...— Cette misère, dois-je laisser mon âme comme un mouchoir tombé à terre, qu'un passant foulera?—L'âme laissée pour compte.—La faute de Psyché.—Il m'aimait pour mes culottes bleues.—La belle âme que j'ai forgée au courant des heures dures, la belle âme, il s'en moque!— O femmes, votre corps c'est votre âme. Quelle mise à mal des pauvres vérités éternelles, le temporel pour vous c'est l'essentiel. Le miroir prime Dieu et la marmite la vie spirituelle; femelle, femelle. Sainte Soupe et Saint Ventre, qui te délivrera de la liste de courses? Dompteuses ou servantes.—O Abraham, ton partage est injuste, laisse-moi dépasser la maison. Car l'annonce faite à Lilith se chuchote partout. Des âmes en gésine pleurent sous le linge rose.—En ce lieu de combat, l'androgyne ne sait pas arbitrer.

Mais je continuais à sourire, les deux natures avaient enfanté une médiatrice qui gardait un seuil inconnu. Nouvelle madone, quels maladroits t'apporteraient des cadeaux sans étoile des Mages? Attendons cette étoile.—Mais un jour l'androgyne décida une absence, à son tour, pour diriger une succursale. Et la nature mâle avait délivré un blanc-seing: tu t'offriras qui te plaira...Mais pour les avoir commandés, ces hommes que son enfance prenait si dévotement au sérieux, voilà qu'ils lui apparaissaient de tout petits garçons, les subalternes sans prestige, voilà qu'aucun regard ne faisait signal, déclic, pour la mise en marche de la Belle Amour.

Androgyne, tu avais perdu sur les deux tableaux. Mais les astres te consolaient, effaçant tes discours: question de transition, quand tu auras grandi, tu seras placée au-delà des gagnantes. Et pourquoi regretter les coeurs de midinettes? Parce que dans la jeunesse, les gar-

silence seemed monstrous, suspect, contrite. The silence of a hostile man, for in handing him the keys of iron I had lost the keys of gold. He offered sarcastic praise, dismayed congratulations.—And we proceeded through murderous gold. Fine, perfect, said the rival to his competitor. In my work clothes I had changed worlds, from bed to barricades. He remembered rumpled lace, the soft silk of blue panties, he remembered: at night, he couldn't.

Can you make love with a man? asked his balking flesh. And the androgyne wept, saying, "What must be mutilated? Which of the two natures?" Abraham's sacrifice, which part was the most fruitful? Which rose to the heights?—It's cold up there on the heights.—Guilty of what sin?—The slogans go by; truth is reborn.—How can you go back to being a half? asked the pretentious woman. But the other answered:—You, people everywhere, don't you understand that the grandest thing of all is to remain young and small?...But this misery, must I drop my soul on the ground like a handkerchief, to be crushed by a passerby?—A soul left on account.—Psyche's mistake.—He loved me for my blue panties.—He laughs at the beautiful soul I shaped in difficult hours.—O woman, your body is your soul. What a blow to poor eternal truths: for you, the temporal is the essential. The looking glass is above God, the stew-pot above the life of the spirit; female, female. With Saint Soup and Saint Belly, who will deliver you from the shopping list? Hen-peckers or servant maids. O Abraham, the division is unjust, let me go beyond the house. For the annunciation to Lilith is whispered from ear to ear. Souls in labor weep under pink linen. In this field of combat, the androgyne cannot call the play.

But I went on smiling. The two natures had given birth to a mediatrix guarding an unknown threshold. Latter-day Madonna, what oafs would bring you gifts without the star of the Magi? Let's await that star.—But one day the androgyne herself decided to leave and head a branch office. And the male nature gave carte blanche: you can have anyone you want...But once they were subordinates, those men that dutiful childhood had taken so seriously began to seem like little boys, underlings without prestige, and their eyes made no signal, no click to get the Great Love going.

Androgyne, you lost both ways. But the stars consoled you, erasing your words; it's a question of transition; when you're grown up, you'll be placed ahead of the winners. Why mourn over a work-girl's heart? Because when you're young, the boys that could bring you a drink are masked in a rosy glow, like lanterns on Bastille Day. They seem larger than life, until later you see them in broad daylight. The light of day will reestablish Justice.

cons qui pourraient vous apporter à boire sont fardés par des lumières roses, comme aux lampions du quatorze juillet, ils apparaissent plus grands que nature, mais ensuite on les voit à pleines lumières. La lumière du jour remettra les choses en Justice.

En justice, répéta d'une voix implacable l'amie qui me voulait à d'autres fins. Et elle disait: «Parce que tu as détecté, lorsqu'une femme veut vivre avec son âme, qu'elle recontre toujours l'ombre de l'homme qui l'aime pour lui barrer la route et réclamer cette âme, ils ont mis les mots contre toi. Ignorants!

«Tu méprisais les ismes et les histoires sordides, on ne t'intéressait, nous autres, que pour stationner à un carrefour éventé de l'Histoire, pour nous engager sur la plaque tournante... Et moi je t'aimais pour ces choses qu'on refoulait en toi, j'aimais cette jeune fille préservée des orages, qui mourait jour après jour comme d'une tuberculose morale, pour abriter un monde qui ne trouvait pas de sortie.»

La lutte des femmes contre l'homme ressemble assez à la lutte des anges contre Dieu, parce qu'elle est à base d'amour.

(1957)

Justice, repeated the implacable voice of the girl friend who wanted me for other reasons. She said: "Because you figured out that, when a woman wants to live with her soul, she always runs into the shadow of the man who loves her, blocking her way and demanding that soul, they turned their words against you. Idiots!

"You scorned 'isms' and horror stories; you cared for us only because we stopped at an open crossroad of History, ready for commitment on the whirligig...And all the while I loved you for those things they repressed in you; I loved the young girl sheltered from the storm, dying day by day of a sort of moral tuberculosis, for harboring a world that had no way out."

Women's struggle against man is rather like the angels' struggle against God, because it is based on love.

—*Barbara Johnson*

LA RENARDE

Le maître de meute caresse son fouet
Il ordonne à ses chiens aux abois
De lever l'orgueil de la renarde
Dans son terril ourlé d'effroi

5 Renarde le vent cruel t'a trahie
Il a livré ta senteur féline
Ton chauffoir de terre est illusoire
Et tu n'as déjà plus d'abri

Tout n'était que mensonge
10 Sous rayons de lune meurtrie
Tes bruyères mauves étaient rêvées
Seul vrai le féroce hallali

O ma jeune soeur renarde
Sauvage feu courant comme moi
15 La balle froide nous cherche partout
Pauvres hors-la-loi

Avant d'esquisser la fuite
Nous sommes déjà condamnées
Le maigre bonheur d'être vivantes
20 Pour nous n'a guère existé

(1969)

CHANSON

Je veux que ma Danse
Ne soit qu'imprudence...
Marcher tout au bord
De ce précipice
5 Ce n'est qu'un caprice
Pour qui sait être ivre,
Mais si tu veux vivre

CLAIRE GOLL (1891–1977)

THE SHE-FOX

The pack-master strokes his whip
Orders his dogs at bay
To prick the pride of the she-fox
In her hole rimmed with fright

5 She-fox the cruel wind betrayed you
Releasing your feline smell
Illusory is your warm earth refuge
Your shelter already gone

All was but deception
10 Under rays of a bruised moon
Your mauve briars were dream-stuff
Only the wild death call is real

O she-fox my young sister
Savage quick-running fire like me
15 The cold bullet hunts us everywhere
Poor outcasts that we are

Before attempting flight
We are already condemned
The meager delight of living
20 For us has scarcely been

—*Mary Ann Caws*

YANETTE DELÉTANG-TARDIF (1907–)

SONG

I want my dance
To be careless, rash...
Though walking the edge
Of this precipice
5 Is only caprice
If you know how to drink,
If you want to live

C'est danger de mort!
Ivre du dédale
10 Qu'un hasard subtil
Fait prendre à ce fil
Où l'intelligence,
La noble démence,
Pointe sa sandale...
15 Les profonds arcanes
Ne sont que miroirs
Où le désespoir
Grimace et ricane,
O métaphysique
20 Et mensonge affreux,
Ma danse vaut mieux
Que vos gymnastiques!
L'homme au cerveau noir
Prône la clarté...
25 Sais-tu ce que c'est?
C'est ce qu'il peut voir
Aveugle à moitié
Sans se fatiguer!
Lacis compliqués
30 Où mon pas me mène,
Visages masqués
Des beaux phénomènes
Je n'aime que vous,
Figures secrètes
35 Que mon oeil pénètre
Au delà de tout...
Voyez, je suis femme
Enceinte d'un fruit,
Un plus beau produit
40 Que leurs mélodrames...
Et je danse encore
Malgré ces problèmes
De vie et de mort
Qui font de moi-même
45 Leur fatal décor!

(1930)

It's the risk of death.
Drunk in that maze
10 Which subtle chance
Grasps with this thread,
Where intelligence,
Nobly crazed,
Points its sandal...
15 Deep mysteries
Are only mirrors
In which despair
Grimaces, sneers.
O metaphysics
20 And frightful lies,
My dance is as fine
As your gymnastics.
The dark-brained man
Preaches light...
25 You know what that means?
It's what he can see
In his laziness
And half-blindness.
Labyrinths
30 My footsteps trace,
Masked faces
Of beautiful things,
I love only you,
Hidden forms
35 My eyes look through
And see beyond...
I'm a woman, you see,
Pregnant with fruit,
More richly produced
40 Than their tragedies...
And I dance all the more,
I dance despite
The problems of life
And death of which I
45 Am the fatal decor.

—Martha Collins

MA MÈRE EST MORTE

Ma mère est morte. Cette simple phrase (si c'est une phrase, elle n'a pas besoin d'être simple, ni si simple) qu'il est enfin donné d'écrire ne paraît ici qu'à la faveur de sa mort: vivante, je n'eusse jamais pu la présenter. Elle est morte à mes yeux, à mes tâtonnements effrayés, à mes chemins rétrécis, à mes hypothétiques circuits. Allongée là, elle ne respire plus, elle ne sera désormais ni véhicule ni communication. Meurt la mère de chacun, c'est entré dans les moeurs, mais meurt également l'écriture avec la mort de la phrase ici présentée. Ce n'était qu'autant que je pouvais noyer mon angoisse dans une rivière de grasse encre bleue qu'il me fallait, à son sujet, explorer des lexiques, dresser des échafaudages, construire des châteaux de papier, les renverser de la main, ingurgiter ces longs mots qui sillonnent la lymphe, parler de tout et de rien, jamais de la mort de ma mère, ratrouper mon troupeau, accoucher mes brebis, vaquer en somme, être vide, m'emplir alors de ces fongus, de ces sargasses, de ces détritus, de ces marines, qu'il devient loisible ensuite de présenter sous forme de poèmes. Je n'ai pas crié. Si je l'avais fait c'eût été lugubre haleinée, gémissements de roseaux. J'ai vaticiné sans qu'on le sache autour du sombre empire d'une phrase enfouie sous des chambardements chirurgicaux, d'une carcasse qui régentait ce qu'il me semblait ne pas dire au sujet de l'indicible, jusqu'au moment où, butant contre elle-même, elle a métamorphosé en continents boueux ses eaux, et enfin, émergée, a pu se dissoudre et disparaître, engloutissant avec elle la mort de ma mère.

(1974)

THÉRÈSE PLANTIER (1911–)

MY MOTHER IS DEAD

My mother is dead. That simple sentence (if it is a sentence, it doesn't have to be simple, not so simple) which can finally be written appears here thanks only to her death: I could never have presented it had she been living. She is dead to my eyes, to my terror-filled groping, to my narrowed paths, to my hypothetical circuits. Stretched out there, she breathes no longer; from now on she will be neither vehicle nor communication. She dies, everyone's mother; it's become part of the custom, but writing also dies, with the death of the sentence here presented. Only insofar as I could drown my anguish in a river of thick blue ink did I need to explore lexicons in speaking of her, erect scaffolding, construct paper castles, knock them over with my hand, ingurgitate these long words that furrow the lymph, speak of everything and nothing, never of my mother's death, herd up with my herd again, give birth to my sheep, in short, be vacant, empty, then fill myself with these fungi, these sargassos, this detritus, these seascapes, that can finally be presented in the form of a poem. I have never cried out. It would have been a lugubrious breath, a moaning reed. I have hesitated, no one knowing, around the somber empire of a sentence buried under a surgical din, a carcass ruling what it seemed to me was not said about the unsayable, until the moment when, butting up against itself, it transformed its waters into muddy continents, and, once emerged, could dissolve and disappear, swallowing up in itself the death of my mother.

—*Mary Ann Caws*

HOMMES PO HOMMES À LUNETTES

hommes po hommes à lunettes
hommes politi
méphipolitimemphi
                limemphi
5   tiques
vous êtes de farce pleins
de mère-patrie dans vos nombreux trous
nous on veut que ce soit l'armée qui décide
sacré putain de bordel de dieu
10 de nous envoyer à l'université oui ou non
après deux ans automatiques de mépris pour nos
parents passés à ne rien faire
nous étions si tendancieux en naissant
tous ces bras ces nez ces couilles
15 ça vous apriorise une femme en moins de deux et vaginades
il nous faudra pratiquer pendant des heures
le métier de ne rien faire
et par ce critère professionnel
sera effectué notre tri dans la masse
20 des Comités Guerriers
nous aurons un rôle effectif
d'éliminés planifiés
notre pipi usé sera rectifié
on saura notre adresse à peine à cause du climat
25 nous serons raccourcies (les femmes) par acte notarié
et tondeuse humiliante
nous monterons la garde au pied du retour
en Alsacélorraine ne l'oubliez jamais!
hommes popo hommes titi
30 mes Shihanouk mes Princes
tous indépopo indépenpen dants
Cachemiris sikhs kikis
en ce moment chez eux
pas de décroissance mographique
35 ils sont si bien les prin par les po Etios reçus
mon Chou:
problèmes essentiels résolus.

(1974)

MEN PO MEN WITH GLASSES

men po men with glasses
men politi
mephipolitimemphi
        limemphi
5   tics
you are stuffed full with farce
with the mother-land in your many holes
as for us they want the army to decide
brothel of a damned whore god
10 whether to send us to college yes or no
after two years of requisite scorn for our
parents spent doing nothing
we were so tendentious at birth
all these arms these noses these balls get you
15 à priori a woman in two shakes and a vagina-deal
we'll practice for hours on end
the craft of doing nothing
and by this professional criterion
we'll be classified in the mass
20 of Warrior Committees
we will be efficacious
as the planned-out eliminated
our used peepee will be rectified
they'll barely know our address for the climate
25 we will be shortened (we women) by a notarized act
and a humiliating shearer
we will keep watch at the foot of the return
in Alsacelorraine iust don't forget it!
men po po men titi
30 my Sihanouk my princes
all indepopo indepenpen dents.
Cashmeris sihks kikis
at this moment in their country
no mographic shrinking
35 they are so nice the prin received by the po Etios
my Chou:
major problems solved.

—*Mary Ann Caws*

PARLER JE NE SAIS OÙ

Je veux revivre
L'ange muet je veux le mordre au cou
afin qu'il crie et qu'il me nomme
à la face ouverte du vent.
5   Quelqu'un m'a retirée malgré moi de mon sang
Pour donner ma parole en pâture à ses fauves
Mais le temps brisera ses os dans le miroir
qui défendait le fruit perdu
sous l'éternité chaste du feuillage.
10   Ai-je parlé tout haut jadis du mal d'amour
sur cette terre de lilas blessée par les orages
Ai-je jadis plombé tout le regard de l'homme
avec des mots
pour qu'il oublie la chasse à courre
15   et nous enferme ensemble sous sa tente
toute la nuit d'une saison.
Nous avons subvenu derrière le nuage
pendant longtemps à la chanson de nos délires.
L'espace d'un parfum, le nôtre
20   nous suffisait pour enterrer les morts
et pour mûrir notre dialogue en serre
sous les auspices du vin noir.
Tout s'est détruit
quand ton regard a recouvré sa propre loi
25   pour accoucher de l'astre mâle
qui frappait ma lèvre d'exil.
Et le silence a fait blêmir nos entretiens sur ton visage
Et je n'ai plus que mon fantôme entre les dents pour tout bagage.
Je sais, nulle parole encore n'a pu rayer la pierre.
30   Je veux revivre
Je veux chanter à mon amour
le poids du sang
le fruit des vagues.
Je veux mordre cet ange au cou
35   Je veux parler je ne sais où.

(1970)

ANGÈLE VANNIER (1917–)

TO SPEAK I KNOW NOT WHERE

I want to live again
That mute angel, I want to bite him in the neck
to hear him scream and name me
in the open face of the wind.
5 Someone took me from my own blood against my will
And gave my word to feed his savage beasts
But time will break his bones in the looking glass
that forbade the wasted fruit
in the chaste eternity of leaves.
10 Did I ever say out loud the pain of love
upon this earth of lilacs wounded by the storm
Did I ever plumb entirely a man's eyes
with words
to make him leave aside his hunting
15 and enclose us in his tent
a whole season's night long.
Behind the cloud, we have long provided
delirious melodies of our love.
For the space of a perfume, our own
20 was enough to bury the dead
and ripen our dialogue in the hothouse
under the auspices of ink-black wine.
All was destroyed
when your eyes retrieved their own law
25 and gave birth to the male star
that struck my lip with exile.
And the silence made our talk grow pale upon your face
And all the baggage that remains is my own ghost between my
      teeth.
I know, no word has ever yet crossed out a stone.
30 I want to live again
I want to sing to my love
the weight of blood
the fruit of waves.
I want to bite that angel's neck
35 I want to speak I know not where.

—Barbara Johnson

FEMMES DE TOUS LES TEMPS

Ancestrales et pourtant fraternelles
Lointaines et pourtant proches

Elles viennent à notre rencontre
Ces Femmes d'un autre âge

5 Dans la pulpe éphémère de leurs corps
Dans la beauté d'un geste périssable
Dans les brefs remous d'un visage neuf ou vieilli

Ces Femmes immémoriales
        à travers argile et pierres
10   écartant les écorces du temps
Se frayent passage jusqu'ici.

Hors du tréfonds des siècles
délivrant l'esprit

Non plus *femmes-objets*
15 Mais objets devenus Femmes

Elles lèvent échos paroles
et questions d'aujourd'hui.

(1976)

JE PENSE À LA MORTE DANS UN POÈME

Je pense à la morte dans un poème
à la patience d'une statue
je suis la morte
je suis le poème dans une tombe
5 l'objet
rêvant de rêver l'objet
je suis la morte dans moi-même
je suis la morte dans mon poème

(1966)

ANDRÉE CHÉDID (1920–)

WOMEN OF ALL THE AGES

Ancestral and still fraternal
Distant and yet near

They come to greet us
These Women from another age

5 In the ephemeral flesh of their bodies
In the beauty of a gesture bound to perish
In the brief swirls of a face new or aged

These immemorial Women
                    through clay and stones
10   parting the husks of time
Clear a path to the present.

From the subsoil of centuries
delivering the spirit

No longer *women-objects*
15 But objects become Women

They raise echoes words
and questions of today.

—*Mary Ann Caws*

MARIE-FRANCOISE PRAGER (1925?–)

I THINK ABOUT THE DEAD WOMAN IN A POEM

I think about the dead woman in a poem
about the patience of a statue
I am the dead woman
I am the poem in a tomb
5 the object
dreaming of dreaming the object
I am the dead woman in me
I am the dead woman in my poem

—*Carl Hermy*

NOYÉE AU FOND D'UN RÊVE ENNUYEUX

Noyée au fond d'un rêve ennuyeux
J'effeuillais l'homme
L'homme cet artichaut drapé d'huile noire
Que je lèche et poignarde avec ma langue bien polie
5 L'homme que je tue l'homme que je nie
Cet inconnu qui est mon frère
Et qui m'offre l'autre joue
Quand je crève son oeil d'agneau larmoyant
Cet homme qui pour la communauté est mort assassiné
10 Hier avant-hier et avant ça et encore
Dans ses pauvres pantalons pendants de surhomme

(1960)

LE TRAIN D'ENFER

Passagère occasionnelle de vos trains de luxure,
prisonnière clandestine des barreaux du désir,
complice momentanée de l'accession à vos pouvoirs imbéciles
(et non compagne de la longue route, avec le respect dû à ceux
5 qui apportent ce qui manquait dans vos paniers),
vous ne me faites, de vous, que le complet-menteur
de vos envie désordonnées
et rien ne me sert de désespérément chercher
en vous ce complément à ma nature,
10 attribut divin
que vous vous croyez trop grands pour porter
et que vous avez jeté aux orties
comme une défroque dont vous vous moquez...

Hommes, je vous aimais.
15 Hommes-Sexe, je vous hais!

Homme, qu'as-tu fait du sceptre-initiateur,
doigt qui devait montrer la voie?

JOYCE MANSOUR (1928–)

DROWNED AT THE BOTTOM OF A BORING DREAM

Drowned at the bottom of a boring dream
I'd strip the leaves off man
Man that artichoke draped in black oil
That I lick and stab with polished tongue
5 Man whom I kill man whom I deny
This unknown man who is my brother
Who offers me the other cheek
When I split his eye of lachrymose lamb
This man who for the common good has been assassinated
10 Yesterday before yesterday before that and again
In his poor droopy drawers of superman

—*Albert Herzing*

MONIQUE BURI (1928–)

THE TRAIN TO HELL

A passenger at times in your trains of vice,
clandestine prisoner in your courts of desire,
momentary accomplice to the rise of your imbecilic powers
(and not a fellow traveler, with due respect to those
5 who replenish your baskets),
you have only made me the best-suited liar
of your dissolute urges
and I get nowhere desperately searching
in you for my other half,
10 divine attribute
that you think you're too grand to wear
and that you've thrown away among the thorns
like the frock of a dead priest...

How I loved you, men!
15 How I hate you, man-sex!

Man, what have you done with your initiating scepter,
the finger that was to show the way?

une baudruche, une enflure grotesque
dans laquelle tu t'es réincarné!
20 Pantin dérisoire au bout de tes propres ficelles
où tu gigotes comme une queue séparée de son tronc.
Tu t'es fabriqué un monde
où l'enfant n'a plus droit d'innocence
ni la femme à la douceur d'aimer,
25 et ce monde va mourir comme tout ce qui pourrit,
et ce monde meurt, entraînant dans sa chute
tout le troupeau aveugle
qui vous avait pris pour des chefs...

O soleil électrique,
30 monde artificiel
O vie qui s'étrique
d'avoir perdu le ciel.

Etre l'objecteur de sa conscience propre
dans son fort intérieur,
35 ne se pas laisser dégrader de son proper chef
fut-ce un chef d'accusation,
militer pour un désarmement devant la douceur
et ne s'armer que de patience à la douleur.
Général, qu'as-tu fait des particuliers?
40 La tunique
du chef est unique.
Mieux vaut la raccommoder
que d'en emprunter
une neuve de soldat d'opérette
45 à parader devant des minettes.

O monde de polichinelles,
tu meurs de ta mort belle,
trop belle encore
pour te foutre dehors!

50 A quand le recommencement?
C'est pas bientôt fini de jouer sérieusement
à se prendre au sérieux,
nom de Dieu!

(1976)

a condom, a ludicrous swelling
in which you've been reincarnated!
20 Laughable marionette hanging at the end of your strings
where you twist like a tail split from its body.
You have made a world
where the child has no right to innocence
nor woman to gentle loving
25 and this world will die like all things rotten
and this world is dying, dragging the blind horde
in its fall
which took you for its leaders...

O electric sun
30 artificial world
O life on the run
for having lost the sky.

To be the objector to one's own clear conscience
in one's innermost fort,
35 and not willingly degrade oneself
even by the hand of a master accuser,
to struggle for disarmament in face of gentleness
and arm oneself only with patience when pain invades.
General, what have you done to particulars?
40 The master's tunic
is unique.
Better mend it
than borrow
a new one from a toy soldier
45 to strut about before coquettes.

O world of jokesters,
you die your fine death
still too fine, in fact,
to boot you out!

50 When will there be a new beginning?
Aren't you through seriously pretending
to take yourself seriously,
damn it to hell!

—*Serge Gavronsky*

LE POÈME D'A

êtres humains
vous voici dans la brume du soir
des blocs de pierre plats posés sur vos rivages
ordonnent votre monde

5   ce jeu de cartes perforées
              dont vous dressez la liste
              exacte
              tremblant de peur quand l'ordre est inversé
tremblez

10 l'ordre n'est pas notre langage
nous dormons sur la terre ignorée
nos corps faits en berceaux par les têtes amies
protégées
par des bras millénaires

15   ne vous réveillez pas
              car nous serons plus vivantes que la pierre
ne me réveillez pas
moi qui suis la mémoire
des voix endormis de silence

20 tendre chanson
tissée de chaque instant qui passe
le noeud qu'on fait au fil des jours
pour ne pas oublier le temps
et le café

25 fumant dans la cuisine basse
              un peuple de servantes aux mains vides et
                soumises
              qui relèvent interminablement
              les draps sur la tête des morts
a pour ces apparences

30 et les miroirs sans tain
que sont les visages de femmes
l'image ne fait plus les gestes du réel
les voleuses de feu dansent dans vos ténèbres
impunément.

(1972)

CATHY BERNHEIM (1946–)

THE POEM OF A

human beings
there you are in the night mist
stone blocks posed flat on your shores
command your world
5   this game of perforated cards
               whose list you compose
               exact
               trembling with fear when the order is reversed
10 tremble
order is not our language
we sleep upon the earth ignored
our bodies changed to cradles by friendly heads
protected
15 by age-old arms
               do not wake
               for we shall be more lively than the stone
do not wake me
I who am memory
20 voices sleepy with silence
tender song
spun from each passing moment
the knot made in the thread of days
so as not to forget time
25 and the coffee
steaming in the low kitchen
               a people of maidservants empty-handed and docile
               ceaselessly drawing the sheets
               over the faces of the dead
30 has for these appearances
and unsilvered mirrors
which women's faces are
the image no longer makes the gestures of the real
fire-stealers* dance in your shadows
35 fearlessly.

—*Mary Ann Caws*

*Translator's note—Feminine in the original.

V

Au M.L.F.

O femmes
lorsqu'au petit matin, auprès des hommes, nos amants,
nos fils et nos pères
comblées ou déçues dedans le creux du ventre
5　en chaînes de générations
enchaînées ou charmées

le ventre au beau milieu de moi
qui je? moi...toi...je—moi...L'ESPÈCE?

Avant le souffle,
10　le verbe
cette folle du logis dedans l'homme
ô ma soeur Anne tu restes en tour de guet pour explorer
le retour des hommes nos fils, nos amants et nos pères

moi...je
15　la lune aussi violée au petit matin
la terre qui tourne dans les oracles de l'homme
le cerveau coule comme du sperme, oh oui coule le cerveau
comme du sperme fou dans de l'encre et la politique

Allons-nous, au-delà de l'amour,
20　dans les eaux de nos accouchements, allons-nous
retrouver le verbe dans des antennes d'une aube où la
première lettre attend?

la lune bleue, pourquoi
la femme au noir d'un continent diurne
25　du soleil viendra
du soleil et du jour
dedans le ventre, les CONSONNES
les VOYELLES à la place du sang et de la chair

pourquoi, cybernétique,
30　pourquoi la parole
lorsque virginale en nous, femmes, attend la genèse?

(1977)

CHARLOTTE CALMIS (?–1970)

V

*To the M.L.F.**

O women
when in the early dawn, near men, our lovers,
our sons, and our fathers
fulfilled or disappointed in the hollow of the womb
5 in the chains of generations
shackled or charmed

the womb in my very center
who I? me...you...I—me...THE SPECIES?

Before the breath,
10 the word
that madwoman, imagination, in man
O my sister Anne you take your turn watching
for the return of men our sons, lovers, and fathers

me...I
15 the moon too raped in the early dawn
the earth turns in the oracles of man
the brain flows like sperm, ah yes flows the brain
like sperm gone mad in ink and politics

Shall we, on the other side of love,
20 in the waters of our giving birth, shall we
find the word in the antennae of a dawn where
the first letter awaits?

the blue moon, why will
the woman in black from a diurnal continent
25 from the sun
from the sun and the day
come inside the womb, the CONSONANTS
the VOWELS instead of blood and flesh

why, cybernetics,
30 why speech
when virginal in us, women, genesis awaits?

—*Mary Ann Caws*

*Translator's note—M.L.F. is the acronym for the Movement de Libération des
Femmes, the women's movement in France.

NE SUIS-JE DENTELLIÈRE DE L'OMBRE

Ne suis-je dentellière de l'ombre
qu'araignée au tissage secret
peau tatouée (façon que j'ai de broder-main la connaissance)
sur ma chair de clair-obscur destin

5   Qu'est-ce qui
DORT NOIR AU COEUR DE MES DENTELLES
Pourquoi élucider   si
à travers corps pénètrent pierres vos mots
là où d'autres mots stagnent
10   cette pamoison de mots ma chair stigmatise
pourquoi élucider   Méditation de chouettes aveugles

Que périssent les saisons rousses de nos passions
automnes fous
temps des mal-aimés
15 Crissements-cris à fleur de mots de pierres et
de stigmates

Pourquoi élucider
Je t'interroge   jour de trop soleil
Quel secret dort noir au coeur de mes dentelles?

(1977)

AM I NOT THE LACEMAKER OF SHADOW

Am I not the lacemaker of shadow
only a spider with secret weave
tattooed skin (how I hand-embroider knowledge)
chiaroscuro fate upon my flesh

5 What
SLEEPS BLACK AT THE HEART OF MY LACE
Why elucidate   if
through the body penetrate stones your words
there where other words stagnate
10   this swooning of words stigmatized by my flesh
why elucidate   Meditation of blind owls

Let the seasons perish russet with our passions
crazed autumns
time of the unbeloved
15 Grating-cries on top of words of stones and
of stigmata

Why elucidate
I question you   day of excessive sun
What secret sleeps black at the heart of my lace?

—*Mary Ann Caws*

NOTES ON THE POETS

Louise Ackermann (1813–1890)
Louise Ackermann, née Victorine Choquet, began writing poetry in her childhood, a period she would describe in her autobiography (1877) as solitary and fearful. Her many volumes of published work, the first of which, *L'Homme*, appeared in 1830, comprise short stories (*Contes*, 1855, 1862) and a journal covering the period 1849–1869 (*Les Pensées d'une solitaire*, 1882). By and large, her poetry is not feminist in inspiration; it is best known for an emotional and intellectual pessimism that is rooted in philosophical and scientific preoccupations, notably positivism and Hegelianism. *Poésies philosophiques* (1871, 1874) is the best introduction to Ackermann's work.

Natalie Clifford Barney (1877–1972)
Natalie Clifford Barney was a wealthy American heiress and expatriate who spent most of her adult life in Paris. The openness with which she rejected certain social and sexual conventions and, in particular, her lesbian affairs and lasting friendships with such women as Renée Vivien (q.v.), Lucie Delarue-Mardrus (q.v.), Gertrude Stein, and Colette made this "Amazon," as she dubbed herself in *Pensées d'une amazone* (1920), a legend in her own time. Barney's salon attracted the leading European and American intellectuals, writers, and artists of her day. Her verse, drama, fiction, essays, epigrams, and memoirs span more than a half-century—from *Quelques portraits–sonnets de femmes* (1900) to *Traits et portraits* (1963). Barney, however, insisted that her writing was only a byproduct of her real work of art: her life.

Camille Bélot (n.d.)
No biographical information is available on Camille Bélot, the late-nineteenth-century author, whose works include *Les Pruneaux*, a monologue (1882), *Elégie sur la mort de Gambetta* (1883), *La Résurrection* (1885), *Les Secrets du magnétisme* (1884), and *La Fille-Mère* (1901), the representation of the trial of an unwed mother, from which the selection in this volume has been taken.

Cathy Bernhein (1946–)
Cathy Bernheim wrote "le poème d'A" for the feminist paper *Le Torchon Brûle* in 1972. She has published poems in the journals *Alternatives* and *Change*, and since 1974 has contributed articles to *Les Temps Modernes*. Bernheim is also the author of *Perturbation, ma soeur* (1983), a memoir of the women's movement in the early 1970s, and of the forthcoming *Bye Bye Baby*, a narrative on "post-feminism" in France.

Monique Buri (1928–)

Monique Buri, who recently left France to return to her native Switzerland, published *Les Chantiers du coeur* in 1975 and *L'Amande double* in 1977. "Le Train d'enfer," the selection in this volume, appeared in an anthology of women poets, *Femmes poètes de notre temps* (1976).

Charlotte Calmis (?–1970)

Charlotte Calmis is the author of *Les Chants roux de la femelle* (1973). The two poems chosen for this anthology were first published in *Le Nouveau Commerce*, nos. 36 and 37 (1977).

Mlle Certain (n.d.)

Nothing is known about the author and poet Mlle Certain, not even her first name. *Nouvelles Poésies ou Diverses Pièces choisies, tant en vers qu'en prose* (1665) is the only work published under this name.

Andrée Chédid (1920–)

An Egyptian of Lebanese origin, Andrée Chédid has had a markedly diverse and productive literary career, beginning in 1943 with the publication of her poems in English, *On the Traits of My Fancy*. She has written several novels, a collection of short stories (*L'Étroite Peau*, 1965), three plays, and some fifteen volumes of verse. In 1972–1973 alone, three volumes of her poetry were published: *Visage premier*, *Têtes et lubies*, and *Prendre corps*. In a book of notes on poetry, *Terre et poésie* (1956), Chédid expressed her opposition to overtly philosophical messages and verbal acrobatics. "Femmes de tous les temps" was selected for this volume from *Fraternité de la parole* (1976).

Louise Colet (1810–1876)

Literary historians have cited Louise Colet chiefly for her celebrated liaisons with Victor Cousin, Flaubert (as recorded in their correspondence, c. 1846–1855), and Alfred de Musset. Her fictionalized biography of the latter romantic poet and dramatist is entitled *Lui: Roman contemporain* (1859). The author of several other novels and of a one-act play in verse, *La Jeunesse de Goethe*, Colet wrote many volumes of poetry that are notable for their concern with women and the working class. She signed her first verses "une femme," and published her first book of poetry, *Fleurs du midi*, in 1835. Her other volumes of poetry, which appeared over a thirty-year period, include *Penserosa* (1840), *Le Chant des vaincus* (1846), *Ce qui est dans le coeur des femmes* (1852), and *Le Poème de la femme* (1856) in three parts ("La Paysanne," "La Servante," and "La Religieuse").

Comtesse de Die (Twelfth Century)

Mystery and conjecture surround the little that is known about the life of the Comtesse de Die, the most famous of the four recognized *trobairitz* (women troubadours). She may have been the wife of William of Poitiers. More important, she was perhaps the lover of the troubadour Raimbaut d' Orange, about whom her four extant *canzos* are said to be written, and with whom she has a dialogue in the *tenson* (dialogue or debate song), "Estat ai en gran cossirier," which is sometimes attributed to her. The Comtesse de Die's poetry has a stylistic directness and sexual frankness (often labeled "sincerity") that contrast with male troubadour poetry, in which the speaker typically seeks a mystical union with an inaccessible and idolized lady of his imagination.

Lucie Delarue-Mardrus (1880?–1945)
Lucie Delarue-Mardrus was a writer, painter, sculptor, musician, and composer, and an indefatigable traveler and lecturer in Europe, Brazil, and the United States. She practiced a variety of literary genres: tragedy (*Sapho désespérée*, 1906; *Prêtresse de Tanit*, 1908); fictionalized biography (on William the Conqueror, 1931); the novel (virtually one a year after *Marie, fille-mère*, 1908); and poetry (her first volume, *Occident*, appeared in 1900). Most popular as a novelist in her time, especially for *L'Ex-voto* (1922), Delarue-Mardrus is primarily remembered today for her lyric verse. Her lesbian poetry, which has never before been included in an anthology, can be found in *Nos Secrètes Amours* (1951).

Yanette Delétang-Tardif (1907–)
The first published works of Yanette Delétang-Tardif, *Éclats* (1929) and *Générer* (1930), from which the selection in this volume is taken, reveal the influence of Valéry's prosody, as does her *Chants royaux* (1956), a study in complex metrical form. Delétang-Tardif's *La Colline* (1936), *Morte en songe* (1937), *Les Séquestrés*, a novel, and much of her later work are notable for their surrealist imagery.

Christine de Pisan (1364–c.1430)
Widowed at the age of twenty-five, the Italian-born Christine de Pisan became a writer to support her family, the first French woman of letters to live by her pen. Among the many political, moral, philosophical, and historical treatises of this erudite woman, *Le Livre de la mutacion de la fortune* (1404) is perhaps the most notable. Although her shorter poems usually treat traditional themes of love, *Le Dit de la rose* (1402), *Le Livre de la cité des dames* (1404–1405), and especially *Epistre au Dieu d'amours* (1399) denounce the secondary status of women in the Church and the misogyny of medieval satires and romances, in particular the celebrated *Roman de la rose* by Jean de Meung. Pisan, moreover, argues for the right to education of her sex and for the legal rights of widows and unmarried women. To date, she may be considered the first feminist critic and theorist.

Catherine Des Roches (1550–1587)

Catherine Des Roches was the only child of Madeleine Des Roches (q.v.) and was schooled by her in the study of Greek, Latin, and Italian texts. Catherine Des Roches is said to have refused numerous proposals of marriage so as not to be separated from her mother; in fact, mother and daughter succumbed to the plague on the same day and are buried in a single tomb. Their work, always published together, is collected in two volumes. The first, *Oeuvres* (1578, 1579), contains some of Catherine's sonnets and epistles and her tragicomedy, *Tobie*. Their *Secondes Oeuvres* (1583) features her translations, songs, sonnets, quatrains, and, among others, two prose dialogues that argue the benefits of learning for women.

Madeleine Des Roches (1530?–1587)

Madeleine Des Roches elicited attacks from her contemporaries for her "unseemly" erudition and her poetic practice. With her daughter, Catherine (q.v.), Madeleine Des Roches created a salon that was the literary center of Poitiers. Whereas most of her poetry treats subjects associated with the Petrarchan traditions of her time, her "Ode première" attacks the prejudices that condemn women to silence, ignorance, and servitude.

Marie-Anne Du Boccage (1710–1802)

From her first literary effort, an imitation of *Paradise Lost*, written at the age of thirty-six, Marie-Anne Le Page Du Boccage was the object of public acclaim. During her lifetime, her work was celebrated in verse by Voltaire and Fontenelle and was honored by literary societies. The most notable of Boccage's many texts are *La Colombiade*, perhaps the first French work of literature to use Christopher Columbus as its subject; *Les Amazones* (1749), a tragedy in verse; and two volumes of correspondence recording her travels in England and the Continent. Most of her work has been translated into English, Spanish, German, and Italian.

Adelaïde-Gillette Dufresnoy (1765–1825)

As a young woman, Adelaïde-Gillette Dufresnoy enjoyed considerable fame and fortune in Parisian literary circles. The Revolution, however, brought about her husband's financial ruin and forced her to write for a living. Her work covers a broad spectrum: verse, including three volumes of erotic poetry (*Elégies et poésies diverses*, 1807, 1813, 1821); two plays; numerous novels; a history of modern Greece; translations from English; manuals of education; and an autobiographical novel, *La Femme auteur, ou Les Inconvénients de la célébrité* (1812). During the Restoration, Dufresnoy remained personally loyal to the royalists, although her salon was a center of liberal opposition to the régime. Some romantic poets cited her as their precursor.

Pernette Du Guillet (c. 1520–1545)

Pernette Du Guillet, Maurice Scève, and Louise Labé form the triad of what is called the Lyonnaise school of poetry. Situated in a city of great literary activity in the sixteenth century, this "school" helped promote the Petrarchism and neo-Platonism of the Italian Renaissance in France. Guillet is often cited as the inspiration for Scève's major work, *Délie* (1544), but her own poetic accomplishments, founded on her knowledge of Greek and Latin, of Italian, Spanish, and French literature, were considerable in her short life. Her *Rymes*, a collection of epigrams, songs, and elegies dedicated "to the ladies of Lyon," was published posthumously in 1545 and augmented in 1552.

Claire Goll (1891–1977)

Born in Germany, Claire Goll began publishing her work in the 1920s in Paris, where she met the leading surrealist painters and poets. Her first literary influence, however, came from Rainer Maria Rilke, with whom she maintained a correspondence that was eventually published in 1944. Her earliest volumes of poetry—*Poèmes de la jalousie* (1926), *Poèmes de la vie et de la mort* (1927), and *Poèmes d'amour* (1930)—were written as dialogues in collaboration with her husband, the poet, novelist, and translator Yvan Goll. Works solely her own include four novels, published between 1926 and 1933, and four volumes of poetry: *Les Larmes pétrifiées* (1951) and *Chansons indiennes* (1952), which are inspired by pre-Colombian culture; *Le Coeur tatoué: Chants peaux rouges* (1958); and *L'Ignifère* (1969). The year before her death, she published *La Poursuite du vent* (1976).

Marguerite Grépon (n.d.)

Marguerite Grépon, founder and editor of the journal *Ariane* since 1953, is an essayist, novelist, and poet. Her writing often combines all three genres and reflects her disregard for traditional distinctions among literary forms. "Story in Poetic Form," the subtitle of the text selected for this volume, is also the subtitle of her *Dialogues de la nuit* (1957). Her diverse works comprise *Journal* (1960); *Médiumnité, fardeau*, poems followed by short plays (1965); *Une Croisade pour un meilleur amour: Une Histoire des Saint-Simoniennes: Récit* (1967); *Anti-poèmes et paraboles à partir de l'infinitif* (1972); *C'était un grand amour: Correspondence avec une morte* (1974); *Décoordonnées* (1975); *La Voyageuse nue*, a novel; and *La Servante poète* and *Poétique de la servie*, both poetic prose.

Anne de La Vigne (1634–1684)

Anne de La Vigne frequented the salons of her day and especially the company of Madeleine de Scudéry, the celebrated novelist to whom she addressed the ode, "Les Dames à Mademoiselle de Scudéry." Although her correspondence with the religious orator Fléchier has been published separately, La Vigne's poetry has never been collected in a single volume.

Her work might be characterized as *galant* or *mondain*, with the notable exception of ambitious poems on Descartes, one of which appears in this anthology.

Joyce Mansour (1928–)
Joyce Mansour, an Egyptian born in England and living in Paris, has been considered a leading member of the postwar surrealist movement. Her texts are often marked by a nightmarish quality and erotico-macabre imagery that is both undercut and heightened by humor. Her many volumes of poetry, beginning with *Cris* in 1953, include *Les Gisants satisfaits* (1958), *Carré blanc* (1965), *Phallus et momies* (1969) and *Ça (1970)*. *Faire signe au machiniste* (1977), like some of her most recent work, contains illustrations by contemporary artists.

Thérèse Plantier (1911–)
Thérèse Plantier associated herself with the surrealists and contributed to the journal *La Brèche*. She subsequently broke with that movement and became, in her words, "strictly feminist and expressed it in lyric poetry." She has published French translations of modern British poetry and the following volumes of prose and poetry: *Chemins d'eau* (1963), *Mémoires inférieures* (1966), *C'est moi Diego* (1971), *Jusqu'à ce que l'enfer gèle* (1974), and *La Loi du silence* (1975). Plantier has described her most recent prose work, *Le Discours du mâle*, as "a diatribe against masculine domination."

Marie-Françoise Prager (1925?–)
The poetry of Marie-Françoise Prager had been admired by such critics as Gaston Bachelard, Roland Barthes, and Jean Rousselot even prior to the publication of her first two volumes: *Narcose* (1966), from which the selection in this anthology is taken; and *Rien ne se perd* (1970). Her third volume, *Quelqu'un parle*, appeared in 1979. Prager now lives in Italy.

Adine Brabart Riom (1818–1899)
The literary salon of Adine Brabart Riom in Nantes hosted notable Breton authors. Her writing, often signed "Louise d'Isole" or "le comte de Saint-Jean," comprises novels, a comedy in prose, and numerous poetic works that span more than half a century. While her poetry evokes various romantic themes associated with Lamartine and Marceline Desbordes-Valmore, Riom also celebrated the legends and lyrical forms of her Breton heritage in such works as *Mobiles et zouaves bretons* (1871), *Histoires et légendes bretonnes* (1873), and *Les Adieux: Poésies bretonnes* (1895). "Révolte," the poem selected for this volume, is taken from *Passion* (1864).

Anne de Rohan (1584–1646)
Like her mother, Catherine de Parthenay, Anne de Rohan was a woman of letters, versed in Latin and Hebrew, who staunchly defended Calvinism

against its critics. Both daughter and mother refused to capitulate to the forces of Cardinal Richelieu during the siege of La Rochelle in 1627, and they were taken as prisoners of war. Rohan's writing, entirely in verse, features elegies to her mother, to her sister, and to Henriette de Savoie. *Stances sur la mort de Henri IV* (1616) was admired by poets of her time and remains her best-known verse.

Marie de Romieu (1545?–1590?)
Little is known about the life of Marie de Romieu. Her published work consists of a prose dialogue, *Instruction pour les jeunes dames* (1573), and a collection of odes, sonnets, and elegies, which was edited by her brother Jacques in 1581. Her "Brief Discours," a response to her brother's satire against women, seeks to prove women's moral, physical, intellectual, and artistic superiority to men by citing as evidence celebrated female writers, poets, and heroines in history and mythology.

Louise Geneviève de Sainctonge (1650–1718)
Although little is known of the life of Louise Geneviève de Sainctonge, wife of a Parisian lawyer, the variety and audacity of her work leads one to speculate on her freedom from traditional female roles. Translator of Ariosto's *Orlando furioso* and Montemayor's *Diane*, Sainctonge also wrote the librettos for two operas, *Didon* (1693) and *Circé* (1694); two comedies in verse; and a historical study entitled *Histoire secrète de dom Antoine, roi de Portugal* (1696). Her two-volume *Poésies galantes* (1696, 1714) contains, aside from idylls, epistles, and elegies, several satiric epigrams, earthy fables, and ribald drinking songs.

Constance-Marie de Salm-Dyck (1767–1845)
Among the successes that Constance-Marie de Salm-Dyck enjoyed was admittance to literary societies that had hitherto been closed to women. In one of these, she read her "Epître aux femmes" (1797), a passionate defense of women's right to be authors. Salm-Dyck's four volumes of *Oeuvres complètes* (1842) cover a wide range of forms: poetry of diverse genres; an autobiography in verse, *Mes soixante Ans...* (1833); an epistolary novel, *Vingt-quatre Heures d'une femme sensible* (1824); two tragedies, *Sapho* (1794) and *Camille, ou Amitié et imprudence* (1799); a collection of *Pensées* (1828), which she regarded as her most important prose work; a study on *La Condition des femmes dans une république* (1800); and *Opinion d'une femme sur des femmes* (1801). Her most explicitly feminist works include *Epîtres à Sophie* (1801) and an epistle to Napoleon (1810), selected for this volume, in which she attacks the oppression of women, especially in marriage. Some of Salm-Dyck's texts have been translated into English and Greek.

Pauline de Simiane (1676–1737)
Pauline de Grignan, Marquise de Simiane, was the godchild of the Cardinal de Retz, the famous memorialist, and the granddaughter of Mme

de Sévigné, the author of the most celebrated of seventeenth-century correspondences. Indeed, the upbringing and education of Pauline are the focus of many of Sévigné's letters to her daughter, Mme de Grignan. Simiane's own correspondence, which contains some letters to Sévigné, was published posthumously in 1773. She spent her married life at court; after she became a widow in 1718, she lived in seclusion. Simiane published a single volume of poetry anonymously in 1715, entitled *Portefeuille de Mme ****, *contenant divers odes, idylles et sonnets*.

Amable Tastu (1798–1885)
Amable Tastu wrote poetry as a young girl, for which she received the praise of the Empress Josephine before age eleven and several prizes before she was twenty-five. She published her complete poetic works in three volumes in 1837, but the financial ruin of her husband in the 1830s forced her to abandon poetry for children's literature, pedagogical treatises, and translations from English. The thirty volumes of her work rarely reveal a feminist orientation, although Tastu did edit the letters of Sévigné and wrote a long, appreciative essay on the renowned seventeenth-century *epistolière*.

Angèle Vannier (1917–)
Angèle Vannier, blind since the age of twenty-two, is the author of a novel, *La Nuit ardente* (1969), and several volumes of poetry: *Les Songes de la lumière et de la brume* (1947); *L'Arbre à feu* (1950), with a preface by Paul Eluard; *A hauteur d'ange* (1955); *Le Sang des nuits* (1966); *Théâtre blanc* (1970), from which the selection in this volume is taken; and *L'Atre utérin* (1975).

Philippine de Vannoz (1775–1851)
At the age of eight, Philippine de Sivry, the future Madame de Vannoz, was the toast of Parisian literary salons, where she read her poetry to D'Alembert, Grimm, and La Harpe. With the completion of her lyrical drama, *Calypso*, at the age of 15, she gained admission to the Académie des Arcades. Although Vannoz never enjoyed a comparable celebrity in later years, two volumes of her poems were published in 1812 and 1845; these contain the elegiac poem, "Profanation des tombeaux de St. Denis en 1793" (1806) and "Conseils à une femme sur les moyens de plaire dans la conversation" (1812), in four cantos. Her "Réponse aux vers de M. Lebrun...," which appears in this anthology, was published in the *Almanach des Muses* (1806), an annual anthology of literature published in France from 1765 to 1833.

Marie de Ventadour (?–c. 1222)
Marie de Ventadour (or Ventadorn in Provençal), daughter of a viscount of Limousin, was married to Ebles V, whose family had long been patrons of the troubadours. Ventadour herself supported and inspired many

troubadours, including Gui d'Ussel, with whom she exchanged her only known work, the *tenson* selected for this volume. In keeping with the conventions of this type of verse, the two poets espouse opposite views on an aspect of love in alternate stanzas. Reigning lady of one of the most active courts of Occitania, Ventadour was judge of several of the famous "Cours d'amour" debates.

Renée Vivien (1877–1909)

Born in London, Pauline Tarn took the name Renée Vivien after she had published her first collection of verse, *Etudes et préludes* (1901). Dedicated to Natalie Clifford Barney (q.v.), with whom she had a brief but crucial erotic and intellectual relationship, this work, from which the poem "Nocturne" is taken, was the first of ten volumes that she would write in French. The other selections in this anthology are to be found in *La Vénus des aveugles* (1904) and *A l'heure des mains jointes* (1906). In her poetry and in her autobiographical novel, *Une Femme m'apparut* (1904), Vivien, like Barney, evokes Sappho as inspiration for her lyrical depiction of lesbian love; some of her poems are in fact translations and amplifications of the extant fragments of Sappho's work. The texts of this fin de siècle poet, who died at the age of thirty-two, are haunted by a persistent preoccupation with death.

ACKNOWLEDGMENTS

For permission to reprint and translate the poems in this anthology, grateful acknowledgment is made to the following:

ANONYMOUS: "En un vergier lez une fontenele," translated by Patricia Terry, from *An Anthology of Medieval Lyrics*, ed. Angel Flores (New York: Modern Library Editions, 1962). © Angel Flores. Reprinted here with minor changes by the translator and by permission of Angel Flores.

BERNHEIM, CATHY: "le poème d'A" from *Le Torchon Brûle*, no. 4, 1972. By permission of the poet.

BURI, MONIQUE: "Le Train d'enfer" from *Femmes poètes de notre temps* (Paris: Éditions Grassin, 1976). By permission of the poet.

CALMIS, CHARLOTTE: "V" and "Ne suis-je dentellière de l'ombre" from *Le Nouveau Commerce*, nos. 36 and 37, 1977. By permission of the poet.

CHÉDID, ANDRÉE: "femmes de tous les temps" from her volume *Fraternité de la parole* (Paris: Éditions Flammarion, 1976). © 1976 by Éditions Flammarion. By permission of Flammarion.

COMTESSE DE DIE: "Estat ai en gran cossirier," translated by Muriel Kittel, from *Medieval Age*, ed. Angel Flores (New York: Dell Publishers, 1963). © Angel Flores. Translated here with minor changes by the translator and by permission of Angel Flores.

DELARUE-MARDRUS, LUCIE: "L'Injustice" and "Refus" from her volume *Horizons* (Paris: Éditions Fasquelle, 1904); "Si tu viens" from her volume *Nos Secrètes amours* (Paris: Éditions Les Isles, 1951). By permission of the estate of Lucie Delarue-Mardrus.

DELÉTANG-TARDIF, YANETTE: "Chanson" from her volume *Générer* (Paris: Éditions Aristide Quillet, 1930). By permission of the Société des Gens de Lettres de France.

DE PISAN, CHRISTINE: "Ne trop ne pou au cuer me sens frappée," translated by Naomi Lewis, from *Medieval Age*, ed. Angel Flores (New York: Dell Publishers, 1963). © Angel Flores. By permission of Angel Flores.

GRÉPON, MARGUERITE: "Histoire en forme de poésie, L'Androgyne" from her volume *Dialogues de la nuit* (Paris: Éditions Hautefeuille, 1957). By permission of the Société des Gens de Lettres de France.

GOLL, CLAIRE: "La Renarde" from her volume *L'Ignifère* (Paris: Librarie Saint-Germain-Des-Près, 1969). By permission of the estate of Claire Goll.

MANSOUR, JOYCE: "Noyée au fond d'un rêve ennuyeux" from her volume *Rapaces* (Paris: Éditions Seghers, 1960). By permission of the poet. Translation, by Albert Herzing, reprinted by permission of Joyce Mansour.

PLANTIER, THÉRÈSE: "Ma mère est morte" and "hommes po hommes à lunettes" from her volume *Jusqu'à ce que l'enfer gèle* (Éditions Pierre Jean Oswald, 1974). By permission of the poet.

PRAGER, MARIE-FRANÇOISE: "Je pense à la morte dans un poème" from her volume *Narcose* (Paris: Éditions Chambelland, 1966). By permission of the poet. Translation, by Carl Hermey, reprinted by permission of the translator.

VANNIER, ANGÈLE: "Parler je ne sais où" from her volume *Théâtre blanc* (Paris: Éditions Rougerie, 1970). By permission of the Société des Gens de Lettres de France.

Unless otherwise noted above, all translations were made for this anthology and are used by permission of the translators.

The Feminist Press at the City University of New York offers alternatives in education and in literature. Founded in 1970, this non-profit, tax-exempt educational and publishing organization works to eliminate sexual stereotypes in books and schools and to provide literature with a broad vision of human potential. The publishing program includes reprints of important works by women, feminist biographies of women, and nonsexist children's books. Curricular materials, bibliographies, directories, and a quarterly journal provide information and support for students and teachers of women's studies. In-service projects help to transform teaching methods and curricula. Through publications and projects, The Feminist Press contributes to the rediscovery of the history of women and the emergence of a more humane society.

FEMINIST CLASSICS FROM THE FEMINIST PRESS

Antoinette Brown Blackwell: A Biography, by Elizabeth Cazden. $19.95 cloth, $9.95 paper.
Between Mothers and Daughters: Stories Across a Generation. Edited by Susan Koppelman. $8.95 paper.
Brown Girl, Brownstones, a novel by Paule Marshall. Afterword by Mary Helen Washington. $8.95 paper.
Call Home the Heart, a novel of the thirties, by Fielding Burke. Introduction by Alice Kessler-Harris and Paul Lauter and afterwords by Sylvia J. Cook and Anna W. Shannon. $8.95 paper.
Cassandra, by Florence Nightingale. Introduction by Myra Stark. Epilogue by Cynthia Macdonald. $3.50 paper.
The Changelings, a novel by Jo Sinclair. Afterwords by Nellie McKay; and by Johnnetta B. Cole and Elizabeth H. Oakes; biographical note by Elisabeth Sandberg. $8.95 paper.
The Convert, a novel by Elizabeth Robins. Introduction by Jane Marcus. $6.95 paper.
Daughter of Earth, a novel by Agnes Smedley. Afterword by Paul Lauter. $7.95 paper.
A Day at a Time: The Diary Literature of American Women from 1764 to the Present, edited and with an introduction by Margo Culley. $29.95 cloth, $12.95 paper.
The Defiant Muse: French Feminist Poems from the Middle Ages to the Present, a bilingual anthology edited and with an introduction by Domna C. Stanton. $29.95 cloth, $11.95 paper.
The Defiant Muse: German Feminist Poems from the Middle Ages to the Present, a bilingual anthology edited and with an introduction by Susan L. Cocalis. $29.95 cloth, $11.95 paper.
The Defiant Muse: Hispanic Feminist Poems from the Middle Ages to the Present, a bilingual anthology edited and with an introduction by Angel Flores and Kate Flores. $29.95 cloth, $11.95 paper.
The Defiant Muse: Italian Feminist Poems from the Middle Ages to the Present, a bilingual anthology edited by Beverly Allen, Muriel Kittel, and Keala Jane Jewell, and with an introduction by Beverly Allen. $29.95 cloth, $11.95 paper.
The Female Spectator, edited by Mary R. Mahl and Helene Koon. $8.95 paper.
Guardian Angel and Other Stories, by Margery Latimer. Afterwords by Nancy Loughridge, Meridel Le Sueur, and Louis Kampf. $8.95 paper.
I Love Myself When I Am Laughing . . . And Then Again When I Am Looking Mean and Impressive, by Zora Neale Hurston. Edited by Alice Walker with an introduction by Mary Helen Washington. $9.95 paper.
Käthe Kollwitz: Woman and Artist, by Martha Kearns. $7.95 paper.
Life in the Iron Mills and Other Stories, by Rebecca Harding Davis. Biographical interpretation by Tillie Olsen. $7.95 paper.
The Living Is Easy, a novel by Dorothy West. Afterword by Adelaide M. Cromwell. $8.95 paper.
The Other Woman: Stories of Two Women and a Man. Edited by Susan Koppelman. $8.95 paper.
Mother to Daughter, Daughter to Mother: A Daybook and Reader, selected and shaped by Tillie Olsen. $9.95 paper.
Portraits of Chinese Women in Revolution, by Agnes Smedley. Edited with an introduction by Jan MacKinnon and Steve MacKinnon and an afterword by Florence Howe. $5.95 paper.
Reena and Other Stories, selected short stories by Paule Marshall. $8.95 paper.
Ripening: Selected Work, 1927–1980, by Meridel Le Sueur. Edited with an introduction by Elaine Hedges. $8.95 paper.

Rope of Gold, a novel of the thirties, by Josephine Herbst. Introduction by Alice Kessler-Harris and Paul Lauter and afterword by Elinor Langer. $8.95 paper.

The Silent Partner, a novel by Elizabeth Stuart Phelps. Afterword by Mari Jo Buhle and Florence Howe. $8.95.

Swastika Night, a novel by Katharine Burdekin. Introduction by Daphne Patai. $8.95 paper.

These Modern Women: Autobiographical Essays from the Twenties. Edited with an introduction by Elaine Showalter. $4.95 paper.

The Unpossessed, a novel of the thirties, by Tess Slesinger. Introduction by Alice Kessler-Harris and Paul Lauter and afterword by Janet Sharistanian. $8.95 paper.

Weeds, a novel by Edith Summers Kelley. Afterword by Charlotte Goodman. $7.95 paper.

A Woman of Genius, a novel by Mary Austin. Afterword by Nancy Porter. $8.95 paper.

The Woman and the Myth: Margaret Fuller's Life and Writings, by Bell Gale Chevigny. $8.95 paper.

Women and Appletrees, a novel by Moa Martinson. Translated from the Swedish and with an afterword by Margaret S. Lacy. $8.95 paper.

The Yellow Wallpaper, by Charlotte Perkins Gilman. Afterword by Elaine Hedges. $4.50 paper.

OTHER TITLES FROM THE FEMINIST PRESS

Black Foremothers: Three Lives, by Dorothy Sterling. $8.95 paper.

All The Women Are White, All The Blacks Are Men, But Some of Us Are Brave: Black Women's Studies. Edited by Gloria T. Hull, Patricia Bell Scott, and Barbara Smith. $12.95.

Complaints and Disorders: The Sexual Politics of Sickness, by Barbara Ehrenreich and Deirdre English. $3.95 paper.

The Cross-Cultural Study of Women. Edited by Margot I. Duley and Mary I. Edwards. $29.95 cloth, $12.95 paper.

Feminist Resources for Schools and Colleges: A Guide to Curricular Materials, 3rd edition. Compiled and edited by Anne Chapman. $12.95 paper.

Household and Kin: Families in Flux, by Amy Swerdlow et al. $8.95 paper.

How to Get Money for Research, by Mary Rubin and the Business and Professional Women's Foundation. Foreword by Mariam Chamberlain. $6.95 paper.

In Her Own Image: Women Working in the Arts. Edited with an introduction by Elaine Hedges and Ingrid Wendt. $9.95 paper.

Integrating Women's Studies into the Curriculum: A Guide and Bibliography, by Betty Schmitz. $9.95 paper.

Las Mujeres: Conversations from a Hispanic Community, by Nan Elsasser, Kyle MacKenzie, and Yvonne Tixier y Vigil. $8.95 paper.

Lesbian Studies: Present and Future. Edited by Margaret Cruikshank. $9.95 paper.

Moving the Mountain: Women Working for Social Change, by Ellen Cantarow with Susan Gushee O'Malley and Sharon Hartman Strom. $8.95 paper.

Out of the Bleachers: Writings on Women and Sport. Edited with an introduction by Stephanie L. Twin. $9.95 paper.

Reconstructing American Literature: Courses, Syllabi, Issues. Edited by Paul Lauter. $10.95 paper.

Salt of the Earth, screenplay by Michael Wilson with historical commentary by Deborah Silverton Rosenfelt. $5.95 paper.

Witches, Midwives, and Nurses: A History of Women Healers, by Barbara Ehrenreich and Deirdre English. $3.95 paper.

With These Hands: Women Working on the Land. Edited with an introduction by Joan M. Jensen. $9.95 paper.

Woman's "True" Profession: Voices from the History of Teaching. Edited with an introduction by Nancy Hoffman. $9.95 paper.

Women Have Always Worked: A Historical Overview, by Alice Kessler-Harris. $8.95 paper.

Women Working: An Anthology of Stories and Poems. Edited and with an introduction by Nancy Hoffman and Florence Howe. $8.95 paper.

For free catalog, write to The Feminist Press at the City University of New York, 311 East 94 Street, New York, N.Y. 10128. Send individual book orders to The Feminist Press, P.O. Box 1654, Hagerstown, MD 21741. Include $1.75 postage and handling for one book and 75¢ for each additional book. To order using MasterCard or Visa, call: (800) 638-3030.